EAST SEA OR SEA OF JAPAN

HISTORY AND TRUTHS

EAST SEA OR SEA OF JAPAN

HISTORY AND TRUTHS

SOH JEONG-CHEOL & PARK YOUNG-MIN

HU:iNE

East Sea or Sea Of Japan – History and Truths
By Soh Jeong-Cheol & Park Young-Min

Cover design by Design Pub (+82 2-2254-4308)
Edited by Sunho Shin, Inwoo Choi, and Design Pub

Published by Hankuk University of Foreign Studies Knowledge Press
107 Imun-ro
Dongdaemun-gu, Seoul 02450

http://press.hufs.ac.kr

First printing, November 30th, 2015

Printed in Republic of Korea

ISBN 979-11-5901-040-8 03910

Preface

When I was an elementary school student, I always went to school earlier than the other students because I lived nearby. When I arrived at the classroom, I looked up and down the Korean map on the wall everyday and read the names of the mountains, mountain ranges, and seas on it. I could see that the East Sea was larger than the Korean peninsula. The East Sea, along with the Yellow Sea to the west and the South Sea to the south, made a deep impression on me.

Then, the Korean War broke out in the year when I started middle school and the school closed. The next day, I went to a coffee shop with one of my relatives and found a

Korean map in English for the U.S. armed forces on a chair near the stove. I had nothing to do, so I sat and opened the map. Surprisingly, I saw "Sea of Japan" in the East Sea. It was not the same name that I had seen every day when I went to elementary school. I assumed that the name must be a misprint. "The American soldiers are ignorant and don't know that the proper name is the 'East Sea.'" I resolved to learn English more and tell them that they had made a mistake.

It was not a particularly great shock to me, and I was so engrossed in my studies that I completely forgot about it. Then, about 15 years later in the late 1960s when I was about to finish my studies in France, I visited Versailles. There, in a living room of Louis XIV, I noticed an old terrestrial globe. I saw the small country Korea with the marking "Mer Orientale" beside it. At that moment, I screamed at myself, "That's it! The French knew the proper name. I'll study this!" However, I was studying French language and literature and the new topic seemed too removed from me. I, therefore, decided to tell Korean students studying Korean Studies in France what I had found when I met them at a meeting. Contrary to my expectations, they were completely indifferent. They were only interested in their research papers.

When I returned to Korea, I told of my discovery to friends of mine who were newspaper reporters. They responded much more positively. One of them printed the story. It gave me a stronger sense of responsibility of a kind, and I felt obliged to prove to them that what I told them was true. I visited France during my summer vacation that year and tried to get a copy of the map that I had seen. I talked with a French student who was studying geography, and he told me that there were some map shops along the Seine. I went there and asked for an old map of Korea. What they brought me was a map with the notation "Sea of Korea" instead of "East Sea." I bought the map anyway and showed it to the geography student. He told me that he didn't know much about the map and proposed that we go to the library and find a catalogue of maps. After some searching, we found a record that the map that I had bought was one which was influenced by D'Anville and did not have much original content. I then decided that I would have to find a map by D'Anville.

That decision led me to the hard life of collecting old maps. I visited France every year to collect old maps under the pretext of everything that I could think of. This was costly to me, but I could not get out of the swamp of the old maps that I happened to fall into.

While collecting old maps with the notation of the East Sea, I began to wonder if calling the sea to the east of Korea the "East Sea" was Korea-centric since such a name was obviously based on Korea's geographical position. If every country named a sea this way, wouldn't that be a cause of confusion? A linguistic major myself, I consulted a scholar who was versed in nomenclature about this problem. He explained that, when a common noun is used as a name and then is turned a proper noun, the noun loses the etymological meaning of the common noun and is treated as a proper noun. However, when the noun contains a proper noun in the first place, the noun retains the value of the proper noun even after the name becomes a proper noun. Therefore, such names as "Sea of Korea" and "Sea of Japan" are exclusive and thus inappropriate, but "East Sea" is not: Once it becomes a proper noun, it drops the meaning of a common name, or the meaning "a sea in the east," and remains a simple proper noun. Wherever it is seen in the world, the name "East Sea" is a proper noun, whether it is seen in the United Kingdom to the west of Korea or in Russia to its north, and not a sea to their east. To foreigners who do not know the meaning, he added that all that is needed is a note that it refers to "the sea between Korea and Japan."

I collected old maps from the late 1960s to the 1990s. I joined the Society for East Sea and continued my research. In the early days, I thought that the "East Sea" was the right name and it should be used on maps in place of the "Sea of Japan." However, I gradually changed my mind: As the "Sea of Japan" has recently come into more frequent use and is supported by vested interests, it would be more rational to use both names. I then started to research the maps with the notation "Sea of Japan" in addition to those with the "East Sea." I wrote this book with the conviction that the "East Sea" and the "Sea of Japan" should be used together. To this end, I studied the notations of the sea between Korea and Japan on maps of many countries of the world and attempted to relate the truths about the "East Sea/Sea of Japan" as objectively as possible.

I did the overall organization for the original Korean edition of this book. However, as the problem of the name "East Sea" involves many fields, I could not do everything all by myself. I am greatly indebted to Professor Kim In-Whan for sponsoring my collection of old maps and writing the chapters on Europe in this book.

For this English edition, I decided that the original Korean text needed to be revised and supplemented throughout. This work was done by Park Young-Min, who also assisted greatly in the translation of this book.

I would like to thank Gimmyoung Publishers, the publisher of the original Korean book, for gladly permitting the publication of its English edition, and the Korea Foundation for sponsoring the publication of this book. I would like to express my deepest gratitude to Kim In-Chul, the president of Hankuk University of Foreign Studies, for making the publication of this book possible. I also extend my appreciation to the director and staff of Hankuk University of Foreign Studies Knowledge Press. I express my thanks to Professor Suh Min-Suk for making every effort to organize the draft, despite his busy schedule.

I also hereby extend my great thanks to the Society for East Sea for their substantial help in such matters as my relationship with international organizations, historical study of the name of the East Sea, and the notations of the East Sea in foreign countries, including China, Russia, and Japan. I frequently referred to the papers presented at the annual International Seminar on Sea Names hosted by the Society for the last 20 years.

Finally, I earnestly hope that the East Sea will become not

a flashpoint of dispute between Korea and Japan but a sea of friendship and peace between them. I have great confidence that it will.

Nov. 2015
Representing the two authors,
Soh Jeong-Cheol

Contents

Part I: In Search of the Lost Name, "East Sea"

Part II: Notation of the Name "East Sea" in the World

Part I

In Search of the Lost Name, "East Sea"

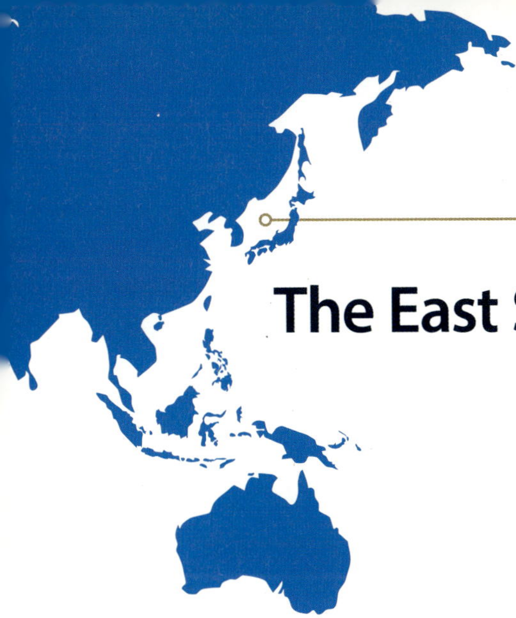

Chapter 1

The East Sea at a Glance

The lyrics of the Korean national anthem start with “Until the day when the East Sea’s waters and Mount Baekdu are dry and worn away, God protect and preserve us; Long live our nation.”

Undoubtedly, the East Sea has been so deeply rooted in the hearts of the Korean people and has become an integral part of their lives. It is therefore hardly surprising that they must have been shocked and disappointed at the fact that the sea is internationally being called “Sea of Japan,” rather than “East Sea.” Setting aside what the sea means emotionally to the Korean people for a moment, however, we need first to know what the sea is about in several dimensions –

physically, historically and culturally.

The word "East Sea" contains three different elements: The first is the appellation itself, the second is what it refers to, and the third is its physical features. Anyone who has never even been to the sea still can call it by a name. To those who have come to the sea, "East Sea" is the physical entity that they can point to. The contents of the sea, including its physical features, are also part of what comprises the sea. Lying to the east of the Korean Peninsula, the coastline of the body of water is shared by South Korea, North Korea, Russia and Japan. China – which also owned a territory, Sakhalin and its vicinity, but was forced to cede to Russia – also cannot afford to be indifferent to the naming of the sea. Geopolitically, then, the East Sea is an area where the continental and oceanic forces can meet and confront each other in their pursuit of regional hegemony, with the Korea Peninsula in-between.

Now, let us examine some basic facts about the East Sea based on the summing-up by Park Chan-Hong, former director of the East Sea Research Institute, Korea Institute of Ocean Science & Technology.

1. Physical Features

The major axis of the East Sea, from the northern tip of Hokkaido, Japan, to Tsushima Island is about 1,500 km and the minor axis, from the vicinity of Sokcho, Korea, across the sea to Niigata, Japan, is some 1,000 km. The total sea area comprises about one million km^2, which is about ten-times larger than the territory of South Korea. The area under the jurisdiction of Korea is approximately 85,000 km^2, which is about 8.5% of the total area of the East Sea. The sea depth averages 1,684 meters, over four times deeper on average than the West Sea, with the deepest point reaching 4,049 meters, which is about 40 times deeper than the West Sea. The capacity is estimated at 1.7 million km^3.

Oceanographically, the yearly average water temperatures range from 8.6 to 15.9 degrees Celsius. Over the past 100 years, the surface water temperature of the East Sea has risen by some two degrees, which translates into an annual 0.06-degrees increase since the mid-1890s. This is twice the temperature rise in the oceans of the world. The surface of the East Sea has also risen by 6.5 mm over the past nine years, eroding over 130 sections of the coastline.

The currents of the East Sea can be divided into surface layer currents and deep sea currents. The surface currents consist of cold currents and warm currents, with different maritime plants and marine products in each. In contrast, the deep currents have a mixture of cold and warm currents.

2. Resources

The various resources contained in the East Sea can be divided into fishery resources, mineral resources, energy sources and seawater resources. A confluence of the clean cold and warm currents, the East Sea is abundant with marine products, including squid, sardines, mackerel, oysters, octopuses, shrimps, crabs, eels and anchovies. The mineral resources include phosphate, natural gas, methane gas and oil. The offshore wind power can be an important source of energy. As for the seawater resources, the sea has a great deal of potential for developing the clean, deep seawater rich in minerals due to eutrophy.[1]

3. East Sea, Yesterday

Since prehistoric times, the East Sea has formed a vital part of the lives of the residents on its shores. It was also a confluence where the two forces, one from the north and the

1) Park Chan-Hong, "Donghaewa Dogdoui Jayeongwahagjeog Gachi" ("The Value of the East Sea and Dokto Island in Natural Science"), *Donghaewa Hanguginui Salm (The East Sea and the Life of the Koreans)*, Society for East Sea and Korea Institute of Ocean Science & Technology, 2011.

other from the south, meet, have exchanges, and confront each other. For example, Goguryeo attempted to expand its territory through the East Sea and Silla conquered Usanguk, a state which governed Ulleungdo and the adjacent islands. Japan also used the sea when it invaded and abducted people during the Silla period.

Balhae, the successor to Goguryeo, maintained cordial ties with Japan through the convenient access of the East Sea, leaving behind many historical materials. From the Goryeo Dynasty onward, Korea made efforts to protect Ulleongdo Island from Japanese pirates. During the Joseon Dynasty, people engaged in fishing operations around Dokdo Island, an island annexed to Ulleungdo Island under the jurisdiction of Gangwon Province.

4. East Sea, Today and Tomorrow

Over the centuries, the East Sea has been a stage for exchange, cooperation, and conflict among South Korea, North Korea, Russia, Japan and even China which once secured a territory on its shores for future expansion to the sea.

The neighboring countries of the East Sea have taken advantage of the sea to promote their respective interests. The clashes of interest in areas of fishing, resource development and territorial disputes among the countries have produced many conflicts and made the sea a potential "powder keg" for wider conflicts.

The following is a summary of what each country has done and is expected to do with regard to the issue of the East Sea:

A. Japan

With the longest coastline among the coastal states of the East Sea, Japan has traditionally called the East Sea the "North Sea." Historically, while the areas adjacent to the Pacific have made rapid development as centers of foreign trade, the areas facing the East Sea have traditionally fallen behind for circumstantial reasons, even in the presence of some large cities and the Port of Niigata. However, Japan worked out a plan to invigorate major cities on the East Sea, such as Niigata and Toyama which have had exchanges with South Korea, North Korea, China and Russia, respectively. It was part of its scheme of what it called the "Japan Sea Rim Economic Bloc" which it formulated in 1988 in an effort to develop an economic bloc connecting Japan, South Korea, North Korea, Primorsky Krai of Russia and Northeast China.

In such exchanges, Japan aims to accomplish several

goals. First, as the coastal countries of the East Sea grow in importance as trade and defense partners, Japan wants to take the initiative by building on the Japan Sea Rim Economic Bloc. Second, Japan is keen to maintain the name, "Sea of Japan" for the East Sea. Above all, it has Japan Sea Rim Institutes at over ten universities along the East Sea coastline. The institute at Niigata University, the largest among them, holds a seminar twice per month. Japan also runs a nationwide Association of the Sea of Japan. Incidentally, some employees at the Niigata City Hall who speak Korean say "East Sea" instead of "Sea of Japan" when they talk to Koreans, presumably not to displease the Koreans. In sum, Japan seems to have decided to promote development of the entire country through the development of the East Sea coastline as the leader of the Japan Sea Rim Economic Bloc.

B. Russia

After proclaiming exchange and cooperation with the Pacific Rim states, including the East Sea Rim countries, through Gorbachev's Vladivostok Speech in 1986, Russia implemented an openness policy beginning in 1992 and through its decision to participate in the "East Sea Rim Economic Bloc." When it was made an issue, Russia stopped dumping nuclear waste clandestinely into the East Sea, a practice from the former Soviet Union. It took part in the Northeast Asia Regional Cooperation Program, UNDP, where the estuary of the Tumen River, including Russia's Hasan, China's Hunchun, North Korea's Rajin-Sonbong areas, was designated as a free trade zone. In 2000, the Putin government decided to develop Primorsky Krai under the slogan of "rebuilding a strong Russia."

Russia decided to build the Siberian gas pipeline to sell Siberian gas to large consumers, such as Korea and Japan, and connect the TSR (Trans-Siberian Railway) and the TKR (Trans-Korean Railway). It plans exchanges with Japan and China in this regard.

Vladivostok, where a naval base is located, was closed at first and only its neighboring Nakhodka was open. As Vladivostok became increasingly known to Korean tourists, it now has an ocean liner service to Sokcho, Korea, and an airline connection to Busan. Since the opening of the city, an increasing number of Russian tourists visit Korea as well as peddlers for suitcase trade.

C. China

Historically, China had to cede its territory of Sakhalin and Primorsky Krai to Russia in 1860 when it was under the Xianfeng Emperor after defeat in a war with Russia. Since then, China has been keen to gain access to the East Sea again. From the economic perspective, it aims to form what has been conceptualized as the Greater Chinese Economic Bloc by developing areas near the East Sea, including special economic zones. Ultimately, it sets the goal of forming the Chinese Federation. This is an approach based on the new Chinese imperialism. Specifically, China plans to gain access to the East Sea through the estuary of the Tumen River as part of its Southeast Project. Signing a contract in 2006 with North Korea on the joint management of Rajin-Sonbong of North Korea for 50 years, China also intends to make investments and station a naval fleet there. Some Chinese scholars are conducting studies on the East Sea with such intent in mind.

D. North Korea

Seeking to promote the foreign investment it so badly needs, North Korea declared Rajin-Sonbong a free trade and economic zone in 1991 to attract suitable Chinese investments. North Korea then laid a careful but solid foundation when it enacted the Free Economic and Trade Zone Act in 1993. For a variety of reasons, apparently North Korea also desires enhanced cooperation and exchanges with the East Sea Rim states and is poised to take part in such a movement.

E. South Korea

Korea has sought exchanges and expansion through the East Sea since the Goguryeo and Silla periods. It now plans to form the East Sea Rim Economic Bloc connecting ports along the middle part of the eastern coast of Korea with Tsuruga and Niigata on the island of Honshu, Japan. Even with a liner from Sokcho and air link from Busan, both to Vladivostok, Russia, the east coast of Korea has not seen much development except Ulsan and Pohang. However, as the east coast areas, especially Gangwon Province, has many spots favored by tourists, it is expected that tourist facilities will continue to be built.

In the 21st century, the East Sea has been undergoing probably its most significant transition. At this very moment, when new paradigms are being called for in every area, all East Sea Rim countries are being called upon to design and built a new political, economic, and human exchange model. Historically, the East Sea Rim has often been marked with strife and conflict among the relevant countries. Currently, it features territorial disputes between Russia and Japan, Korea and Japan, and China and Japan. In the future, however, it should be more characterized by international cooperation and mutual benefit.

Chapter 2

The Name "East Sea"

Cratylus, by Plato, records the argument between Cratylus, a student of Socrates, and Hermognes, on two theories of language that confronted each other in Greece. In the former, the naturalists, argued that language, or specifically names, are something called naturally in reflection of the inherent properties of the natural objects – hence, naturalism. In contrast, the latter, the conventionalists, held that names are determined on agreements in society – hence, conventionalism. Socrates is known to have agreed with naturalism at first and then leaned toward conventionalism later. Naturalists say that the "rocking stone" on Mt. Seorak has naturally been called by that name because it sways whenever visitors rock it.

Conventionalists say that a person should be called by a different name when he/she changes his/her name. In fact, both naturalism and conventionalism have a point.

It would be true to say that both theories reflect part of the truth, but not the whole truth. On the other hand, they do not necessarily conflict with each other. A name that came into being naturally by people calling it by the same name may undergo change when people start to call it by a different name. Then it can satisfy both naturalism and conventionalism. Therefore, the two theories are complementary and there is linguistic "motivation" between them. For example, "China" is called that way from the name of one of its ancient dynasties, Chin (or Qin in the current Romanization system), with an attachment of the female noun ending –a. Likewise, "America" derived from the Italian explorer Amerigo Vespucci with an attachment of the female noun ending –a. The "Pacific Ocean" was named that way because the ocean was peaceful. The "Indian Ocean" was named after India, the country dominantly sharing the coasts of the sea – a name that came into being reflecting both natural properties and people's agreements.

According to these arguments, what can be said about the naming of the "East Sea" or the "Sea of Japan"?

Lying east of Asia in general and the Korean Peninsula

in particular, the East Sea has been called that way for a long period of time by the Koreans and the residents of Manchuria. It thus reflects aspects of both naturalism and conventionalism. By contrast, the "Sea of Japan" began to be called that in the 19th century and gained international recognition following Japan's registration with the International Hydrographic Bureau (IHB) when Korea was under Japanese colonial rule. With Japan being only one of the countries sharing the sea, the name "Sea of Japan" is deemed neither natural nor of historicity that can draw agreements from other relevant countries.

In Semiotics, all names comprise three elements: To take the example of "East Sea," the first is the expression "East Sea" itself, which is called "signifiant"; the second is what signifiant means, or "signifé"; and the third is what they refer to, or "referent." Combined, these three create a name.

Names, therefore, not only distinguish and refer to all things in the world, but they also conjure up certain images and cause psychological modulations. The reason why we feel better when the name of our favorite object, being a person or thing, is mentioned is because the signifiant of the name brings up all the positive associations and make it present in our heart. The presence of the signifiant subrogates, substitutes and represents the object. When we cast a vote, we mark our choice beside or below of the name of the candidates, which allow us to reconstruct the characteristics or properties of the candidates. This is what the English verb "represent" or the French verb "représenter" does as part of its function.

In a broader sense, the name of an object, especially natural objects, also fulfills other functions as well. Natural objects are, in a manner of speaking, witnesses of historical events that take place while they exist. The name of the natural objects "tells" what they have witnessed to the later generations of people by way of bringing up all the images and stories that they know of through the readings. When the natural objects are handed down to the next generation, their name and what their name entails – the historical, cultural and emotional meanings – are also handed down.

For many Korean people, for example, "Miari Hill" is not just the name of a hill, it is a strong reminder of the tragedy of the Korean War. Mt. Baekdu is often associated with Dangun, the legendary founder of Korea. The East Sea is often cited as a place where King Munmu of the Silla Dynasty was buried according to his will that he wanted to become a dragon after death and protect the country. Handing down a name, therefore, is handing down the historical, cultural and emotional meanings that the name contains. Losing the name, then, means losing an important part of their raison d'être and their meanings along with it. The Korean people suffered such an experience of losing their personal names when they were forced to change their names to Japanese names under Japanese colonial rule. Now they find themselves in a situation where the name "East Sea" has been replaced internationally by "Sea of Japan," and many parts of the functions and meanings that the name has traditionally conveyed cannot be handed down to the next generation.

Then, how has the name East Sea been handed down to us historically? *Samguk sagi* (*History of the Three Kingdoms*) records important events mostly of the ancient Three Kingdoms, but also of some dating back to the founding of Korea. It mentions the East Sea in an episode about the dream of King Dongmyeong, the first ruler of Goguryeo (37 B.C. – A.D. 668), which corresponds with 59 B.C. This suggests that the name "East Sea" must have been used from the earlier time. It is almost certain that the name existed far earlier than 2,000 years ago. Chinese classics, including *Hou Hanshu* (後漢書, *Book of the Later Han*) and *Shan hai jing* (山海經, *Classic of Mountains and Seas*) recorded that the Jurchens called the sea to the south of Manchuria the "East Sea," an occurrence of over 2,000 years ago. *Goryeosa* (高麗

史, *History of Goryeo*) and *Joseon wangjo sillok* (朝鮮王朝實錄, *Annals of the Joseon Dynasty*) described natural disasters and unusual weather related to the East Sea.

To note the notation of geographical names in foreign countries in ancient times, place names – mostly inland ones – are not very often mentioned in historical books except in case of important historical events. The place names are often shown on old maps. The rivers, mountains, mountain ranges and large fields in foreign lands were mostly marked following the local names. However, the names of the seas were often given by map-makers and geographers of the times on the basis of the knowledge and information that they possessed. Sometimes, when there was more than one name for the same sea, they decided on the most reasonable name among the candidates. In those days when there was no international organization like the International Hydraugraphic Organization (IHO), sea names were often established in such a way. Just like such country names as Korea, China, Japan and America, sea names like the Pacific Ocean, the Atlantic Ocean, the Indian Ocean, the Bering Strait and the Magellan Strait went through the same process, sometimes with some modulations, to have today's name. The study of the name of the seas thus necessarily involves the research of the notation of the names on old maps. In the study of place names, the study of old maps is indispensable.

A close look at the notation of sea names on old European maps reveals that there were several principles in naming remote foreign seas. The most common principles include:

First, the names were determined in terms of their bearings from Europe. In the past, the Pacific Ocean was named "Mer du Sud" ("South Sea") for a long time because it was the sea that European sailors reached after going on a long voyage southward. Until the early 17th century, the East Sea and the sea area off the south of Japan were collectively called "Oceanus Orientalis" or "Mare Orientalis" because the body of water lay to the east of Europe. In the early 17th century, some European maps showed the East Sea as "Oceanus Occidentalis" because, after the discovery of the American Continent, it was deemed that the sea could then be reached by sailing west from the new continent.

The second principle is to name a sea by the name of the most important country in the neighborhood. The Indian Ocean, the Persian Gulf and the Arabian Sea are some of the examples. During the time when Korea did not yet appear on the maps, some maps marked the West Sea and the East Sea together as "Mare Cin" ("China

Sea") and the sea off the south of Japan as "Mare Cin" sometimes and "Mer du Japon" at other times. In the 18th century, some French and British maps labeled the East Sea as the "Sea of Korea" because geographically it was deemed to be the most appropriate.

The third is to name the sea after the name of its first known discoverer or navigator. The Strait of Magellan, the Bering Sea and the Bering Strait are some examples. The fourth is to give a name according to some characteristics of the sea, as exemplified by the Black Sea and the Red Sea.

In the area of study on names, including geographic ones, the study of sea names can be divided into two steps: The first is Onomasiology and the second, Onomastics.

Almost all names start with a common noun. Nouns comprising the onomasiological level are based on their etymological meanings. The "North Sea" was named that way because it was "the sea in the north" as a common noun. When it moves to the onomastic level and becomes a proper noun, it sheds off the etymological meaning on the onomasiological level and starts to function simply as a proper noun. It now refers to the sea in the vicinity of Scotland and being called "North Sea" by Norway, Island and Greenland to the north, Denmark, Lithuania and Latvia to the east, or anywhere in the world. By the same token, the

“East Sea,” in a shift from the onomasiological to onomastic level, loses its etymological meaning of “the sea in the east” and becomes simply a proper noun.

This principle holds even when the noun has a modifier and the linguistic value of the name does not change even on the onomastic level. For example, on the onomastic level too, the “Bering Sea” is a sea with a special relationship with Vitus Bering, a Danish navigator, and the “Indian Ocean” closely relates with India. In this light, the “Sea of Japan” can be said to be a misnomer, because Japan is neither a country dominantly neighboring the sea area nor does it have a special relationship with it. The sea area is shared by South Korea, North Korea, Russia and Japan and the name “Sea of Japan” has a history of only over 100 years. That is why the Korean people regard it unfair to call it with the country name of Japan and demand the name “East Sea,” which has a history of over 2,000 years, should at least be used as well. It is not understandable that the IHO, which has published *Limits of Oceans and Seas*, a special publication (SP-23), has evaded using both names citing procedural reasons, but in fact for no justifiable reasons, when it has corrected and changed the names of other seas.

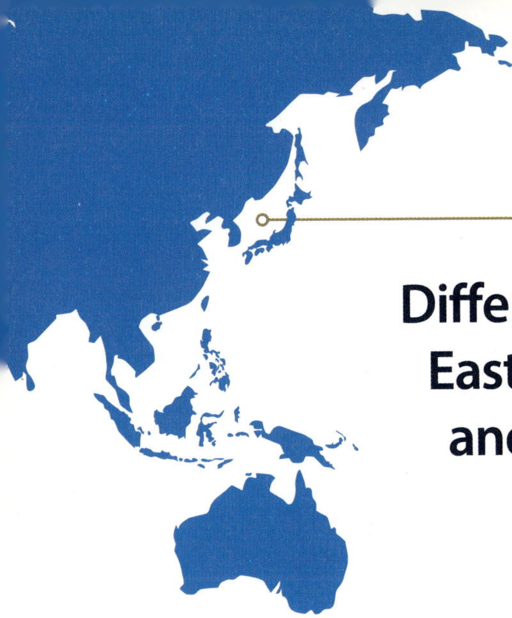

Chapter 3
Different Names of the East Sea/Sea of Japan and Their Toponymy

Korea and Japan have been in dispute over the naming of the East Sea over the past 20 years. Unlike in the case of Dokdo Island, however, regarding the issue of the naming of the East Sea, Japan has stuck to the notation of the Sea of Japan only, while Korea has worked to break the practice. During recent years, an increasing number of international news media has adopted the use of both names, the Sea of Japan and the East Sea. However, it is still hard to have major countries change their position on this issue until agreement is reached with Japan. The UN Conference on the Standardization of Geographical Names (UNCSGN) adopted a resolution, recommending that "when countries sharing a given geographical feature do not agree on a common name, it should be a general rule of cartography that the name used by each of the countries concerned will be accepted" and an endonym should be given priority over an exonym. Notwithstanding the resolution, Japan has refused to negotiate. Under these circumstances, in order to find a solution to this conundrum, both Korea and Japan need to review the historical background and toponymy of the names related to the East Sea/Sea of Japan and the names themselves.

According to a Russian study, there are about 400 names for the Caspian Sea. Historically, the East Sea has about 12 names with nine epithets, which can be classified into four groups as follows:

Group	Name	
Group I	1. Oriental Ocean (I)	(i) Ocean Eoum (East Ocean) (ii) Oceanus Orientalis Indicus (East Sea Beyond India)
	2. Oriental Ocean (II)	
	3. Oriental Sea	(i) Eoum Mare (East Sea) (ii) Mare Oriental Minus (Small East Sea) (iii) Kleine Orientalische Meer (Little East Sea)
	4. Donghae (East Sea)	(i) So Donghae (Small East Sea)
	5. East Sea	(i) Eastern Sea
Group II	6. Sea of Korea	(i) Gulf of Korea
	7. Josen Kai (Joseon Sea)	

Group	Name	
Group III	8. Riben Hai (Japan Sea)	(i) Oceanus Chinensis / Mare della China (China Ocean)
	9. Sea of Japan / Japan Sea	
	10. Nihon Kai (Japan Sea)	
Group IV	11. Septentrionale Sea / Boreal Sea (North Sea)	
	12. Hok Kai (North Sea)	

1. Oriental Ocean (I)

Denominated by Alberto Cantino of Italy in 1502 for the sea area of Southeast Asia and the East Sea, the name was used in Italy, the Netherlands and France. “Ocean Eoum” or “Ocean Eous” was used as an epithet and simply means the same, Oriental Ocean, which was only marked in Greek to give an exotic nuance. Martin Behaim and Laurent Friese of Germany used “Oceanu Orientalis Indicus” because the two seas were, as they saw, beyond India.

2. Oriental Ocean (II)

Although indicated the same, “Oriental Ocean (I)” and “Oriental Ocean (II)” refer to different seas: Oriental Ocean (II) refers only to the East Sea. Pierre Briet was a French Jesuit priest who came from the same hometown as Nicolas Sanson, a famous cartographer, and worked in cooperation with him. He came to know from his colleagues who had been to Beijing that the Manchus were calling the sea off the south of Manchuria the "East Sea." When he made a map of Japan in 1655, he translated it as the "Oriental Ocean." Today, an ocean means something larger than a sea (*mer* in French), but at the time, the two terms were used interchangeably. In the 1660s, Sanson had Briet supervise the two atlases that he was about to publish. Afterwards, Sanson and his successors applied this name only to the East Sea. It may be questioned whether Oriental Ocean (II) can be regarded as an endonym because it is a translation of an endonym. However, it certainly is a loanword because it was used in France for the French-speaking people. After Briet, others who used this name included Alain Manesson Mallet and Jean Baptiste Tavernier.

3. Oriental Sea

In his 1528 *Isolario*(*Book of Islands*), Benedetto Bordone of Italy marked the South Sea of Korea and the sea areas that include part of the Pacific Ocean as "Mare Orientale," which, however, excluded the East Sea.

In the late 17th century when it was known to France that the "East Sea" was the endonym for the sea area, however, Guillaume Delisle first used the name in the translation, "Mer Orientale." As the chief royal geographer geographer, he could acquire plenty of information and have exchanges with missionaries. He stuck to the name after he gained the knowledge that the "East Sea" was the endonym and started to identify it as such, beginning with his "L'Asie" in 1698. However, as more and more people perceived the East Sea as "Mer de Corée," he made it clear that "Mer de Corée" and "Mer Orientale" refer to the same sea in *Carte des Indes et de la Chine* (*Map of India and China*) in 1705.

The map-maker who lent support to the notation of Guillaume Delisle was Nicolas de Fer. Having published over 700 kinds of maps and atlases during his lifetime, he was a successful map seller and a great source of information. De Fer seems to have obtained from missionaries his information that the "East Sea" was the endonym. At the top of an East Asian map of 1703, he added a very unusual note: "Mer peu ou point connue des Européens. Les Tartares l'appelle [sic] Orientale" ("The sea is little or not known to Europeans. The Manchus call it [sic] Oriental"). Here, the "Oriental Sea" cannot be an endonym for the same reason as the "Oriental Ocean."

The epithet "Eoum Mare" is a combination of a Greek word meaning "East" and the French word meaning "Sea." It is a translation of what Father Antoine Thomas heard from the Kangxi Emperor when he accompanied the Chinese emperor to Manchuria in 1690 and heard him describing the sea to the south of Manchuria as the "East Sea." Johann Homann of Germany indicated the East Sea as "Mare Orientale Minus" in the meaning of a "small sea" on his 1707 map of Asia. Hasius, a student of Homann, also used the name. However, Franz Ludwig Güssefeld labeled the East Sea as "Kleine Orientalische Meer" ("Little East Sea") with an addition of a diminutive on the map of "Russische Reigh" ("Russian Empire") in 1786.

4. Donghae

As previously noted, the name "Donghae" (or "Tonghae" according to the former Korean Romanization system, meaning "East Sea") is mentioned in the episode about King Dongmyeong, the founder of Goguryeo, in *Samguk sagi*, which corresponds to A.D. 59. The East Sea is mentioned 15 times in the book and 14 times in *Samguk yusa* (三國遺事, *Memorabilia of the Three Kingdoms*). The name, therefore, can be said to have always been part of the history of the Korean people. The biggest misunderstanding about the name is that because it is a name based on a bearing and thus too common and general, it is not appropriate as a proper noun for a sea. This is part of the reason Japan has not been considering the name seriously.

The truth, however, is that the name of seas has been determined based on the bearing regardless of the East and the West. Etymologically, the East Sea too means the sea to the east of the Korean Peninsula. However, it is long before that the name has lost its etymological meaning on the onomasiological level and taken the simple function of referring to the specific sea area on the onomastic level – a name that is called as such wherever in the world, be it Americas in the east, Australia in the south, Russia in the north or Europe in the West. The only time when such a name becomes a problem is when it includes the name of a certain individual, organization or country.

The name "East Sea" was known even to Japan early on. When Korea sent to Japan some Buddhist Sutras during the Joseon Dynasty, Japan responded with a letter of gratitude where it mentioned the "East Sea" in expressing its appreciation.

Many historical documents attest that the name "East Sea" was known to China too from a long time ago. It is generally known that the name started to be used after the Sui and Tang Dynasties and came into wider use from the establishment of the Qing Dynasty, mostly by the Jurchens, to the end of the 19th century. However, such Chinese scholars as Wu Songdi, Gu Renhe and Liu Xin

Jun state that the name "East Sea" was already used in *Hou Hanshu* and *Shan hai jing* in relation to the Dongyi, or "Eastern Barbarians" referring to ancient peoples living in eastern China and in lands east of China. *Hou Hanshu* was published in the 5th century and covers the history of the Han Dynasty from A.D. 6 to 189. The present version of *Shan hai jing* is of the early Han Dynasty and its earlier forms are known to have existed a few centuries earlier. Cheng Long asserts that the use of the term "East Sea" has never ceased since the Jurchens existed. Whether from the Korean records or from the Chinese testimony, the name "East Sea" is a complete endonym, which is also recognized by Japanese scholars.

The "So Donghae" ("Small East Sea"), an epithet of the East Sea, is a notation that Giulio Aleni, a Jesuit priest, used for the East Sea when he made a map of East Asia in 1623 with a view to revising and supplementing the map of Matteo Ricci, also a Jesuit priest. It is considered that Father Aleni knew that the "East Sea" was the endonym. The question is, why did he then add the diminutive?

According to Chinese scholars, the sea area that China had interest in was mostly the northern part of the East Sea where its easternmost territory met the sea. However, after China ceded the land on the north of the East Sea, including

Sakhalin, to Russia during the reign of the Xianfeng Emperor, some Chinese called the northern part of the East Sea "Small Sea" and the southern part "Great Sea." Therefore, the name "Small East Sea" can be interpreted as a combination of "Small Sea" and "East Sea."

5. East Sea

On the onomasiological level, the "East Sea" is an English name derived from the combination of "East" and "Sea" to refer to the sea area to the east of the Korean Peninsula. As it is an English name and English is not the native or official language of Korea, some experts on geographical names might consider it to be an exonym.

If native speakers of a foreign country called Donghae "East Sea," it would certainly be an exonym. However, the "East Sea" is a term that the Korean government made by means of translating the Korean name "Donghae" for the understanding of foreigners. Another factor that should be taken into consideration is the status of English education in Korea. In the past, English was a second language that was taught starting from middle school. Now it is taught from the third grade in elementary school and by native speakers in many cases. In large cities, many kindergartens provide English-only service. These circumstances should be considered in determining whether the name East Sea is an endonym or an exonym.

If a native people, of whom only some can communicate in English with each other, has changed the name of a place in their country to English for the benefit of native English speakers, then is the name an exonym or an endonym? We believe that one of the basic dividing lines between the endonym and the exonym would be drawn between whether a name was given in a foreign country for the convenience of themselves and whether it was made within a country for the convenience of foreigners.

The epithet "Eastern Sea" came into being when John Senex, an active map-maker in the 18th century, gave the name to the East Sea on his map "Asie" in 1721. There is little chance that he knew the endonym of the sea area and translated it into English. Considering the influence of French maps on the maps of the Great Britain, Senex seems to have referred to the maps of Guillaume Delisle or de Fer. Later, Senex marked the East Sea as the "Eastern Sea," "Korea Sea" or "Oriental Sea."

6. Sea of Korea

The map-maker who identified the East Sea as the "Sea of Korea" for the first time was Manuel Godinho de Erédia.

He used the term on a map of East Asia that he published in Macau in 1615. Probably because it was published in Macau, the map seems to have not been received very well in Portugal, the author's home country. The next one who marked the East Sea with the country name Korea was Arnoldus Montanus, a former Dutch Protestant minister. On a supplement map to his 1669 book on Japan, he indicated the East Sea as the "Sea of Korea." This book was very popular in Europe and was translated into many European languages. It is estimated to have laid a foundation to make the 18th century the golden age of the "Sea of Korea." Following him, Tavernier, Chambon and Jacques-Nicolas Bellin also marked the East Sea as "Mer de Corée" ("Sea of Korea"). The notable fact is that the books of Montanus and of Tavernier were both about Japan. There is no doubt that they had no relationship with Korea and knew almost nothing about it. Still, the marking of "Sea of Korea" was possible supposedly because of, above all, Korea's geographical location. From the late 17th century, Korea was depicted on European maps as a Peninsula stretching straight from north to south, while Japan was a series of islands from northeast to southwest. If map-makers had to include the name of a country in the name of the East Sea on the basis of the geographical locations of the two countries, they would would supposedly prefer Korea to Japan as a more reasonable choice.

Another reason relates to their linguistic habits. In contrast to the way many Asian peoples at the time wrote, the Europeans wrote from left to right when using a pen. Important parts of the sentences, like verbs, objects and complements appear on the right but their gender and number are governed by the subject on the left. From this perspective, for the name of the sea on the right hand side of the Korean Peninsula, Korea would have naturally taken precedence over Japan.

However, the Sea of Korea is not the best name because Korea is not the only country that borders this sea area. In addition to South Korea, the sea is also shared by Japan, Russia and North Korea; and China too is a close neighbor. It would be an egocentric attitude to assert that only the name of Korea should be used as part of the sea name.

The epithet "Gulf of Korea" for the East Sea was first used by Thomas Kitchin of Great Britain in his map, "Asia According to the Sieur d'Anville" in 1772. Later, J. Hinton and Robert Sayer used the name and it also appears on the maps of others. Here, "Gulf" may have been used in the same manner as "Minus" or "Kleine," taking the sea as relatively small. Otherwise, it simply came into being as the first user noticed what is now the Donghan Gulf on the east coast of Korea.

7. Josen Kai (Joseon Sea)

The first map-maker who marked the East Sea as "Josen Kai" ("Joseon Sea") was Takahashi Kageyasu. He was in charge of cartography of the Shogunate of Japan at the time. On "Nippon henkai ryakuzu" (日本邊界略圖, "Simplified Map of Japan's Periphery") that he made in 1809 at the request of the Shogunate, Takahashi indicated the sea off the east coast of Korea as "朝鮮海" ("Josen Kai" in Japanese pronunciation, meaning "Joseon Sea"). Since there is no other name on the map for what is now the East Sea, the name is taken as a marking for the entire East Sea. There is no chance that the marking was an individual one that Takahashi made on his own initiative against the official position of the Shogunate.

Some infer that Takahashi made the indication because European maps at the time had the marking of "Sea of Korea" for the East Sea. However, the same author's "Shintei bankoku zenzu" (新訂萬國全圖, "New and Revised World Map") that he made the following year may give a better clue. On the map, he marked the sea east of the Korean Peninsula as "Josen Kai" and the sea south of Japan as "大日本海" ("Dainihon Kai" or "Great Japan Sea"). Quite a lot of European maps, of course, also indicated the sea off the south of Japan as the "Sea of Japan," including Robert Dudley's map of 1646. But the marking of "Great Japan Sea" on the Pacific Ocean side seems to represent what may be described as the "Japanese Shogunate's spirit to expand to the world." In this situation, it must have been difficult for Takahashi to mark the East Sea area too as the Japan Sea. Anyway, Takahashi and his students marked the East Sea as "Josen Kai" until the 1870s.

8. Riben Hai (Japan Sea)

As is widely known, the East Sea was marked "日本海" ("Riben Hai" in Chinese pronunciation) for the first time in the world on Matteo Ricci's "Kunyu wanguo quantu" (坤輿萬國全圖, "A Map of the Myriad Countries of the World") of 1602. However, as it was too large and the markings were made in Chinese, the map did not have much influence on Europe. It did not do much either to the way Japan labeled the East Sea, although it opened the eyes of the Japanese people to the world. Some Japanese scholars say that when he arrived in China, Ricci might have met missionaries on their way home from Japan and acquired the information about the "Japan Sea." However, if he did meet the missionaries, there is no chance that he heard the name

"Riben Hai" from them because it was only in 1802 that the name "Japan Sea" was first indicated for the East Sea in Japan by Ine Takago, 200 years after Ricci.

Supposedly, Ricci used the name Riben Hai for some good reasons. First, Japan was known to Europe as it had trade with European countries, including Portugal and the Netherlands, from early on. A number of books on Japan had been published in Europe and many countries were seeking trade with Japan. As Japan wanted to receive missionaries from European countries, the Europeans had a good image of the Japanese. Accordingly, regarding the sea area between Korean and Japan, the chances were that the Europeans choose Japan over Korea if they had to put the name of a country in the sea name as the trend in Europe at the time dictated.

Second, by contrast, Korea was known to Europe only as a Peninsula until the mid-17th century and its closed-door policy prevented contact with or access to foreigners even when European countries wanted to trade with or send missionaries to Korea. Ricci wanted to introduce Europe to Korea, a completely unknown country there, using information from China. So on his map, he made the unusual but tactful note about facts on Korea, including its history, in the east of the Korean Peninsula. Under these circumstances, it might have been not easy for him to give the sea area the name Korea.

Third, there is no possibility for Ricci to hear from the Manchus that the sea area to the east of the Korean Peninsula was called the "East Sea" because he arrived in Beijing via Zhongyuan from southern China. If he had landed on Sakhalin, which was part of the Chinese territory at the time, and arrived at Beijing via Manchuria, it is most likely that he would have obtained the information that the sea was called the East Sea, not Japan Sea, while passing settlements of the Jurchens and marked that way on his map. Nonetheless, Ricci made the marking of "Riben Hai" not at the center of the East Sea but closer to Japan, implying the possibility that if he did not provide the note on Korea in the space of the East Sea on his map, he might have put "Sea of Korea" there.

Be that as it may, while further research is necessary on how the East Sea was indicated on the maps in Japan that copied Ricci's map, the name "Japan Sea" did not attract any attention in Japan. Meanwhile, to the missionaries stationed in China, Ricci's naming was a hot potato: Following it meant hiding the truth and following the truth meant denying the naming of Ricci, one of the founders of the Jesuit China missions.

Father Aleni, who came to know the endonym, marked the East Sea as the "Small East Sea" when he revised and supplemented Ricci's map in 1623. Other missionaries reached different conclusions of their own. When he published *Nous Atlas Sinensis* (*New Atlas of China*) together with Joan Blaeu in 1655, Father Martino Martini left the East Sea blank. Father Ferdinand Verbiest, who is known as Nan Huairen (南懷仁) in Chinese, embraced the two names and used the name "Mer Orientale ou du Japon" ("East Sea or Sea of Japan"), with the East Sea first, on a world map of 1669. However, Father Atoine Thomas, who arrived in China in 1686, went further to label the East Sea as simple "Mare Coreanum" ("Sea of Korea") on in his 1690 map of East Asia. The four years in China may not have been long enough for him to get acquainted with the affairs of the host and neighboring countries. How then was he able to call the East Sea "Sea of Korea" without hesitation? One hypothesis is that Father Thomas read a book by Arnoldus Montanus, who came from Flanders like himself, and saw the marking of the "Sea of Korea" on the "Map of Japan," an appendix to the sensational bestseller in the Netherlands. Until then, no one called the East Sea "Sea of Korea" except Montanus. Later, Father Thomas kept a journal of accompanying the Kangxi Emperor where he said he learned that the East Sea was the endonym from the emperor. However, he did not publish a revised edition of the map.

As another epithet of the East Sea, there was "Oceanus Chinensis" or "Mare della China." In the names used for the East Sea in the 17th century, "ocean" and "sea" were synonyms. Reckoning that the sea areas of Southeast Asia, including the East Sea, were under the Chinese influence, Abraham Ortelius in 1570 and Gerardus Mercator in 1587 used "Mare Cin" (China Sea) and Johannes Janssonius also used "Oceanus Chinese" in 1658.

9. Sea of Japan/Japan Sea

Father Christopher Blancus, a missionary to Japan, was the first in Europe to use the name "Sea of Japan." The Japanese say that the marking "Mare de Japâ" that Diogo Homem made on his map "Asia" in 1568 was the first, but this is far from the actual depiction of the map. Portuguese merchants arrived in Japan in 1543 and started the intermediary trade. And true, there was a country marked "Iapan" on the map made by Lopo Homem, father of Diogo Homem, in 1554. However, there is neither Japan nor any country that looks like Japan on Diogo's map. Under these circumstances, the marking of the "Sea of Japan" on the sea areas of Southeast Asia cannot be considered to have any serious meaning.

After Ricci and Blancus, Jean Baptiste Nolin named the East Sea as "Mer du Japon" on his map "L'Asie" in 1704. As is widely known, Jean-François de La Pérouse indicated the East Sea as the "Sea of Japan" on his "Carte générale des Decouvertes" ("General Map of Discoveries") in 1797. It had a great influence on the markings of other maps in the 19th century. In Great Britain, Laurie and Whittle used the name "Sea of Japan" on their "Asia" in 1799. Later, Codell and G. Thomson made the same marking. In the Netherlands, Philipp Franz von Siebold, a German physician, naturalist and cartographer who married a Japanese woman, indicated the East Sea as "Japanisches See" on his map "Nippon" in 1832.

With regard to the use of the name "Sea of Japan," Japan makes an implausible claim that any markings that include "Japan," whether it be the "Sea of Japan," the "West Sea of Japan," the "North Sea of Japan" or the "East Sea of Japan" in the sea areas of Southeast Asia and near the Bering Sea refer to the Sea of Japan. In fact, however, until La Pérouse there was only a small number of indications of the Sea of Japan; and it has been just over 100 years since the use of the name increased under his influence: Simply put, the name is by no means a match to the East Sea.

10. Nihon Kai (Japan Sea)

"Nihon Kai" is the Japanese translation of the Chinese transliteration "Riben Hai." Since Shiba Kokan used the name "Inland Sea of Japan" in 1792, Ine Takago used "Sea of Japan" on his map of 1802 but it was 200 years later than Matteo Ricci.

Some experts on place names infer that, because the "East Sea" is an endonym, "Nihon Kai" is also an endonym as it is a Japanese name used by the Japanese in Japan. However, it is a misunderstanding stemming from the lack of knowledge on the formation of the name "Sea of Japan." More than anything else, the "Sea of Japan" was a name that had not been used in Japan and that the Japanese accepted 200 years later than Ricci's "Riben Hai," 185 years after the term appeared in Europe. In addition, while the "East Sea" has become a proper noun, losing its etymological meaning and only implementing the function of referring to the sea area to the east side of the Korean Peninsula, "Nihon Kai," with the name of a country in it, maintains the etymological value and makes it Japan's or a sea with a special relationship with Japan. In the end, this will make the sea area irrelevant to South Korea, North Korea and Russia, which share the sea. The name reflecting a Japanese monopoly would not be easily accepted by the sea's neighboring countries.

11. Septentrionale Sea/Boreal Sea (North Sea)

"Septentrionale" derived from the mythology about the seven plow oxen working at the North Pole. "Boreal," originating from the ancient Greek mythology meaning the north wind, came from an adjective meaning, "of the natural conditions in the north." Both relating to the north, they form an almost complete synonym. After Bernardino Ginnaro, who had been to Japan, marked the East Sea as "Mare Boreal" on a map of Japan in 1630, Robert Dudley marked on the map of Korea and Japan in his book *Dell'Arcano del Mare* (*Secrets of the Sea*) of 1646, "Mare Di Corai" ("Sea of Korea") in the middle of the East Sea in large square type, and "Oceano Boreale del Giappone" ("North Sea of Japan") in the sea off the north of Japan, and "Mare di Iezo" ("Hokkaido Sea") in the sea off the northeast of Japan, both in cursive type. After Dudley's death in 1649, the book was re-published in 1661 with a slight change in the markings. First, a cartouche appeared in the middle of the East Sea, pushing the large-typed "Mare di Corai" closer to the Korean Peninsula with the marking "Il Mare Settentrionale di Iappone Ō Giappone" ("The North Sea of Japan") off the north of Japan in cursive type for the "North Sea of Japan." Here, "Mare di Corai" can be considered as the name of the sea area while "Oceano Boreale del Giappone" and "Il Mare Settentrionale di Iappone Ō Giappone" can be regarded as explanatory notes to the sea. De Fer also used the same name, "Mer Septentrionale du Japon" in 1896. The two cartographers seem to have attempted to explain what North Sea it was by supplementing the name of the country with the information that the sea area was called the "North Sea" in Japan.

12. Hok Kai (North Sea)

Surrounded by the seas on all four sides, Japan did not traditionally name the seas, and instead made only bearing marks on maps. Of course, it would have been obvious to them which sea they referred to even when they simply said, "North Sea," "East Sea," "South Sea" and "West Sea." Since it would have been enough for them to avoid confusion, they seem to have been used as substitutes for proper names of the seas. Among them, the "North Sea" apparently functioned almost as a proper name. According to Dr. Shim Jeongbo, until the end of the 19th century, many Japanese textbooks, dictionaries, newspaper articles and history and geography books used "North Sea" where "Sea of Japan" should supposedly have been used, suggesting that the Japanese were accustomed to the term.[2] However, Japanese

2) Shim Jeongbo, "Ilboneseo Ilbonhae Jimyeonge Gwanhan Yeongu

scholars tend never to mention the name "North Sea" supposedly in an attempt to conceal the truth and maintain the current name "Sea of Japan."

Ultimately, the "East Sea" is a complete endonym, while the "Sea of Japan" ("Nihon Kai/Japan Sea") is clearly an exonym. In the past, the Japanese explained that foreign countries used the term "Sea of Japan" first and they simply accepted it. However, realizing that such a claim meant that the East Sea had not been called "Sea of Japan" in Japan and was nothing but a confession that the term is an exonym, they recently changed its stance and started to argue that the name was used in Japan prior to being used in foreign countries and was later known to them – a groundless and absurd argument. And those with the opinion that the East Sea is an exonym because it is a translated name will find that it is different from other place names of seemingly the same construction once they understand the origin of its English name and the reality of the use of English in Korea.

Donghyang" ("Research Trends in Japan on the Place Name 'Sea of Japan'"), *Journal of the Korean Cartographic Association*, 2007, no.2, p.18, Korean Cartographic Association.

Chapter 4

International Organizations and the Name " East Sea"

As explained above, the name "East Sea" has been used in Korea for over 2,000 years without any changes during the period. When they noticed the markings of "Sea of Japan" on the maps used by American soldiers during the Korean War – probably the first time Koreans encountered Western maps collectively in modern times – most Koreans simply thought that it was a wrong marking, a mistake, or something on the part of the map-makers who did not know the local situation. To them, it was too obvious that there was no chance the sea was called by any other name than "Donghae" or "East Sea." However, in 1990, the Korean president, learning that the sea area was marked "Sea of Japan" internationally, instructed the relevant government agencies to do the necessary research.

It was found that during the time when Korea was a Japanese colony, Japan registered the name of the sea as "Sea of Japan" with the IHO before the Koreans were aware of it, and thus it came into common use on the international scene. Moreover, Japan not only took the Koreans' personal names by forcing them to change their names to Japanese names during the colonial period, it also took the name of a natural heritage, the East Sea, that had been with the Korean people for a very long time. The Koreans did not know that the name was stolen during the colonial period and, after their liberation from Japan in 1945, they could not afford to take much interest in the matter, amidst the chaos immediately after the liberation under the U.S. military administration – in addition to the unstable political situation after South Korea established its first modern government in 1948, followed by the devastating Korean War in 1950-1953 and the May 16 coup in 1961.

The notation of the East Sea involves two problems: The first is linguistics as it is a name and the second is hydrography as it concerns ships navigating the sea. In linguistics, the issue of the standardization of geographical names was raised by Albrecht Penck of Germany at the International Geographic Congress held in Bern, Switzerland, in 1891.[3] It was, however, after World War II

3) Peter E. Raper, "The UN and Standardization of Geographical Names," The International Seminar on the Standardization of Geographical

that his proposal was accepted by the UN and discussed in detail. Prior to this, the name "Sea of Japan" was registered with the IHO, which, organized in 1919 to ensure safer navigation of vessels on sea, formalized it as an international name through its publication *Limits of Oceans and Seas*. Now, let us take a look at the IHO and the issue of the East Sea based on the research by Lee Ki-suk, honorary president of the Society for East Sea.

1. IHO

The increase in the number of ships in the world in the 19th century made it necessary to unify business on international navigation and waterways. Preliminary meetings were held in Washington in 1899 and St. Petersburg in 1912 and based on the meetings, the International Hydrographic Conference was held in London, the center of the world's maritime business, in 1919. A total of 24 countries participated in the IHC, including 18 major countries, such as the UK, the USA, France and Japan, and colonized countries of the UK, such as Australia, India and Egypt. Korea, a colony of Japan at the time, did not know about the conference and if it did, Japan would not have allowed Korea to participate in it.

The IHC aims to ensure that all the world's seas, oceans

Names, Session I, 1997, The Society for East Sea.

and navigable waters are surveyed and charted in a unified form and that information be exchanged on waterways-related affairs in forums for experts. Although designating names of the seas was not its main purpose, it was required to publish atlases to ensure navigation, and the general meeting of the IHC established the IHO in 1919 and set up the International Hydrographic Bureau (IHB) in 1921 to oversee maritime affairs.

The London Conference in 1919 passed an important resolution regarding the notation of oceans and seas. The notation would be made primarily by literal transcription and avoid phonetical transcription. The member countries of the IHB would prepare alphabetic notations of their relevant bodies of waters.

Together with this, the 1919 Conference also adopted a resolution on the limits of the oceans (Resolution, Section IV-B) or "Recommended plan for providing for the notice of geographic navigation so that waterway charts and indication of lighthouse can be coincided." According to this Resolution, the member countries presented to the IHB the data on the limits of their respective seas. With the data thus collected, the IHB drew up a plan and distributed it in the form of a circular (No. 1-H of 23) to the member countries to inquire if they had any dissent about the plan. The plan clearly stated the notation of "Japan Sea" and the limits of the sea area. The proceedings of the 2nd IHC, held in Monaco in 1926, recorded the feedback of the member countries but not a single discussion was held on the name "Japan Sea."[4]

In reply, Japan asked the IHC to add "Naikai or Inland Sea" to the list of the sea areas written in two names and partially corrected the Northeast limit of the "Japan Sea." The IHB then made adjustments to the limits of the sea areas at issue and distributed the final publication "Spec. Pub. No. 23" at the Complementary International Hydrographic Conference held in Monaco in 1929 for official authorization. The name "Japan Sea" was thus established. Although the *Limits of Oceans and Seas* was revised in 1937, 1953 and 1986, the issue of the "Japan Sea" was never raised during the time and the name has been used on most charts and many world maps.

In 1972, the IHB adopted a resolution on the notation of place names as a guideline in giving geographical names. According to the resolution:

A.4.2 International Standardization of Geographical Names

A.4.2.6 It is recommended that where two or more countries share a given geographical feature (*such as a*

4) IHB, Report of Proceedings, p.47, 1926.

bay, strait, channel or archipelago) under different names, they should endeavor to reach agreement on a single name for the feature concerned. If they have different official languages and cannot agree on a common name form, it is recommended that the name forms of each of the languages in question should be accepted for charts and publications, unless technical reasons prevent this practice on small scale charts.[5]

Admittedly, the IHO, currently not an affiliated organization of the UN but an intergovernmental organization, does not have compelling powers over countries that do not follow its resolutions. But it is a entirely different matter when the organization does not comply with its own resolutions. Korea joined the IHO in 1957 as a regular member and has sent a government delegate to the regular IHO general meetings, starting from the 8th meeting in 1962. In 1997, Korea pointed out to the IHB that the notation of "Japan Sea" could not be justified and demanded correction thereof. It also explained to the IHO member countries that "East Sea" was the proper name.

---

5) Lee Ki-Suk, "Gugjesulogiguwa Ilbonhae Pyogiui Gongsighwa Gwajeong" ("IHO and the Formalization of the Name 'Sea of Japan,'") *Donghaeyeonguhoe Hagsul Balpyo Daehoe Nonmunjib (Collection of the Papers Presented at the Academic Conference of the Society for East Sea)*, The Society for East Sea, 1997.

At the recommendation of the IHO, Japan had some perfunctory meetings with Korea where they did nothing but attempt to justify the notation of "Japan Sea" to the Korean representatives and refused to heed Korea's proposals. If both names are used, Japan argued, it could create confusion for the navigation of ships. It further argued that Korea's demand ran counter to the spirit of the IHO because it was a political one when the organization is responsible for technical problems in maritime affairs. Based on these unreasonable arguments, Japan has denied any possibility for compromise in the first place.

2. UN Conference on the Standardization of Geographical Names (UNCSGN) and (UN Group of Experts on Geographical Names (UNGEGN)

After World War II, many new countries emerged all around the world. One of the problems that these newly independent states faced was getting rid of the geographical names that were determined during their colonial years and regain their original names. During the process, many disputes and conflicts occurred when the places in question were beyond a single sovereignty. The disputing countries went to the UN seeking a settlement, and the United Nations Economic and Social Commission (UNESCO) became the venue for discussion on this mater. The UN had acknowledged the necessity for standardizing georgaphical names before the war when it was the United Union and had interest in the problem. In 1948, the UNESCO adopted the Resolution 131 (*vi*) to provide a foundation for geographical experts to gather together and discuss this matter. In 1949, they met at Lake Success and discussed the problem. In 1956, the UNESCO adopted a resolution for the standardization of geographical names in an effort to standardize them internationally. In 1959, the UNESCO adopted Resolution 715 (*XXVII*) Part A to form the UNGEGN and hold regular meetings for the standardization of place names. As a result, it was decided that a meeting of the UNGEGN would be held every two years and the UNCSGN, every five years.

In the 1st UNCSGN in 1967, the meeting adopted the resolution that recommends countries to set up an organization solely responsible for geographical names. According to the reports sent to the UNGEGN and relevant subcommittees, many countries had not had such an organization until then and it was about time when they started to show interest in the matter. In 1977, the 3rd UNCSGN passed the Resolution III/20 where it strongly urged consultation, mutual recognition, agreement and acceptance of different names from one's own in standardizing geographical names.

However, according to Professor Peter E. Raper,[6] former chairman of the UNGEGN, the top priority in the standardization of geographic names at the early meetings was the need to reduce the exonyms and replace them with endomyms. The UNCSGN's definition of the exonym and endonym was devised by Brahim Atoui, then Vice Chair of the organization. He defined the exonym as "a name used in a specific language for a geographical feature situated outside the area where the language has official status and differing in its form from the name used in the official language or languages of the area where the geographical feature is situated" and the endonym is "a name of a geographical feature in one of the languages occurring in that area where the feature is situated."[7]

In light of these definitions, which are contained in the UNGEGN's Glossary of Terms, "Nihon Kai" and "Japan Sea" are both exonyms because they are the translation of "Riben Hai" (日本海), the Chinese name for the geographical feature situated outside the area where the Chinese language

---

6) Raper, "The UN and Standardization of Geographical Names."

7) Brahim Atoui, "'Donghae,' 'Nihon Kai,' 'Sea of Japan' or 'East Sea': Is it a Question of Qualification and Categorization in Exonym, Endonym, Allonym or Translated Name?" The 17th International Seminar on Sea Names, 2011, The Society for East Sea/Northeast History Foundation.

has official status. By contrast, "Donghae," with its history of over 2,000 years, is an endonym because it is the Korean name of the geographical feature occurring in that area where the Korean language has official status and the feature is situated. "East Sea" is what the Korean government translated the endonym "Donghae" for the convenience of foreigners, it can also be considered as a psedo-endonym. Regarding this matter, however, Paul Woodman, former member of the UNGEGN and former Secretary of the United Kingdom Permanent Committee on Geographical Names, says that "Tong Hae" is an endonym in Korean and, likewise, "Nihon Kay" is also a Japanese endonym because it is Japanese.[8] This is, however, a perspective from those who do not know about the historicity of the place names. How can "Sea of Japan" be an endonym when it is the translation of what Matteo Ricci marked as "Riben Hai" in Chinese in 1602 and Blancus marked as "Mare Japonicum" in 1617, which Ine Takago translated in 1802? By contrast, Tong Hae is a 2,000-year old Korean name and the "East Sea" is a word not imported but devised in Korea – a name of a completely different nature to "Sea of Japan."

According to Raper, "Each country has territorial

8) Paul Woodman, "The See of the Three Endonyms," The 15th International Seminar on Sea Names, 2009, The Society for East Sea/Northeast History Foundation.

waters of 12 nautical miles in extent under its jurisdiction, measured from the low-tide baselines. Beyond the territorial waters the sea extending to a distance of 24 nautical miles from the baselines are the Contiguous and Maritime Cultural Zones of the country. The sea beyond the Territorial Waters to a distance of 200 nautical miles is the Exclusive Economic Zone. Beyond these limits are international waters, falling beyond the jurisdiction of any one country, and sometimes called the high seas ... There is no official language in areas covered by the high seas, the term exonym is also appropriate to refer to high seas."[9] And, "the Korean name Tong Hae has the terminological status of an endonym in the territorial waters of Korea and acquires the status of an exonym in the territorial waters of Japan, while the Japanese name Nihon Kai has the terminological status of an endonym in the territorial waters of Japan and becomes an exonym in the territorial waters of Korea."[10]

---

9) Peter E. Raper, "Interpreting United Nations Resolutions on Geographical Names," The 16th International Seminar on Sea Names, 2010, The Society for East Sea/Northeast History Foundation.

10) Naftali Kadmon, "Endonym or Exonym – is there a Missing Term in Maritime Names?" 9th United Nations Conference on the Standardization of Geographical Names, New York, 21 - 30 August 2007; United Nations, New York, E/CONF.98/ 6/Add.1, quoted in P. Jordan, "Is 'Exonym' an Appropriate Term for Names of Features Beyond any Sovereignty?" The 16th International Seminar on Sea Names, 2010, The Society for East Sea/ Northeast History Foundation.

If the IHO, following the interpretation by international laws, give the name "East Sea" to the territorial waters of Korea on its east and "Japan Sea" or "Sea of Japan" to the territorial waters of Japan to its north and publish a new edition of *Limits of Oceans and Seas* accordingly, it would naturally be in the form that Gilles Robert de Vaugondy used both names in his "L'Empire du Japon" in 1750. At least, it would be an expression of fairness and Korea would have no reason to refuse it because its primary objective is the use of both names.

The resolutions that the IHO and the UNCSGN have adopted provide some important principles that can relate to the problem of East Sea/Sea of Japan. For example, Resolution III/20, one of the resolutions adopted at the 3rd UNCSGN, states: [It] 1. Recommends that countries sharing a given geographical feature under different names should endeavor, as far as feasible, to reach agreement on fixing a single name for the feature concerned; 2. Further recommends that when countries sharing a given geographical feature do not succeed in agreeing on a common name, it should be a general rule of international cartography that the name used by each of the countries concerned will be accepted. A policy of accepting only one or some of such names while excludingg the rest would be inconsistent in principle as well as inexpedient in practice.[11] This Resolution clearly shows that Korea's argument is valid and and Japan's argument denies the UN's principles on the use of geographical names. The resolution also completely corresponds with IHO's Technical Resolution A.4.2.6.

Regarding the UNCSGN Resolution III/20, Woodman says, "[It was] intended to consider shared or divided features on land, and to ask the international community to accept on an equal basis all the endonyms for that feature."[12] However, if he really thinks that "a given geographical feature" in the Resolution relates to such features on land only, we cannot help wondering what he would think about the IHO Technical Resolution A.4.2.6. where "a given geographical feature" is specifically qualified by "such as a bay, strait, channel or archipelago." One may argue that the Technical Resolution A.4.2.6. does not relate to the naming issue of the East Sea because it is not a geographical feature under the sovereignty of any country. However, the sea area fits well the definition of the geographical features as provided in both UNCSGN Resolution III/20 and IHO Technical Resolution A.4.2.6. Also, the sea area is not the

---

11) Statues, Rules of Procedure and Resolutions on Geographical Names, 2002, UNGEGN.
12) Paul Woodman, "Maritime Feature Names: The Role of UNGEGN during its First Decade," The 16th International Seminar on Sea Names, 2010, The Society for East Sea/Northeast History Foundation.

high seas as one may question but falls under the definition of a "semi-enclosed sea" as set out in Article 122 of the UN Convention on the Law of the Sea (UNCLOS) as it is a sea "surrounded by two or more States," "connected to another sea or the ocean by a narrow outlet" and "consisting entirely or primarily of the territorial seas and exclusive economic zones of two or more coastal States." Further, "A bay, strait, channel or archipelago" as stipulated in the IHO Technical Resolution A.4.2.6 are provided simply as examples of a given geographical feature and are not limited to them.

While different experts of place names offer different interpretations of the resolutions that the IHO and UNCSGN-UNGEGN have adopted, the problem is that those organizations have failed to put into practice what they have taken as reasonable and fair solutions. They may first urge the countries concerned to work out a mutually acceptable agreement, but when this fails, they should make a decision on their own on the basis of the principles they made clear through the resolutions that were adopted.

Chapter 5
The Name "East Sea" in the World

Korea did not take much interest in the issue of the notation of the East Sea until quite recently because it was so obvious for them to call the sea area by the name "Donghae" (East Sea) that it was almost unimaginable for them to call it by any other name; and if it was marked by any other name on maps, it was a "mistake" by the map-makers that could be corrected simply by notifying them of their mistake. When this issue started to be brought to public attention, the reported response by a Korean scholar specializing in Korean history encapsulates such attitude of many Koreans at the time: "Why bother with it? East Sea is East Sea whatever others may call it."

If they thought things would take their course in due time, however, it was not long before many Koreans realized that they were living in a world where things do not always turn out as they wish. They were awakened to the fact that when, for example, the Dokdo islets became a territorial issue with Japan, it would be awkward to persuade the international community that the island has traditionally been a Korean territory when people find it marked on maps as being in the "Sea of Japan." What the East Sea was called in foreign countries was thus found to be, in fact, a very important matter.

As Korea has been increasingly affected by the winds of globalization, more Koreans realized that things uniquely Korean too should be recognized by peoples of the world, including the name of the East Sea. Recognition and use by foreign countries were a prerequisite for the justification of the name. In the 1990s, Korea therefore launched an active campaign directed at the international community to rectify the name, "Sea of Japan" and assert the legitimacy of the name "East Sea." In 1992, the Korean government petitioned the 6th UN Conference on the Standardization of Geographic Names (UNCSGN), requesting that the erroneous name "Sea of Japan" be replaced with "East Sea." Since then, Korea has advanced the goal of restoring the rightful name with a lance, which Japan has dodged with a shield, refusing to address the issue directly and not engage in any serious discussions on the issue with Korea.

Among the Korean scholars who started to work on this issue, Professor Choo Sungjae studied notations of the East Sea by different countries. According to his study, the Japanese government surveyed 392 maps, which were in use in the year 2,000, of over 60 countries, excluding South Korea and North Korea as well as Japan. It was found by Professor Choo that only 11 maps, or 2.8% of the total, marked both "East Sea" and "Sea of Japan." However, the Japanese government's survey on 331 maps of 67 countries in 2005 found that 34 maps, or 10.3%, used both names. Regarding the commercial maps among them, excluding school textbooks and maps for educational purposes, 60 maps, or 18.1%, used both names. Afterwards, no statistics released by the Japanese government are obtainable.

Recently, the Korean government performed a survey of 351 maps of the East Sea area made in 75 different countries. The survey revealed that maps using both names numbered 83, accounting for 23.6% of the total.[13] The steadily upward trend in the statistics made the Japanese government uneasy and it thus changed the way it had handled the problem.

13) Choo Sungjae, "Recent Progress for Restoring the Name East Sea and Future Research Agenda," The 13th International Seminar on the Naming of Seas and East Sea, 2007, The Society for East Sea.

The Japanese government's shift in policy can be summed up by two changes: Following the moves by Korea from the 1990s to restore internationally the name of the East Sea, the Ministry of Foreign Affairs of Japan started to translate important academic papers and news reports of Korea into Japanese and sent them to major new media and academic institutions of Japan. And Japan set up over ten institutes dedicated to the problem at universities along the East Sea coastline. Internationally, however, as the single marking of "Sea of Japan" was in the absolute majority, it ostensibly ignored Korea's moves and did not make any conspicuous response. Toward the end of the 1990s, then, the raised recognition and agreement on the name "East Sea" prompted Japan to start changing its policy. From ignoring Korea's argument externally, it shifted toward defending the use of "Sea of Japan" alone in an active diplomatic offensive. The 7th UN Conference on the Standardization of Geographical Names in 1998, in which one of the authors of this book, Suh, participated, is regarded as the first international venue where Japan's policy shift came to the fore. As many delegates, especially those from newly independent nations, responded positively to Korea's logical arguments, the Japanese delegate felt a sense of crisis and reported the situation to the Japanese government. Accordingly, Japan's Ministry of Foreign Affairs had its diplomatic offices overseas put pressure on the respective governments, which then resulted in them sending urgent messages to their delegates at the UN Conference to change their support in favor of Japan rather than Korea. Japan, a founding member of the IHO, has an internationally strong influence as the provider of a great amount of funding to developing nations with regard to maritime matters, in addition to its contributions to the regular budget of the organization. The next day, the Korean delegates learned of the situation and had to withdraw its plan to urge the UN to confirm and implement what it had already resolved about the naming of the East Sea. Ultimately, it was the power of politics and money that prevailed over a reasonable solution.

Professor Choo analyzes that the use of "East Sea" has gained ground because Korea's consistent logic has worked strongly to persuade the international community. The essence of Japan's argument for the single use of "Sea of Japan" is that, it has a long history after Matteo Ricci's marking of the East Sea as the "Japan Sea" in 1602 and is now in use in almost all countries, except for South Korea and North Korea, through the acceptance of relevant international organizations. It should be maintained as it is in order not to create confusion, they say.

In response to this argument, Korea counters that a

majority of the old maps published in foreign countries used various names, including Sea of Korea, East Sea, and Oriental Sea, from the late 17th century to the end of the 18th century. While the name "East Sea" is a 2,000-year-long endonym, "Sea of Japan" (*Japan Sea*) was not a name used in Japan but an exonym that they started to use in the late 19th century under the influence of foreign countries. Second, the international organizations responsible for the standardization of geographical names authorized the Japanese name because Japan presented the name of the sea area as "Sea of Japan" for acceptance when it solely participated in an international conference during the time when Korea was under Japanese colonial rule and its traditional names were forced to change into Japanese names, including personal names. Third, while UNCSGN Resolution II/29 recommended the reduction of the use of exonyms and the change into endonyms and IHO Technical Resolution A.4.2.6. and UNCSGN Resolution III/20 recommended that if the countries in disputes cannot agree on a common name form, the name forms of each of the languages in question should be accepted, Japan has not complied with the recommendations.

In an effort to prove the validity of its argument, beginning in the 1990s the Korean government attempted to show that the name "Sea of Japan" was used in old European countries only in the 19th century and the use of the name "East Sea" or "Sea of Korea" by far outnumbered "Sea of Japan" in the 17th and 18th century. Korea's overseas information offices visited such places as the British Library, Cambridge University Library, the National Library of France, personal collections in Germany, Southern California University Libraries, Russian State Library and Russian State Archive of Ancient Acts to search old maps there. They also obtained necessary information, including the report by a specialized research agency of the United States on old maps at the U.S. Library of Congress, to prepare statistics. Professor Choo summarized the statistics thus tallied as follows:

<table>
<tr><th>Period / Name</th><th>16th C</th><th>17th C</th><th>18th C</th><th>19th C</th><th>Total</th></tr>
<tr><td>Sea of Korea</td><td rowspan="3"></td><td rowspan="3">39</td><td rowspan="3">341</td><td rowspan="3">60</td><td rowspan="3">440</td></tr>
<tr><td>East (Eastern) Sea</td></tr>
<tr><td>Oriental Sea</td></tr>
<tr><td>Sea of Japan</td><td></td><td>17</td><td>36</td><td>69</td><td>122</td></tr>
<tr><td>Others</td><td>29</td><td>69</td><td>90</td><td>12</td><td>200</td></tr>
<tr><td>Total</td><td>29</td><td>125</td><td>467</td><td>141</td><td>762</td></tr>
</table>

As Korea publicized this statistics, the Japanese government sent scholars to the institutions that Korea visited for the survey and made its own search and, alleging that Korea's statistics were incorrect, came up with the following numbers:[14]

<table>
<tr><th>Period / Name</th><th>16th C</th><th>17th C</th><th>18th C</th><th>19th C</th><th>Total</th></tr>
<tr><td>Sea of Korea</td><td rowspan="3">5</td><td rowspan="3">29</td><td rowspan="3">165</td><td rowspan="3">107</td><td rowspan="3">306</td></tr>
<tr><td>East (Eastern) Sea</td></tr>
<tr><td>Oriental Sea</td></tr>
<tr><td>Sea of Japan</td><td>1</td><td>16</td><td>70</td><td>1,312</td><td>1,399</td></tr>
<tr><td>Others</td><td>5</td><td>56</td><td>39</td><td>67</td><td>167</td></tr>
<tr><td>Total</td><td>11</td><td>101</td><td>274</td><td>1,486</td><td>1,872</td></tr>
</table>

Denying the outcomes of Korea's survey, Japan argued that "Oriental Sea" had nothing to do with Korea and counted "East Sea" and "Sea of Korea" separately. However, as "Oriental" was used with the same meaning as "East" until the middle of the 18th century and substituted for East to exude exotic flavors in the 19th century, "Oriental" and "East" should be considered as a complete synonym. Furthermore, the Korean statistics are the sum of the data obtained from research of the markings on maps country by country and can thus be regarded as quite trustworthy, even if some possible errors are taken into consideration. On the other hand, Japan's statistics, especially about the 19th century are found not easily acceptable. True, since La Pérouse, the shift

14) Choo, "Recent Progress for Restoring the Name East Sea and Future Research Agenda."

to "Sea of Japan" increased continuously in the 19th century, but some French and British maps continued to use "Sea of Korea." Moreover, "old maps" generally refer to those made until the 1850s, but Japan's statistics included the maps that were produced in the late 19th century. However, even when the timeline can be stretched to the end of the 19th century, the statistics look quite suspicious. Again, for more reliable statistics, it is advisable for both countries to agree on the criteria and the method of the survey and entrust the survey to a specialized agency of a third country.

In a situation where Korea and Japan disagree on the statistics about old maps and Japan has refused Korea's demand for its acceptance of the UN resolutions, many countries, albeit they consent to Korea's proposal, are reluctant to change altogether the notations that they have made according to the current names as provided in *Limits of Oceans and Seas* of 1929 by the IHO. Still, changes have been observed. Lee Ki-suk also surveyed how the East Sea is marked on in maps of major publishers in the world. According to his research, Rand McNally, perhaps the largest map publishers in the United States, used both names, Sea of Japan and East Sea, in *Premier World Atlas* in 1997 and *Portrait World Atlas* in 1998. *The Most Comprehensive World Atlas Ever Created* by Encarta, online encyclopedia, used the marking "Sea of Japan (*East Sea*)" in 2000. The Humanitarian Response Planning Map, a publication by the United Nations Environment Program Global References also marked the East Sea as the "Sea of Japan (*Tong Hae*)."

The United Nations Office for Coordination of Humanitarian Affairs used the same marking, "Sea of Japan (*Tong Hae*)." The notation where the East Sea or Tong Hae is placed in parenthesis is not exactly what Korea wants, but it can be regarded as a transitional stage.

More encouraging is Warwick Publishing Inc. of Canada using the marking "Tong-Hae/Nippon-Kai (*Japan Sea*)" in its *Cartographic Satellite Atlas of the World*. The 1990 CD-ROM edition of Encyclopaedia Britannica marked the East Sea as the "East Sea (*Sea of Japan*)" in the entries on Korea and "Sea of Japan (*East Sea*)" in the entries on Japan. *New York Times* and the 2001 *Webster's Dictionary* used the same way of marking.

The Agency for International Development published in 1997 maps that marked the East Sea as the "East Sea" without the notation of "Sea of Japan."

The map of Korean mountains in 1999 "The Bulletin 49 (*2*)" by the International Geographical Union labeled the East Sea as "East Sea (*Sea of Japan*)." Throughout the 2000 new edition of *Geography: Realms, Regions and Concepts*, the authors Harm J. de Blij and Peter O. Muller replaced "Sea of Japan," which they used in the previous editions, with "East Sea (*Sea of Japan*)." A seminar of the U.S. National Council for Geographic Education, held in Indianapolis, Indiana, USA, in 1998, apparently assured both authors that "East Sea" was the right term. The 1997 edition of the book still used "Sea of Japan" only.

The National Geographic Society (NGS) chose a different way. On the Korean maps, they use "East Sea (*Sea of Japan*)" while on other maps in the atlas, they use "Sea of Japan (*East Sea*)." Until 1996, the NGS marked the East Sea as the "Sea of Japan," refusing Korea's request and following regulations of the U.S. Board of Geographic Names. Then it changed its policy when it started to publish the Korean-language edition of *National Geographic* magazine in Korea in 2000. At the time, the NGS announced that it would use both "East Sea" and "Sea of Japan" on all maps in the magazine and put it into practice beginning in 2001.

It is also encouraging to see that changes begin to occur in none other than Japan, especially in tourism maps and other materials on Korea. Some use both "East Sea" and "Sea of Japan" and others use "Sea of Japan" followed by "East Sea" in parenthesis. The number of maps using both names increased after 1998. In 1998, a German atlas marked the sea area as "Japanisches Meer" ("Japan Sea") and "Ostmeer" ("East Sea"). The report of Transboundary Diagnostic Analysis (RAS/98/G31) of the 2002 Tumen River Strategic Action Program by the UNDP/Global Environment Facility used both names. In the same year, International Travel Maps & Books of Canada used the two names "East Sea (*Sea of Japan*)" mostly and "East Sea" only in some pages.

In the process, some map-makers, who had used to identify the sea area as "Sea of Japan" according to the IHO SP-23 of 1929, were now torn between the previous resolution and the later UNCSGN Resolution III/20 and the IHO Technical Resolution A.4.2.6 and decided to leave the sea unmarked. For example, the Economic Research Institute for Northeast Asia (ERINA) in Niigata, Japan, used to use "Sea of Japan" but, in a break from the previous policy, recently started to leave the sea area blank in its publications. The Beijing office of the United Nations Development Programme (UNDP) published three maps in 2000 for a project known as the Tumen River Economic Development Project. All three maps, published in China, bear no name for this sea area. The North Korean map (Map No. 4163), published in 2001 by the UN Department of Public Information Cartographic Section, also gave no name to the sea area. The official map published by FIFA for World

Cup 2002, which was hosted by both Korea and Japan, also did not mark any name in the sea area.

Apparently, the organizations and map-makers leaving the sea unnamed decided that way in an effort to ensure fairness between the two names. It seems that they made the hard decision out of the recognition that maintaining "Sea of Japan" would not be right when they became aware of the historical truth and international rules.

The disputes over how the East Sea should be identified will continue and no one party is likely to win a complete victory. Many factors are involved in the determination of the name. Korea has held more than 20 international seminars and stepped up exchanges with experts on geographical names with experience with international organizations in an effort to help increase Korea's leverage of influence internationally. Many experts, however, tend to remain "neutral" while agreeing with the decisions of the UN and the IHO in principle. Although some important news media have adopted the use of both names, Korea's ultimate goal is that the IHO changes the name of the sea area from "Sea of Japan" to "East Sea" in its publications, thereby making it possible for all countries to follow suit. If Korea continues to make efforts to disseminate the historical truth and urge the implementation of the international resolutions, such change will surely take place.

Chapter 6
Map Road

The name, "Silk Road," originated from the ancient routes for the Chinese silk trade, which was delivered to the West via Central Asia. In a broader sense, however, it was a channel through which things of the East and the West were exchanged and proved to be an important landmark in the history and development of civilization. In Korea, in 2008, a TV program titled "Noodle Road" was aired[15] and enjoyed wide popularity. The documentary showed how the noodle originated in ancient China and was diversified while it was transmitted to Europe through many regions of China and via Korea, Japan and Southeast Asia, along with the development of the machines needed to make noodles.

15) A documentary aired by KBS 1, Dec. 7, 2008 – March 29, 2009.

In 2010, another TV documentary, titled "Paper Road," was broadcast by MBC, which traced the development and dissemination of paper. Now, almost everything about people's daily lives can be illuminated through the name of "Road."

Today, when traced back to their origins, many things that we use in our everyday lives have been modified and supplemented after much meandering through different cultures before reaching us. Interactions between ingenuity and necessity were at work in the process. Ultimately their development and transformation are the epitome of the different phases in the development of our civilizations. Accordingly, can maps perform such a function? If so, then let us find out what could be described as the "Map Road."

The first model of the present-day maps was made by the Greek, Claudius Ptolemaeus, otherwise known as Claudius Ptolemy. Ptolemy's geography and astronomy were inherited by the Arab-Islam civilizations, which, thanks to this, were able to open the beginning of map-making and trade between the East and the rest of the world. However, no specific maps or charts remain, apart from some maps with abstract figures depicting what people at the time conceived as the world.

It was Renaissance Italy that embraced Ptolemy's geography and developed it into modern maps. Since the 1400s when Ptolemy's geographical books were re-published in Bologna, Italy, Venetian craftsmen developed the making and printing of the maps. Building on them, map-makers called cartographers were able to publish maps. At first, they published maps of Italian regions and then started to make maps of the world as the people of the time perceived it to be. As the necessity for maps rose on the Iberian Peninsula, some Venetian craftsmen moved to Barcelona and Lisbon and taught their family's map-making techniques there, making a great contribution to the development of maps.

In the two Iberian states, Spain and Portugal, the impact of map-making had different outcomes. Spain sent Christopher Columbus to discover the Americas and colonized most of South America. But it was mostly conducted by a strong army and it had not much interest in map-making. Portugal, a smaller country with barren lands in the south of the Iberian Peninsula, was different. Producing Vasco da Gama, Bartholomeu Diaz and Ferdinand Magellan, Portugal was ambitious to stand high as a maritime state from early on by concentrating on overseas resources trade and the development of colonies.

With the emergence of Prince Henry the Navigator, it beefed up the naval forces and built a host of ships, necessitating charts for safe and efficient navigation of the vessels. Now as a priority national business, Portugal encouraged and promoted the map-making industry. In a timely manner, it was thus able to invite artisan map-makers from Italy, speeding up the process of map-making.

The discovery of the Americas by Columbus opened the Age of Discovery and Portugal preoccupied and ruled the lion's share of South America, namely, Brazil. As the two Catholic states on the Iberian Peninsula, Spain and Portugal, were at loggerheads over their struggle to win colonies, the Pope stepped in to mediate. As a consequence, the two countries signed the Treaty of Tordesillas in 1494, which gave Spain the priority over the Western Hemisphere and Portugal, the Eastern Hemisphere. Thus, Portugal was recognized for its vested interest in Brazil on the American continent. With the signing of the Treaty, Portugal earnestly set out to explore and develop the East. Occupying Goa of India, Malacca of Malaya and Macau of China as bridgeheads for its advancement to the East and monopolizing imports of spices, Portugal was busily engaged in trade with many countries in the East. At the time, Joseon, however, was inaccessible because of its closed-door policy, while Japan opened its doors to Portugal, allowing exchanges between the two countries from early on. Portugal's advancement to the East, however, hit a snag. The Arab-Islam merchants had maintained trade with the East since a long time ago and it was inevitable that there would be a conflict with Portugal.

Portugal responded with the powerful canons of its fleets of battleships to drive out the Arab-Islam commercial fleets. The Portuguese seized materials on navigation and charts from the Arab-Islam vessels, probably including the maps of Northeast Asia that showed Korea, China and/or Japan. Some Portuguese maps of the 1500s depicted Korea as an island in the shape of an elongated funnel, while others drew it in a quite similar shape. At any rate, these maps are considered to have been copied from the Arab-Islam maps because they marked Korea as "Cori," or "Cory." That is the way present-day Arabic and Middle East countries call Korea and in the Portuguese maps, the name is written roughly in the mid-southern part of the Korean peninsula – a marking apparently made by the copiers who did not know what it referred to.

Monopolizing the trades with the East as a maritime superpower, Portugal enjoyed a golden days before it met a great change. In 1578, King Sebastian of Portugal died without an heir apparent, the Spanish king succeeded the throne with Portugal being annexed to Spain. Even after the annexation, the Portuguese naval forces remained where they had been stationed, protecting the spice trade with Southeast Asia. However, as the Netherlands, which had recently become a federal republic in 1581, leaped into the hugely lucrative spice trade with a view to becoming a maritime superpower for survival. Now, conflict between Portugal and the Netherlands was unavoidable. Eventually, the Dutch navy won two vital sea battles, at the trade port of Bantam and in Makassar,[16] thereby putting an end to Portugal's trading with the East.

With Portugal now placed under Spanish rule, the glory days of the Portuguese maps came to an end. However, the golden age of 100-plus years of the Portuguese maps made a great contribution the history of maps. Taking pride in this, the Portuguese government collected important old maps that Portugal made to publish a four-volume atlas, *Portugaliae Monumenta Cartographica*, in 1960 in commemoration of the 500th anniversary of the death of Henry the Navigator.

---

16) Liang Er Ping, *Segyesaui Unmyeongeul Bakkun Haedo* (*Charts that Changed the Fate of the World History*), tr. Ha Jin-Ee, Myungjin Publishing Co., 2011, pp.306-314.

It was the Netherlands that inherited altogether the tradition of the Portuguese maps and for some reasons. A colony of Spain until the late 16th century, the Netherlands was a high population density country located on a challenging landscape that lay lower than sea-level. In a situation where it had to build embankments along the seashores and reclaim lands to extend its land, advancing overseas was the only strategy that it could choose to survive. Many Dutch youngsters landed jobs overseas, especially at Portuguese companies and organizations. They wrote home the information that Portugal obtained from overseas and those who received the letters delivered the geographical information to map-makers nearby. Such information was reflected in the maps for the benefit of consumers. Some Portuguese map-makers contacted famous Dutch cartographers, such as Ortelius, and published maps jointly.

The changes in the social conditions in the Netherlands and the increased interest in Dutch maps in many European countries fanned an unprecedented boom in the Dutch cartographic industry, producing many master cartographers, such as Ortelius, Mercator, Blaeu and Jodocus Hondius, and other important cartographers, including Petrus Plancius, Vissches, Jan Huyghen van

Linschonten, Jansz and Lucas Janszoon Waghenaer. The heyday of Dutch map-making continued until the mid-17th century. However, like everything else which passes through a period of rise, fall, and then extinction, it could not escape such a fate.

Dutch cartography declined, however, due to factors both within and outside of the cartographic industry. As outside factors, the consumer base was saturated and the public interest in maps subdued. Fewer and fewer people took interest in maps and those who did have interest already possessed atlases and maps. Overseas demand also diminished. Domestically, Dutch map-makers published new editions of their maps in an effort to expand the consumer base but their efforts stalled. In a bid to stimulate imagination and exotic flavors, they included too many decorative drawings which were made out of imagination, which gradually became tedious to consumers.

Seeing through such a changing trend, French cartographers, including Sanson, removed unnecessary elements and brought to a focus those areas where consumers had interest in, resolving their curiosity. That way, they could create new demand in France. A strong interest and intellectual curiosity of the French about overseas countries added fuel to the acceleration of the French map-making industry.

Meanwhile, the winds of the Italian Renaissance blew to the northern Alps beginning in the 16th century. As a consequence, clubs for the study of the classics came into being in Switzerland and Austria, promoting the re-publication of Ptolemy's geography books and some maps. However, little further interest in maps was shown, and maps were reduced to be a "pastime" of a small number of researchers. In these areas, the map-making industry gradually became more active centering on Nuremberg, under the influence of Dutch and French maps.

Sanson first attempted to make maps in a small country village and then moved to Paris to do business in a bigger way. He worked as a driving force behind the rise of the French cartographic industry in the early 16th century. Following the Netherlands' map-making zenith, Sanson led the heyday of French maps, sometimes in cooperation and other times in competition with such people as Pierre Duval, his son-in-law; Father Briet who hailed from the same hometown as he and obtained geographical information on China from colleagues returning home from Beijing; and Alexis Hubert Jaillot who inherited his business after his death. From the late 17th century, the engine of the activities of famous map-makers started to roar. Active and informative, de Fer, Guillaume Delisle, Janvier and, from the 18th century, newcomers flocked into the map-making industry. Notable among them were oceanographer Bellin; Chambon; Jean Baptiste Bourguignon d'Anville, a top cartographer who wielded influence internationally for over a century; A. de Garel; Guillaume Danet; the family of Robert de Vaugondy who inherited the map business of the Sanson family and became a map-making family representing the late 18th century; Philippe Buache, grandson of Guillaume Delisle who studied physical geography; and J. N. Delisle, brother of Guillaume Delisle and astronomer who published maps with Buache that attracted public attention.

The "Atlas of Voyage" by La Pérouse had a direct influence on European cartographers, especially British ones. The atlas recorded the logs of the voyage of La Pérouse who went on an expedition that the French royal family organized on national wealth in the late 18th century before disappearing. In the 19th-century Great Britain, an array of prominent cartographers and map-makers made a monumental landmark. However, the glory days could not continue endlessly just like the Netherlands and Portugal.

As the limelight that was shed on France faded away, Great Britain emerged to take its place to carry the torch.

In fact, Great Britain started map-making at the end of the 10th century, earlier than France or any other European country, through the map titled "Anglo-Saxon." Regardless of Ptolemy's map, this map put the east on the top side and drew Europe, including Great Britain, Africa and the Middle East. The "Hereford Mappa Mundi" ("Hereford Map of the World") of 1280 was the first map that depicted the world of the days and Christopher Saxton drew a map showing the regions of Great Britain in 1583. John Ogilby published in 1675 a map of the roads that connected the regions and cities of Great Britain. In 1588, R. Adams drew a map depicting the Armada Sea Battle between Great Britain and Spain. In 1557, Anthony Jenkinson put into a map the result of his exploration of inland Russia with the purpose of promoting trade with Russia, an obscure country until that time, which Ortelius of the Netherlands included in his atlas. The original map is in the collection of the British Library.

As such, Great Britain produced many great maps from early on and could have been in the forefront of the map-making industry in Europe. What, then, kept it from happening?

That was because those early maps were abrupt, isolated achievements rather than something produced by the continuous development of the map-making industry. In other words, they were exceptional accomplishments, without any predecessors or successors. From the mid-16th century, British maps were heavily influenced by Dutch maps, and well-known Dutch maps were published in Great Britain in translation. Some Dutch map-makers moved to Great Britain and were active. Under these circumstances, the British map industry seemingly fell short of developing on its own. From the late 17th century to the 18th century, it fell under French influence, producing Asian maps in almost complete copying of French maps and concentrating on North America, Australia and New Zealand. For these reasons, the British maps were recognized only belatedly for their originality and contributions.

As a matter of fact, however, Great Britain produced some important maps that contributed to the development of maps from early on. India is a big country but it was not very much known to the outside world. In 1619, William Baffin depicted in detail the entire India, which was called the "Mogul Empire" at the time. In 1627, John Speed published *A Prospect of the Most Famous Parts of World*, a world atlas produced for the first time in Great

Britain. Robert Dudley published in 1646 *Dell'Arcano del Mare* (*Secrets of the Sea*), the first maritime atlas of the world. John Seller, Royal Hydrographer to Charles II and James II, published *Atlas Maritimus* (*The Sea Atlas*) in 1670 and *Hydrographia Universalis* (*A Book of Maritime Charts*) in 1690 in addition to other maps of many places of the world.

In the 18th century too, many map-makers were active. Herman Moll, a Dutch citizen who was naturalized as British, published *A General Atlas* in 1700 and *Atlas Geographus* in 1729. Senex started to make domestic maps of Great Britain with *English Atlas* in 1714 and, gradually widening his vision, went into publishing *Atlas of the World* in 1719. His maps and atlases were popular and went to re-publication many times over even after his death and were published in French in 1759. Emanuel Bowen published an ambitious atlas titled, *Complete System of Geography*, in 1744-1747. He made the vignettes of the maps in an intriguing manner, attracting consumers' attention. Kitchin was an enthusiastic map-maker. He published a lot of individual maps but also produced the *General Atlas* in 1773. In 1773-1774, James Rennell published James Cook's travelogue *Cook's Voyage* in seven volumes, presenting the great voyage in charts. Thomas

Jefferys, a Royal Geographer, usually published large maps of London and British regions. His *America Atlas*, which he made in his latter years, was published by Sayer and Bennett in 1776 after his death. William Faden was handed over Jefferys' map business after his death and produced mostly a variety of individual maps as well as General Atlas in 1815.

In the 19th century, many map-makers were active in Great Britain, in fact too many to enumerate. Among them, Aaron Arrowsmith and his nephew and successor John Arrowsmith comprised a map-maker family which distinguished itself prominently. The two cartographers were famous for not only maps of the United States but also many cities and countries of the world, world maps and especially maps of Asia. In addition, to name a few map-makers who were active until the mid-19th century, J. Cary, who produced a great deal of high-level maps; Thomson, who published maps of Northeast Asia; John Pinkerton; and Henry Teesdale.

In summary, the Map Road was completed as Italy "built the highway" and Portugal "ran on it." The roads leading over the Alps were small ones which were used mostly by a limited number of researchers of classics. The main road, which Portugal ran, was then used by the Netherlands followed by France, which, before passing the milestone of the 19th century, had to yield the use of the road to Great Britain. As Great Britain was almost on a par with France in map-making from the 18th century, it was no wonder that "the empire on which the sun never sets," as a naval superpower of the 19th century, could assume the throne of map-making.

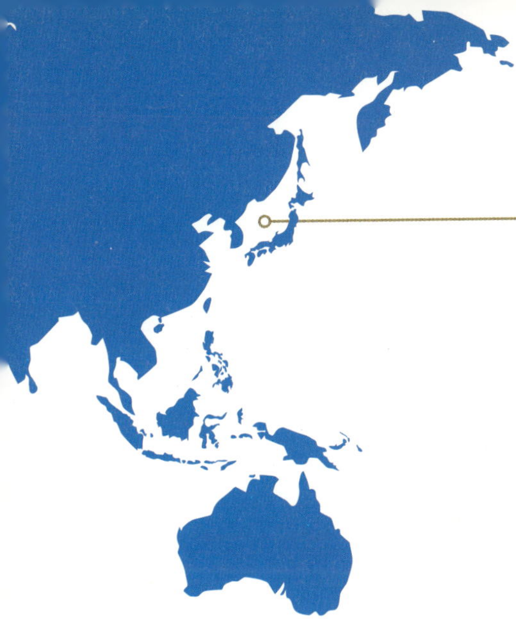

Chapter 7
Korea Road

Of the many branches of the Map Road, our interest is directed toward those related to Korea, and specifically the "East Sea" and the "Sea of Korea." The roads identified in this regard may be called "Korea Road" and now we intend to track the milestones of the maps with the markings of the two names.

On 16th century Portuguese maps, the country that was supposedly Korea first appeared on Homem's world map of 1554, Fernão Vaz Dourado's map of 1573, and Linschoten's map of 1595 that had the former two as an influence. Linschoten's map shows "Costa de Comray" ("Coast of Comray") to the east of the country which is supposed to be Korea. However, Korea neither appears in the 1570 map by Ortelius of the Netherlands, nor in the maps by masters of the late 1500s to the early 1600s — except in some wrong names for the East Sea, such as "China Sea," "South Sea," or "Sea of Mangi." The 1602 map of Asia by Hondius has the name "Oceanus Eous, Fine Orientalis." This, however, is not the translation of "East Sea" but a name with the simple meaning that the sea lies to the east of Europe. In Italy, the world map of 1528 by Bornone depicts Korea quite exactly as a peninsula. But the marking "Mare Orientale" to the south of Korea does not directly relate to the East Sea because it does not refer to the same sea area in spite of the seemingly the same name. Until the early 17th century, it is rarely the case that both the name and what it refers to correspond with the East Sea on the Italian, Portuguese and Dutch maps.

The map that marked the first milestone on the Korea Road would probably be the map of East Asia that Manuel Godinho de Erédia, Portuguese mathematician and historian, published in Macau in 1615. On this map, which was drawn quite exactly, Erédia identified the sea area east of Korea as "Mar Coria." It was 13 years later than Matteo Ricci and he seemingly followed Arab-Islam maps rather than Chinese maps. Unfortunately, the map did not attract much attention probably because it was published in the Far East. However, it still was evaluated as an important map by Portugal and was included in *Portugaliae Monumenta Cartographica.*

Later, when he made a map of Asia in 1623, missionary Aleni named the East Sea "Small East Sea," presumably because he decided that Matteo Ricci's "Riben Hai" was not the proper name. The world's first atlas of charts, *Dell'Arcano del Mare*, which Dudley published in 1646, includes a map titled, "Carta particolare della Grande Isola del'Giapone è di Iezo con il Regno di Corai et altre Isole in torno" ("Detailed Map of the Big Island of Japan and Hokkaido with the Kingdom of Korea and Other Nearby Islands"). Estimated to have been influenced by Dutch maps, this map has the name "MARE di CORAI" ("Sea of Korea") in bold print letters for the East Sea, with the markings of "Oceano Boreale del Giappone" ("North Sea of Japan") to the north and "Mare di Iezo" ("Hokkaido Sea") to the northeast, suggesting that "MARE di CORAI" is another name for the East Sea.

Sanson, the most prominent map-maker of the times in France at the time, marked the sea off the south of Japan and the East Sea combined as "Ocean Oriental" several times. Sonson asked Jesuit priest Briet to look through his atlas. Father Briet proofread Sanson's *Cartes générales de*

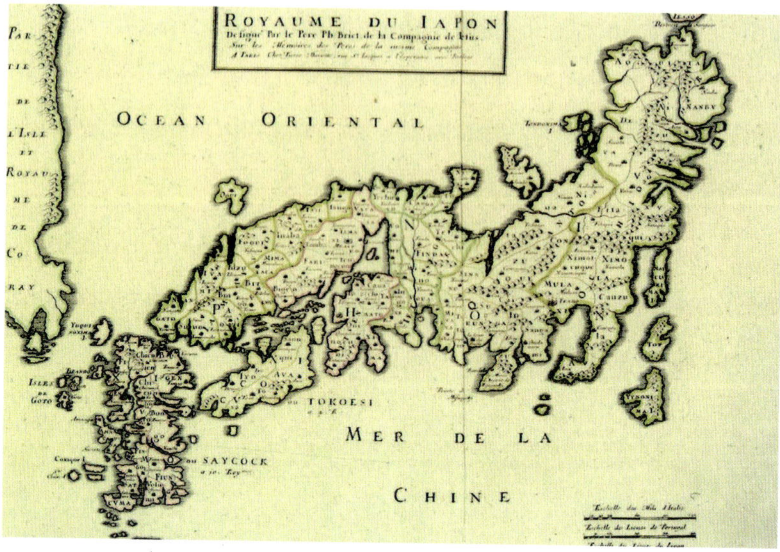

"Royaume du Japon," a map made by Father Briet in 1650. He made this map based on the information that he obtained from his colleagues who had been sent to Beijing and marked the East Sea as "Ocean Oriental."

toutes les parties du monde in 1658 and *Cartes générales de la Géographie ancienne et nouvelle* in 1676. On the "Royaume de Japan" which was contained in the two atlases, Briet identified only the East Sea as "Océan Oriental." His marking bears a different meaning from Sanson's or other "Océan Oriental" notations. He communicated with his colleagues who had been to Beijing and acquired from them information on the geography of the Far East. Learning that Chinese people in Manchuria called the sea area "East Sea," he translated it as "Océan Oriental." At the time, the East was "Oriental" and a sea was sometimes called "Océan" and other times "Mer" regardless of its size. In other words, the two words were used interchangeably until 18th century when they were used separately according to its size, Océan for a larger sea and Mer for a smaller one.

At any rate, from the late 16th century, the name of the East Sea was expressed in two versions of "Sea of Korea" and "East Sea." An important milestone on the Korean Road was erected in 1669 by Montanus, a Dutch Protestant theologian. Due to his close relationship with employees of the Dutch East India Company, he compiled a book with the most fantastic anecdotes from the experiences of the Dutch ambassador and his party on their way from Nagasaki, Japan, to the capital city of Edo to have an audience with the Japanese Emperor. As the bestseller of the day in his country, the book was translated into many languages in Europe, where it also became a sensation. On the map of Japan, which was contained in an appendix to the book, the author indicated the East Sea as "Mer de Corée," laying the foundation for the name's prime time in the 18th century. Following Montanus, Jesuit priest Thomas, a Dutch-born Belgian who was sent to Beijing in 1686, marked the East Sea as "Mer de Corée" on the two maps of Asia which he made in reference to Chinese maps.

After making the map, Thomas accompanied the Kangxi

Emperor of China to Manchuria from 1689 to 1698. In the travelog, he recorded, "The Kangxi Emperor pointed to the sea in the east and said 'Eoum Mare' [Greek and Latin meaning "East Sea" combined] twice."[17] He did not correct his map, though. Priest Jean-Baptiste Du Halde, reading Thomas' travelog, mentioned the East Sea as "Mer Orientale" several times in his *Description de la Chine.*

Meanwhile, the name of the East Sea saw another important milestone in France in the late 17th century. Tavernier, a traveler and researcher of Japan, published a book on Japan in 1679. The map of Japan contained in the book as an appendix was affected by two maps, one by Briet and the other by Montanus. Hesitating between the two, Tavernier, unlike Sanson, mentioned only the East Sea as "Océan Oriental" and marked "Mer de Corée" near the Korea Strait in the south-west of the East Sea. A few years later when he published the reprint of the book, however, he made separate markings, "Océan Oriental" for the East Sea and "Mer de Corée" for the sea between Yeongheung Bay and Japan.

Manesson Mallet, also under the influence of Briet's

17) Philippe Pelletier, "LES CARTOGRAPHES FRANÇAIS et la DENOMINATION de la 'MER DU JAPON' (MER DE L'EST) aux XVIIe et XVIIIe siècles," The 8th International Seminar on the Naming of Seas, Special Emphasis Concerning the North Pacific Ocean, 2002, The Society for East Sea.

maps, marked the East Sea as "Océan Oriental" on his "Isles du Japan" of "De L'Asie" in 1683. However, Guillaume Delisle, the famous chief royal geographer, identified the East Sea as "Mer Orientale" on his map "L'Asie" in 1696, thus acting as a spokesperson for the notation of "East Sea" both within and outside the academic community. This led to "Mer Orientale" being marked on the narrow space of the sea area on the "Mappemonde" in 1700. Given Guillaume Delisle's standing and his exchange with missionaries, the information that Guillaume Delisle had about the "Mer Orientale" must have come from Manchuria via China. In the same year, Chambon marked the East Sea as "Mer de Corée," apparently tipping the balance between the two names on the Korea Road toward "Mer de Corée." Sensing it, Guillaume Delisle wrote that "Mer de Corée" and "Mer Orientale" refer to the same sea on his 1705 "Carte des indes et de la Chine." On "L'Asie" in 1708, he adhered to "Mer Orientale." It was de Fer who buttressed Guillaume Delisle. Acquiring geographic information from a variety of sources like Guillaume Delisle, de Fer also identified the East Sea as "Mer Orientale" on his 1703 map of East Asia. Not only that, but he also added an unusual note in the upper margin, "Mer peu ou point connue des Européens. Les Tartares l'appelle [sic] Orientale" ("Sea little or not known to the Europeans. The Manchus call it [sic] Oriental").

Later, when de Fer learned about different names for the East Sea from Japanese and Chinese sources, his belief that the sea was "Mer Orientale" was shaken. Senex marked the East Sea as the "Sea of Corea" on his "A New and Correct Map of the World" in 1711 but as 'The Eastern or Corea Sea" on "Asia Corrected from the Observations Communicated to the Royal Society at London and Royal Academy at Paris" in the same year.

Moll, who was born in the Netherlands and moved to London, called the East Sea, the "Sea of Korea" on the "Map of Asia" in 1710 and did the same on "A New and Correct Map of the Whole World" in 1719. He maintained the same markings on the maps he published afterwards.

Before his death in 1726, Guillaume Delisle published "Carte d'Asie" in 1723 where he marked the East Sea as "Mer de Corée." On "Mappe-Monde" which was published in his name posthumously in 1741, the same marking was made. In fact, map-makers around him apparently all thought that "Mer de Corée" should be the name of the East Sea. Joseph-Nicolas Delisle, Guillaume Delisle's brother, astronomer and cartographer; Philippe Buache, his daughter's son and famous physical geographer; and Guillaume Danet, his close, junior colleague, all leaned toward "Mer de Corée." It is very likely that the maps published in his final years or posthumously were in fact published by his close acquaintances.

Joseph-Nicolas Delisle, who directed the making of the map of Siberia as head of a Russian astronomical observatory, had influence over Russian maps over 20 years thereafter, resulting in most Russian maps identifying the East Sea as the "Sea of Korea" until ca. 1850. He made the same markings on the maps which he, after returning home, made independently or jointly with Buache. Danet also did the same.

Rigobert Bonne, d'Anville's most faithful student, left the remote sea of the East Sea blank as his teacher until he finally marked it as the "Sea of Korea" on a map of East Asia in 1720.

Gilles Robert de Vaugondy, a relative of Sanson and inheritor of the Sanson family's map materials and Jaillot's map business, formed a prestigious map-making family of his own from the mid- to late 18th century and produced many maps. With just one exception of "L'Empire du Japon" in 1750, de Vaugondy marked the East Sea as the "Sea of Korea" on all of his maps. And his successors, including Didier Robert de Vaugondy, followed suit.

After marking the East Sea as "Mer de Corée" on his 1735 "Carte de l'Empire du Japon," Bellin retained the marking on all the maps that he published until he died in 1772. He left a great legacy as the first oceanographer in France. As a recipient of the royal stipend from 1741 and a founding member of the *Académie de Marine* in 1752, he made maps based on his hydrographic knowledge, which had a great influence on maps of Germany, the Netherlands, and Great Britain as well as France. Adam Friedrich Zürner of Germany labeled the East Sea as "Sin Coreer" on his "Planipharium Terrestris" in 1740. Isaak Tirion also marked the East Sea as "Mare di Corea" on his "Nuova Carta dell'Imperio della China" in 1740. D'Anville did not make any mark for the East Sea on his "Royaume de Corée" in 1737 in compliance with his own principle but on the map drawn manually for the preparation of the 1737 map, he marked "Mer de Corée" on two spots in the East Sea. And most European maps that were modeled after his map of Korea labeled the East Sea as "Sea of Korea." Gilles Robert de Vaugondy also identified the sea as "Mer de Corée" on "L'Asie" in 1739 and other maps afterwards. Kitchin too marked the East Sea as the "Sea of Korea" on "A Map of Quan-Tong, or Lea-Tonge" in 1743.

Although they are found to have been influenced by Guillaume Delisle, German maps exhibited some ingenuity of their own. For example, the successors to Homann called the East Sea "Mare Orientale Minus" ("Small East Sea") on "Imperii Russici et Tartariae Majoris" in 1735. Johann Matthias Hase,[18] August Gottlieb Boehme and Güssefeld, who learned map-making from Homann, all followed the naming. Georg Moritz Lowitz also used the same name on "Planiglobii Terrestris" in 1746.

Just like Gilles Robert de Vaugondy, Saint Robert of France used both "Mer de Corée" and "Mer Mer du Japon" for the East Sea on his "l'Empire du Japon" in 1750, It is not clear if it was mere coincidence or the result of their consultation. However, in France, "Sea of Korea" was dominant in the late 18th century too. Thus, Janvier marked the East Sea as "Mer de Corée" on his 1760 map of Asia and made the same marking on other maps as well. Nicolas Antoine Boulanger also marked the East Sea as "Mer de Corée" on his "Nouvelle Mappemonde" in 1760. Jean Baptiste Louis Clouet did the same on his "Carte d'Asie" in 1764. M. Pocaud's "Carte pour l'histoire générale" of 1763, which d'Anville collected as an important material, was not an exception in intifying the East Sea as "Mer de Corée" and Louis Brion de la Tour also made the same marking on "L'Asie" in 1765. L.C. Desnos and L. Charles also used the same name on "L'Asie" in 1766.

18) He liked to sign his maps with his Latin name, "Hasius."

Turning back to Great Britain, the *Encyclopedia Britannica* marked the East Sea as the "Sea of Korea" on its appendix "Map of Asia" in 1771 and retained the marking in the 2nd edition of the world prestigious encyclopedia in 1783. In 1772, Samuel Dunn made a minor change to the name, calling the sea "Corean Gulf" in his *Scientia Terrarumet et Coelorum* (*Heavens and Earth*). The term "gulf" as used in Great Britain in the late-18th century can be interpreted as an expression that recognizes what is today's Yeongheung Gulf. It can also represent that it is a rather small sea, as the German "Minus" was used. Neale and Jefferys marked the East Sea as the "Sea of Korea" on a map of Asia in 1783 and 1785, whereas C. Bowles used "Korean Gulf" on "Bowles's new Four Sheet Map of Asia."

Thomas Conder identified the East Sea as the "Sea of Korea" on "Asia" in 1790 and J. Palairet made the same marking on "Map of the World" in 1792. A. Keith used the term "Korean Sea" on "The World According to the Latest Discoveries" in 1794, while used "G. of Korae" on "Asia." Another example of two different names for the East Sea in the same year by the same author is Robert Wilkinson, who used "G. of Corea" on "A Map of Asia from the Latest Discoveries" in 1794 and "Sea of Corea" on "China, Drawn from the Latest & Best Authorities" in the same year. In

1799, Thomson called the East Sea "Gulf of Corea" in "New Map of Asia" and John Russell also marked the sea ad the "Gulf of Corea" on "Map of the World Shewing the Tracks & Discoveries of Capt. Cook." Thus, some map-makers made slightly different markings on each of the three maps that they made in the same year, while some others used the same name on different maps. The notation of the East Sea as "Gulf" was a British invention in the late 18th century.

The "golden days" of the "Korea Road" in the 18th century were overshadowed at one stroke by La Pérouse's *Voyage de La Pérouse autour du Monde* in 1797. The text of the travelog made a mixed use of "Mer de Corée" and "Mer du Japan." However, the "Mer du Japan" in the atlas, marked from the mouth of the East Sea in the northeast direction, was seriously received in Great Britain, drawing British maps, which would be on the forefront of map-making in the 19th century, toward "Mer du Japan." Some French cartographers changed the marking of the East Sea in the 19th century editions of their maps, and so did the Arrowsmiths, one of the most famous map-making families of the 19th century. Amidst this new trend, Thomas Illman still marked the East Sea as the "Sea of Corea" on "Asia" in 1835 and James Wyld used the name "Gulf of Corea" and "Sea of Corea" on "Asia" of 1840 and 1845, respectively.

Now let us trace the Korea Road in the maps of Russia which stretches to the eastern end of the European continent. A new development of the Russian maps was triggered by Joseph-Nicolas Delisle, brother of Guillaume Delisle, when he was invited to Russia. There he was appointed head of the St. Petersburg Observatory and placed in charge of supervising the Russian cartography. Most Russian map-makers of the mid-18th century were under the supervision of Joseph-Nicolas Delisle. Though some of them were jealous of him and turned their backs to him, two-thirds of them maintained a good relationship with him. As a result, a majority of the maps which were produced until the mid-19th century, including V. Kirilov's map of Asia in 1734, maps by the Russian Academy, and the atlases made for educational purposes, indicated the East Sea as the "Sea of Korea," "East Ocean" the "The Eastern Sea" like Joseph-Nicolas Delisle. The rest left the sea blank or marked as the "Sea of Japan."

The situations in China and Japan were different. Usually, the Chinese did not name a sea – such names as "East Sea," "West Sea," "North Sea" and "South Sea" are the conceptual ones rather than proper nouns, referring to not the seas themselves but the land in that direction. Korea's East Sea, however, was not such a case. According to the presentations that Wu Songdi, Gu Renhe and Cheng Long made at the seminars of the Society for East Sea,[19] the Jurchens called the sea area "East Sea" as early on as recorded in *Hou Hanshu* and *Shan hai jing*. They affirm that the Jurchens continued to call the sea "East Sea," whether in the period which was recorded in historical documents or not.

Although the mentioning of the East Sea in China was mostly made after the Sui and Tang Dynasties, Cheong Long makes a specific report, "Wei Yuan, a prominent historian and geographer who was active in the mid-19th century, confirmed the location of the East Sea twice through maps."[20]

In Japan, there were no names for the seas and their maps only indicated the bearings of the seas. The Japanese were even not interested in it when Matteo Ricci used for the East Sea the name "Riben Hai" ("Japan Sea" in Chinese) in 1602 because it was not the name that they used in Japan. According to Dr. Shim Jeongbo, in Japan, Shiba Kokan first marked the East Sea as the "Inland Sea of Japan" on his "Map

---

19) Jing Tian, "Recent Research Progress on a Study of the Sea Name on East Sea and Japan Sea in China," The 8th International Seminar on the Naming of Seas, Special Emphasis Concerning the North Pacific Ocean, 2002, The Society for East Sea; other presentations presented at the seminars of the Society for East Sea.

20) Cheng Long, "Yuan Wei (1794-1857), His Research and Maps about East Sea," The 16th International Seminar on Sea Names, 2010, The Society for East Sea.

of the Earth" in as late as 1792 and Ine Takago used the term "Japan Sea" in the *Konyo zenzu setzu* (坤輿全圖說, *Complete World Map with Illustrated Explications*) in 1802. Later, the court astronomer Takahashi Kageyasu, who was responsible for the map-making under the Shogunate, marked the East Sea as the "Joseon Sea" twice, one on the 1809 "Nippon henkai ryakuzu" (日本邊界略圖, "Simplified Map of Japan's Periphery") and the other on the 1810 "Shintei bankoku zenzu" (新訂萬國全圖, "New and Revised World Map"), which he made at the request of the Shogunate.[21] The marking was made primarily because, as the Shogunate had been marking the sea to Japan's Pacific Ocean side as "Great Japan Sea," it would have been nonsensical to call the East Sea "Sea of Japan" also. Takahashi's students too followed his marking of "Joseon Sea." According to Dr. Lee Sang-Tae, from Takahashi to the 1870s, over 20 Japanese maps identified the East Sea as "Joseon Sea" and so did 10-plus official documents, including three from the Daijo-kan (太政官), or the Great Council of State, the highest and central administrative body at the time.[22]

The Map Road is a barometer of civilizations and a visual

21) Shim, "Research Trends in Japan on the Place Name 'Sea of Japan.'"
22) Lee Sang-Tae, "Even Japan Used the Name East Sea and Sea of Joseon, not Sea of Japan," The 13th International Seminar on the Naming of Seas and East Sea, The Society for East Sea, 2007, The Society for East Sea.

representation of the historical books as an indispensible companion. The name "East Sea" is an encapsulation of the lives of the Korean people for over 2,000 years and the Korea Road, comprising "East Sea" and "Sea of Korea," was dominant regarding the naming of the sea area in the West from the mid-17th to the end of the 18th century. There was no dominant name for the East Sea in China until the end of the 19th century and in Japan until the 1870s. Therefore, it is most certainly not understandable and acceptable that the name, "Sea of Japan," which has a history of only 100 years or so, should remain the single, monopolistic name for the East Sea.

Part II

Notation of the Name "East Sea" in the World

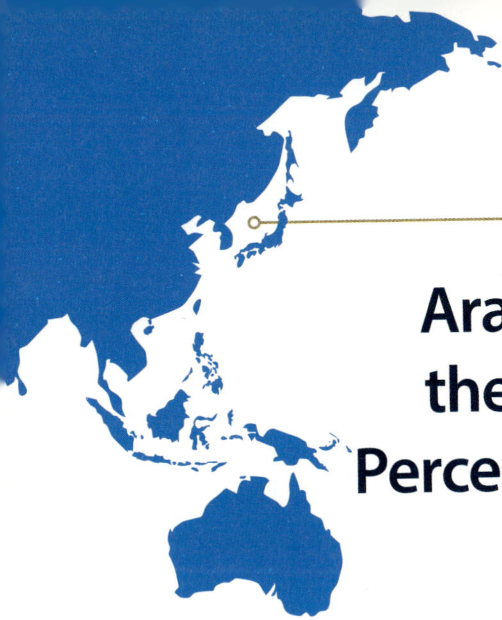

Chapter 1

Arabs' Advance to the East and Their Perceptions of Korea

Many books on the history of human civilizations have been written from the Western perspective. As a result, many readers simply think that the torch of the human civilizations was lit in ancient Greece and passed to Europe via Rome and then to the United States, resulting in today's achievements. On the other hand, the great contributions of the Chinese, Indian, and Arab civilizations are remembered only by some fragmentary relics, such as the Great Wall, the Terracotta Army of Qin Shi Huang, the Taj Mahal, and the Pyramids. The fact is often forgotten that books and achievements by Greek philosophers and natural scientists were introduced to the Western world through the studies and translations of Arab scholars in the Middle Ages and a great deal of them were studied in Alexandria, Egypt. We need to understand how the Arab world bridged Greece and the West, what Arab visitors to Korea in ancient times thought of us, and what records they left.

Although the word "Arab" is of ethnic origin, the regions that we call "the Arab world" are not only today's Arabia, Egypt, Tunisia, Morocco; they also encompass the non-Arab world, including Jordan, Syria, Persia (today's Iran), and Turkey. Harley and Woodward[1] argued that because what connects them all is their faith in Islam, the word "Islam," a religious concept, should be used in place of "Arab." While agreeing with the authors, we also used in this book the terminology "Arab-Islam" in an inertial way of thinking.

Today, Middle-East people who practice Islam are often associated with some negative images, such as abuse of women, terrorism, and drugs, which are regarded as "uncivilized." As is widely known, however, Arabs were inventors of the Arabic numerals, including zero, and had not only highly developed mathematics and sciences but also very sophisticated architecture. The library in Alexandria was the largest center of knowledge and information in the ancient world. Even today, most Middle-East people hold

---

1) J. B. Harley & Woodward, *Cartography in the Traditional Islamic and South Asian Societies*, The University of Chicago Press, 1992.

the belief that all humans are equal and they want to lead peaceful lives just like any other ordinary person in the world.

The Arabs accepted and studied the geography and astronomy of Ptolemy, a Greek-Roman citizen who lived in Alexandria, Egypt (A.D. ca. 90-168). Thanks to the experience-based information that Arab merchants brought home from many Western as well as Oriental countries, they could publish geography books that reflected their knowledge, independent from Greek influence. Among them are quite a number that are related to Korea. We will now examine what they thought of Korea and Korean people at the time based on a study by Dr. Kim Jong-Wee.[2)]

Generally, in the Arab-Islam world, the post office was the confluence of all kinds of geographic information. Information on regions, districts, roads, natural features and climate that were gathered together from direct experience came in handy for postmen to do their job. That was why some heads of post offices published books on geography. It is not known for certain whether post offices had gathered geographic information about the oceans and what happened to the nautical charts that merchants

---

2) Kim Jong-Wee, *Jungse Islam Munheone Bichin Hanguksang* (*Images of Korea as Reflected in Medieval Islam Documents*), Korea International Economics Institute, 1977.

had collected. However, apparently almost all stories of geographic experiences were conveyed to post offices.

The first book where Korea is mentioned in the Islam world is *Kitāb al Masālik w'al Mamālik* (*The Book of Roads and Kingdoms*) by Ibn Khordadbeh, a Persian geographer who worked as an official in the post office business. In this book published in A.D. 846 (second edition in A.D. 885), the author introduced Korea, saying "Silla [an ancient kingdom of Korea] is at the end of China. Silla is a beautiful country with many mountains and abundant gold." With reference to this book, another Persian writer, Ibn Rusta, left a similar description. Arab traveler Sulaiman al-Tajir wrote in his A.D. 851 book *Akhbar al-Sin wa 'l-Hind* (*Notes on China and India*): "Silla lies to [the east of] the Chinese coast. They send gifts to the Chinese emperor. Silla is an island and its inhabitants have white skin." Al-Masudi, a Baghdad-born traveler, mentioned Silla twice in his book *Muruj adh-dhahab wa ma'adin al-jawhar* (*The Meadows of Gold and Mines of Gems*). Under Khordadbeh's influence, he stated that Silla people were descendants of Noah's grandson.

In addition, *Al-Bad' wa-al-tārīkh* (*Creation and History*), a book by Ibn Tahir al-Maqdisi, an Arab who was born in Jerusalem, has a passage mentioning Silla, But it contains nothing new about the country as the author referred to the above writers and wrote more or less the same. Ibn al-Nadim, who managed a bookstore-cum-library in Baghdad, published *Kitāb al-Fihrist* (*Book of the Index*) in 977. In this bibliographical dictionary, he briefly mentioned Silla, but likewise adding nothing new.

Muhammad al- Idrisi was born into an aristocratic family in the city of Ceuta, Morocco, and educated in Córdoba, Spain. He was a geographer who is sometimes referred to as "the Ptolemy of the Medieval Ages." Fond of traveling, he toured Asia Minor early on and further extensively around many regions of southern France, Great Britain, Spain, and Morocco to learn more about the local geography and cultures. In 1138, he was invited as a scholar to the court of the Norman King of Sicily, Roger II. Some scholars postulate that the king invited Muhammad al-Idrisi because the king needed his help in his aim to gain control over North Africa.[3] Whatever the motive behind his invitation, materials about al-Idrisi tell us that Roger II asked him to collect geographic and cultural information on many countries in the world and make a world map. The king

3) S. Maqbul Ahmad, "Cartography of al-Sharif al-Idrisi," *Cartography in Traditional Islamic and South Asian Societies* (David Woodward & John Brian Harley, eds., *The History of Cartography*, vol. 2), Chicago, University of Chicago Press, 1992, p.156.

enjoyed conversations with al-Idrisi about the world. Living up to his job, Al-Idrisi completed in 1154 *Kitab nuzhat al-mushtaq fi'khtiraq al-'afaq* (*The Book of Pleasant Journeys into Faraway Lands*), simply known as "The Book of Roger," and a world map. According to the book, Silla was comprised of several islands beyond China and it was depicted as a utopia with superb nature and abundant gold. The same can be said of his map, on which Silla is marked wrongly as an island to the southeast of China, supposedly in the area of today's Wando Island. Presumably, Korean General Jang Bogo's Cheonghaejin ("Blue Sea Headquarters"), a naval and trading base on Wando, might well have been idealized because it was a flourishing center of international trade of the times. Jang was a powerful maritime commander who controlled Silla's sea trade with Tang China and with Japan. At the time, the sea areas around Silla were known as "China Sea" and the name, "East Sea" was not yet known.

Most authors knew only of Silla, but even after Jang's death and the demise of Silla, the Islamic world continued to trade with Goryeo at the estuary of the Yeseong River. The first author who mentioned Goryeo was Rashid al-Din. He wrote *Jāmi al-tawārīkh* (*Compendium of Chronicles*), a work of world history. Well-acquainted with Mongolia, he introduced the Yuan Dynasty of China and its 12 provinces,

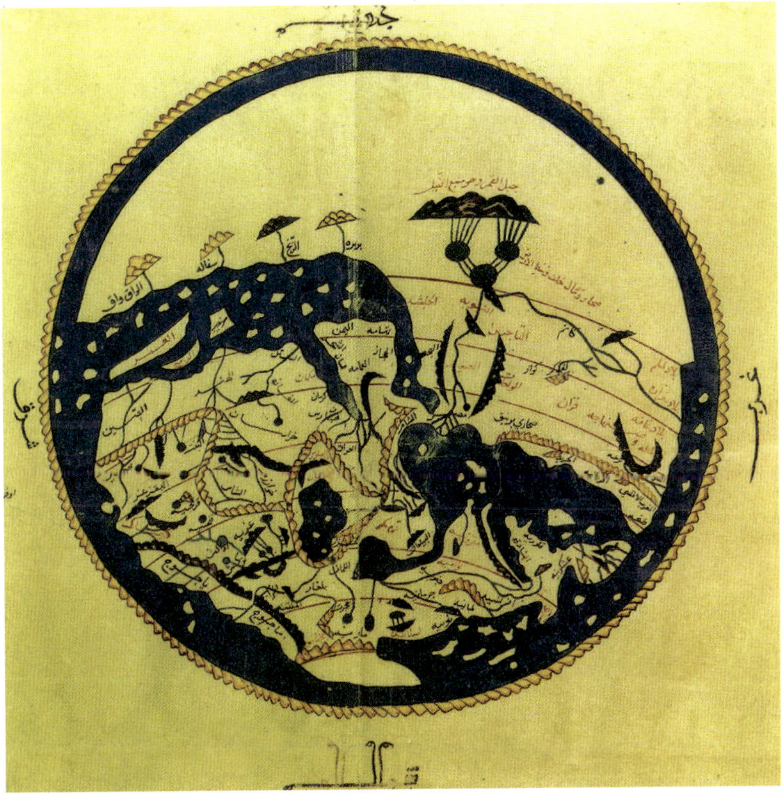

Idrisi's world map depicts the Arabs' world view in ca. 1150.

mentioning the existence of "Kauli" for Goryeo, for the first time in the Middle East. His usage of "Kauli," for Goryeo, which Arab-Islam sailors called "Cory," suggests that he referred to information derived from China: Goryeo (高麗) is pronounced "Gaoli" in Chinese. It is said that for some reason, Rashid al-Din gained the strong confidence of Kublai Khan and became his son-in-law.

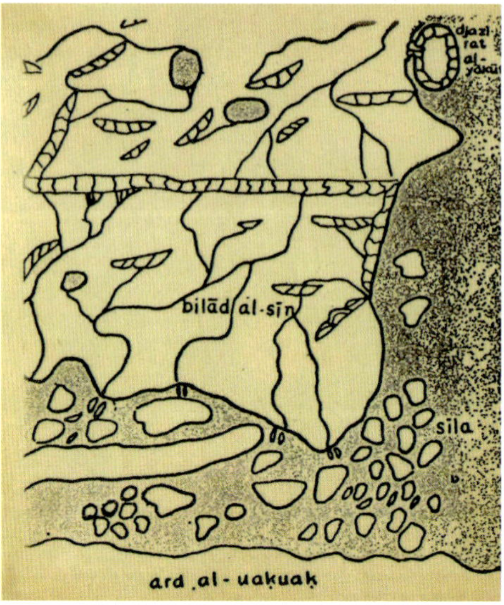

On this map of Southeast Asia by Idrisi in 1150, Silla is comprised of several islands. The author seemingly drew this map on the basis of oral reports received from sailors.

As seen above, in the areas of Islamic culture, the existence of Korea was given merely a brief mention in several books. As for maps, only Silla was marked as an island on al-Idrisi's map. Silla was commonly described almost like a utopia with plentiful resources and rich gold. It leaves a lot to be desired because the authors described it based on what they heard indirectly, through a few acquaintance links, from sailors who had gone to Silla for trade. To identify the actual location of what was depicted as the "island" country Silla, presumablyCheonghaejin, or today's Wando, clearer evidence needs to emerge. It is also desirable that what were described as "Arab merchants" and "Da Shi Guo" (大食國) be more clearly identified.

As the first references to Korea were made in the mid-9th century, it is estimated that the "Arab merchants" first visited Korea during the late 8th to early 9th centuries. But it is yet to be ascertained precisely when it happened. The fact that Rashid al-Din, who was a latecomer among the authors, mentioned Goryeo and the Yuan Dynasty implies that trade with Korea was conducted until a certain point of time during the Goryeo Dynasty. However, likewise, no clear record has been found. Considering Korea is still called "Cory" in the Islamic region, we only assume that the name originated from Goryeo (or Koryŏ according to the former Romanization system). These small traces have further limits in providing us with the necessary information as they were left on only a handful of maps of Portugal, which repulsed Islam, and not in Islamic materials. It is, therefore, strongly hoped that someday ancient Islamic documents will provide more enlightenment on these aspects.

Chapter 2

Old Maps and the Notation of the Name "East Sea" in Italy

Prior to the Italian Renaissance in the fifteenth century, the writings of Greek philosophers and natural scientists were introduced to the Western Roman Empire in the Middle Ages through Arab translations. The Renaissance was made possible in Italy primarily because Greek scholars fled to Italy with cultural heritages after the fall of the Eastern Roman Empire. Basically, however, it was an outgrowth of the favorable environment that Italian city states, especially those in the northern part of the country, such as Florence, Venice, and Rome, provided. It was possible based on the accumulated wealth and the industrial, economic and financial development, which they had achieved through trade with the Orient. The Renaissance, in turn, promoted cultural development in Italy, stimulating the development of the printing industry. In its wake, map-making began to grow as an independent industry.

As studies on Greek classics began to awaken, the achievements of Ptolemy became better known. His *Geography*, in particular, attracted much attention and scholars in cities in northern Italy brought his writings to new light, beginning with the re-publication of *Geography* in Bologna in 1477. Then modified and expanded editions of the book followed because, due to insufficient geographic information at the time of Ptolemy, India had been drawn smaller than Sri Lanka on the world map which was included in the original version of *Geography*.

The Italians came to know about the existence of remote Asian countries, including China, through *The Travels of Marco Polo* (1231). In the 13th century, portolan charts began to be made in Italy to help navigation. Further, the discovery of America by Columbus signaled the start of the Age of Discovery with fanfare, inspiring Europeans' curiosity about distant countries. In Italy, as the map-making industry that flourished following the Renaissance satisfied people's curiosity about the outside world, an increasing number of people also wanted to know more about Italy's own regions and beautiful islands. This interest in local areas led to growing interest in world maps. Benedetto Bordone started his map-making business with the publication of the maps of Italian regions and islands and then came to produce world maps.

One of the earliest Italian maps referring to the name "East Sea" was the "Cantino planisphere" ("Cantino World Map") that Alberto Cantino published in 1502. On this nautical chart, he named the Northeast Asian sea areas, including the East Sea, as "Oceanus Orientalis." Later, Bordone gave the name, "Mare Orientale" to the sea to the south of Korea and Japan in his *Isolario*, which was published in 1528 and republished in 1547. However, Cantino's "Oceanus Orientalis" and Bordone's "Mare Orientale" do not refer to the East Sea only. At that time, ocean (*oceanus*) and sea (*mare*) were used interchangeably and in the European perspective, the two terms simply meant the remote Northeast Asian sea areas, including the East Sea, in the Far East. On his 1561 map "Asia," Giacomo Gastaldi referred to "Mare de Mangi" for the East Sea. B. Zaltieri also labeled the East Sea as "Sea of Mangi" on his map which he made in 1566 with reference to *The Travels of Marco Polo*. G. F. Camocio also used the same name for the East Sea on his map, "Asia," in 1567.

However, on his 1565 "Mappamondo," Bortelli named the

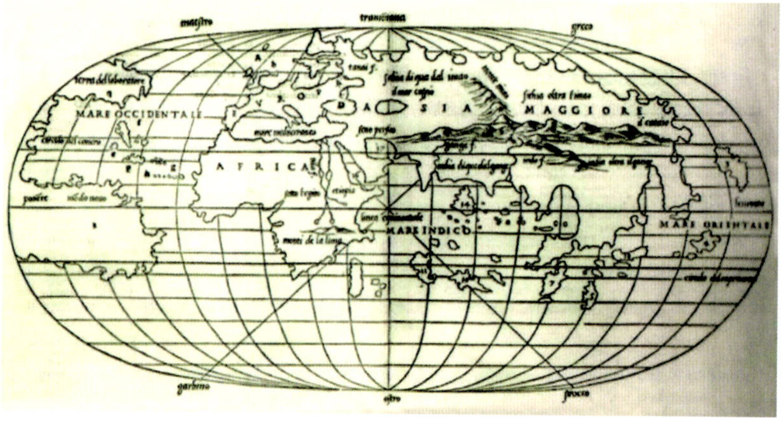

Isolario (1528) by Italian cartographer Benedetto Bordone indicated "Mare Orientale" in the south of Korea.

Southeast Asian sea areas as "Mare della China" and marked "Oceano Orientale" below the Equator. Paolo Forlani, on his 1574 map, "Asia," again named the East Sea as the "Sea of Mangi." It seems that he used the same name after those on the maps that preceded his, except those of Cantino and Gastaldi who first used such epithets as "Oceanus Orientalis" and "Mare de Mangi." On his map, "Asia," in 1580, Giovanni Botero attempted to add a Greek flavor by using the name "Oceanus Eous, Sive Orientalis" ("East or Oriental Ocean") for the East Sea. On the 1596 map, "Tartariae," Giovanni Antonio Magini marked "Mare Chin" ("China Sea") for the East Sea, and Giuseppe Rosaccio made the same marking on his 1598 double hemisphere world map.

In the 17th century, Italy underwent internal conflicts

and monarchical power weakened, diminishing its national competitiveness. Its culture also suffered, thereby adversely affecting the map-making industry. Meanwhile, Spain and Portugal boosted their naval forces and developed colonies, emerging as new powers in Europe. Notably, Portugal's overseas-oriented policy required the aid of maps. The Portuguese were compelled to turn for assistance to the Venetian map-makers in Italy who had experience and expertise in map-making. In spite of declining domestic demand for maps, Italian cartographers did not stop making maps.

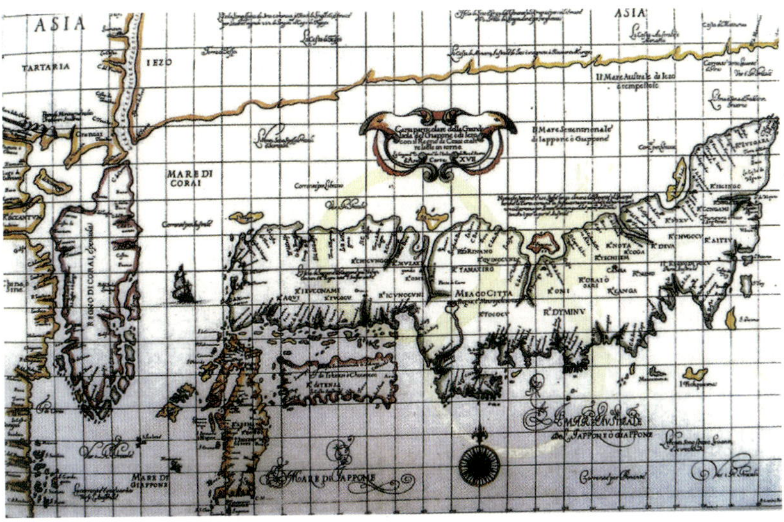

Korea and Japan are shown in this *Dell'Arcano del Mare*, the first maritime atlas to cover the world which Robert Dudley, a British-born, naturalized Italian, made in 1646. In the center of the East Sea, "Mare Di Corai" ("Sea of Korea") is marked in square type, along with "North Sea of Japan" and "South Sea of Iezo" in cursive type.

A map of Asia made by A. Zatta of Italy in 1777. "Mare di Corea" ("Sea of Korea") is shwon for the East Sea.

Robert Dudley's achievements are particularly noteworthy. Born in Great Britain and a devout Catholic, he loved Italy and thus settled in Florence before he published *Dell'Arcano del Mare* (*Secrets of the Sea*) in 1646, the first maritime encyclopedia with a maritime atlas of the world. He included in the book a map covering both Korea and Japan, titled "Carta particolare della Grande Isola del'Giapone è di Iezo con il Regno di Corai et altre Isole in torno" ("Detailed Map of the Big Island of Japan and Hokkaido with the Kingdom of Korea and Other Nearby Islands"), and he wrote "Corai" for Korea. Its first edition in 1647 marked "Mar di Corai" ("Sea of Korea") in large type, at the center of which is the East Sea and "Mare Boreale del Giappone" ("North Sea of Japan") in its northeast. It named the southern sea areas of Japan as "Mare Australe di Jappone O Giappone" ("South Sea of Japan") and the sea in the southwest of Japan as "Mare di Giappone" ("Sea of Japan"). In the second impression in 1661, the author put a cartouche with the title of the map at the center of the East Sea and placed "Sea of Korea" closer to the east coast of Korea, while "Il Mare Settentrionale di Jappone O Giappone" ("The North Sea of Japan") is marked with the definite article "Il" near the cartouche in the northeastern sea areas of Japan. He indicated "Mare di Giappone" in two places, namely, the southwestern and southern sea areas of Japan. "Sea of Korea" and "Sea of Japan" to the south of Japan marked in large type are titles of the seas per se, but "The North Sea of Japan," using the definite article, is an incidental explanation. Kohei Watanabe and Masataka Yaji of Japan argue that the map has four names of "Sea of Japan,"[4] but it only betrays the

---

4) Kohei Watanabe & Masataka Yaji, "Study on the Geographical Name "Japan Sea," The 16th International Seminar on Sea Names, 2010, The Society for the East Sea.

fact that Japanese scholars are susceptible to the bad habit of regarding everything with "Sea" and "Japan" as "Sea of Japan."

In the 18th century, map-making remained a slow business in Italy but a few maps related to the East Sea were still produced. On his 1740 "Nuova Carta dell'Imperio della China," Isaak Tirion named what is the East Sea as "Mare di Corai," presumably because he referred to the name which was in use in Europe at the time. A. Zatta, on "Asiae" in 1777, referred to the East Sea as "Mare di Corea." However, G. M. Cassini made no notation for either the East Sea or the sea area south of Japan on his "Le Isole del Giappone e la Corea" ("The Islands of Japan and Korea") in 1797.

During the 19th century, the map-making industry in Italy suffered an even more serious setback. In making the map, "Asia," in 1830, Bonatti and Pietro indicated "Gulf di Corea" for the East Sea. They probably referred to British maps of the late 18th century, because on most British maps after the 1800s the East Sea was marked as the "Sea of Japan" under the influence of Jean François de Galaup, comte de La Pérouse.

Italy was the first country in Europe to sell and distribute maps, putting map-making into commercial use. As well as Columbus, it produced John Cabot, who explored Canada

Map of Northeast Asia drafted by Bonatti & Pietro of Italy in 1820. It shows the East Sea as "G. di Corea."

for the first time, and Marco Polo. Nonetheless, apparently the Italians had only limited interest in Southeast Asia as their maps lack the local names in the Southeast Asian sea areas and what is the East Sea. However, they established some principles on the naming of sea areas of foreign countries:

First, regarding sea areas distant from Italy, the naming

should be made in consideration of their direction from Italy.

Second, the name of a body of water should be decided upon corresponding to the most important country in the vicinity. For example, the Southeast Asian sea areas, including the East Sea, are named as "Mare della China" and the sea areas to the south of Japan are marked as "Mare Australe di Giapone" ("South Sea of Japan").

These two principles were widely accepted as basic guidelines for establishing sea names on the maps of the Western world. Maps of other countries, including the Netherlands, are also found to have followed these guidelines in establishing sea names.

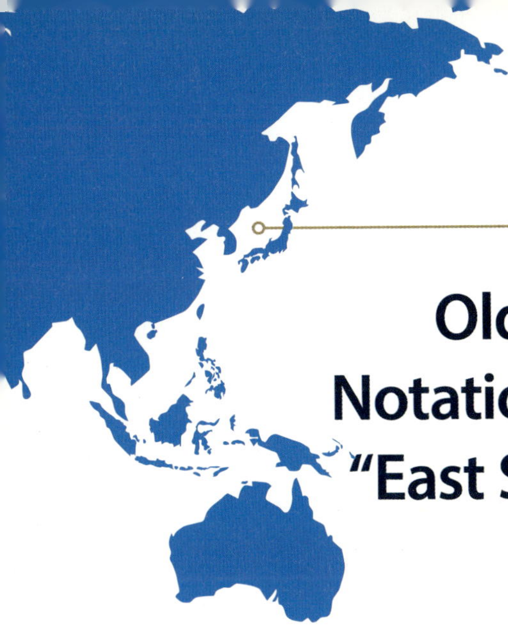

Chapter 3

Old Maps and the Notation of the Name "East Sea" by Vatican Missionaries

Occupying only a small area in Italy's capital city of Rome, the Vatican is the spiritual focal point of the 1.5 billion Catholics of the world. Every year, millions of tourists from across the world visit the Palace of the Vatican. It houses all kinds of rare treasures of humankind and historically important materials. Among them are materials collected and sent by its missionaries working all over the world, which are mostly preserved as confidential. Some missionaries, when they returned home, wrote books about the country of their mission, including maps. Our interest lies in their maps, and especially in how the East Sea was identified, if at all, on them.

China and Japan were the Asian countries in which the Vatican showed the greatest interest among the nations to which Catholic missionaries were sent. While restricting missionary work, China wanted the Vatican to help them manufacture canons and asked it to make a large map of China in a scientific manner. In response, in the selection of missionaries to China, the Vatican gave preference to those who had some knowledge of map-making. The Vatican also had interest in evangelizing Korea, but due to Korea's closed-door policy before the mid-19th century, it virtually excluded the country from its missionary works.

Japan was also preferred by many missionaries. Despite the substantial restrictions that the Japanese imposed on them for political reasons, the missionaries nonetheless favored Japan as a destination for their work. However, obviously they did not accomplish as much as they intended. It was probably because the Japanese, although they are polite and kind in their personal relationships, often refrain from disclosing to others what they really think. In addition, Shintoism and Buddhism were deeply rooted in their culture and everyday life and it must have prevented them from easily accepting a foreign religion. Catholicism was favorably received by local lords and people in some regions in southern Japan, but apparently the exchanges were only superficial and the missionary works there were not truly active. Nevertheless, missionaries to Japan wanted to better understand the country by studying the island country's history, customs and institutions. They also wanted to make Japan more widely known throughout Europe by obtaining locally compiled maps of Japan. Some missionaries to Japan, after returning to Europe, went out of their way to produce maps of Japan themselves. On the maps of Japan that they made, three ways of representing the East Sea can be identified:

First, as they found that Japan had no objective and exact name to refer to what is the East Sea, the missionaries left the sea area blank without giving it any name, as exemplified by António Francisco Cardim's "Iapponia Nova & Accurata Descriptio" ("New & Accurate Description of Japan") in 1612.

Second, Bernardino Ginnaro could not obtain a definite name for what is the East Sea. When he asked local Japanese about the name of the sea areas, what he could get out of them was the answer "Northern Sea" or "North Sea" for the sea area in the north and "Southern Sea" or "South Sea" for the sea area in the south. For this reason, he named the East Sea as "Mare du Boreale" ("North Sea") on his maps of Japan in the 1630s.

Third, meanwhile, Christopher Blancus, on his 1617 map of Japan, labeled the East Sea as "Mare Iaponicum" ("Sea of Japan") and the south of Japan "Oceanus Chinensis" ("China Ocean") probably in consideration of the importance of China. Unlike Ginnaro, Blancus seems to have recognized "Mare" as a smaller sea and "Oceanus," a larger sea. Besides, Ginnaro, like Blancus, used the name "Sea of China" for the south of Japan and "Oceano Chinensis" for the East Sea in 1641.

Missionaries sent to China also experienced difficulties. Besides the many administrative constraints, the Chinese were also not favorably inclined toward foreign religions. Catholicism was accepted mostly as a subject of scholastic endeavor but it failed to take deep root among the general public. Practical Chinese officials and people sometimes asked missionaries to do what they needed to do but hard for them to do themselves. Managing an astronomical observatory and engaging in more scientific map-making were some such areas. Under the circumstances, "Kunyu wanguo quantu" (坤輿萬國全圖, "A Map of the Myriad Countries of the World") made by Matteo Ricci was unexpectedly well received. On this map with markings made in Chinese, the location of China, occupying the middle of the map, presumably satisfied the pride of the

Chinese people.

Matteo Ricci's "Kunyu wanguo quantu" did not have much influence in Europe. The map was introduced into Japan and many copies of it were made there. It is evaluated to have provided the Japanese with an opportunity to open their eyes to the world. However, the notation of the East Sea as the "Japan Sea" was not accepted even in Japan itself. The fact that Ricci's notation of "日本海" ("Japan Sea") did not attract much attention can be interpreted as to mean that such name did not exist in Japan and the Japanese did not care about it. It was presumably because, in view of the maps by missionaries who had been sent to Japan, including Ginnaro, what is the East Sea/Sea of Japan was called the "North Sea" from the days of these maps until the end of the 19th century. Japanese scholars, however, seemingly overlook the heart of the matter by avoiding and not recognizing the name, "North Sea."[5]

Nevertheless, missionaries after Matteo Ricci seemed to have trouble in naming what is the East Sea on their maps. Coming to understand that the East Sea was an endonym, Father Giulio Aleni marked the East Sea as the "Small East Sea" on his 1623 map, "Asia."[6] Father Álvaro

5) Quoted in Shim, "Research Trends in Japan on the Place Name 'Sea of Japan.'"

6) "Small East Sea" was named as such presumably because it was a relatively

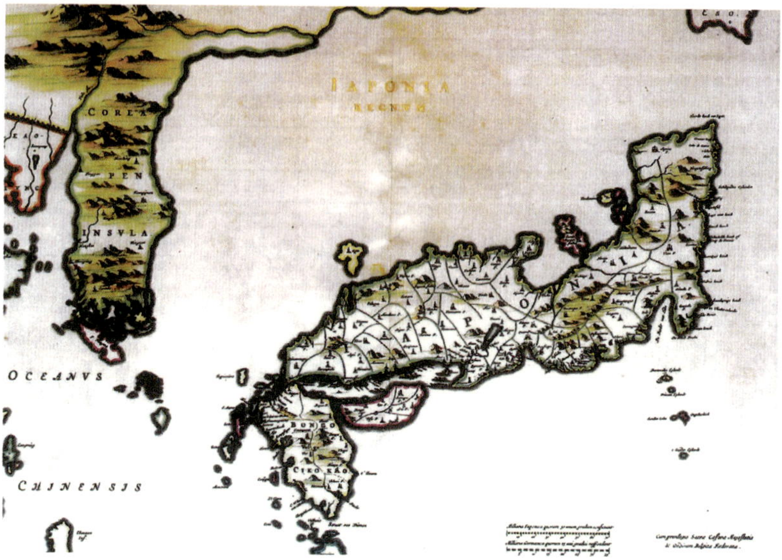

Korea and Japan, part of Novus Atlas Sinensis published by Father Martini of Italy and Blaeu of the Netherlands in 1655. No name is given to what is the East Sea.

Semedo, who had stayed in China before them, returned home to Portugal and in 1655 made "Carta di Asia" in many European languages where he, taking a step further, inscribed "Mare della China" for the East Sea. In the same year, Father Martino Martini left the sea area of the East Sea vacant of any name at all in *Novus Atlas Sinensis* (*New Atlas of China*), which was published by the publisher Blaeu in Amsterdam. Caught in a dilemma where he had to either deny Ricci, a big name who was one of the founders of the

small body of water. On the other hand, because the East Sea was called the "Small Sea" during the Sui and Tang Dynasties in China, "Small East Sea" can also be interpreted as to mean "Small Sea + East Sea."

Jesuit China missions, or conceal what was too obvious, Ferdinand Verbiest, a Jesuit missionary in China, finally decided to retain both "East Sea" and "Japan Sea" by using a compromise name of "Mer Orientale ou du Japon" ("East or Japan Sea") on his 1669 map "Asia."

While engaging in exchanges with priests who had been sent to Beijing, Pierre Briet, a French Jesuit priest himself, came to understand that "East Sea" was an endonym and translated it into "Ocean Oriental" on his "Map of Japan" in 1655. At the time, "Mer" ("Sea") and "Océan" ("Ocean") were interchangeable. Italian Jesuit priest V. M. Coronelli made a map "Isola del Giapone e Penisola di Corea" ("Island of Japan and the Korean Peninsula") in 1692, but it is unclear what maps he had referred to in the making of the map. He marked "Mare della China" across the southern and eastern coasts of Korea and indicated "Oceano Orientale" in the arch-shaped sea area that covers the middle of the East Sea and the south of Japan.

In contrast, Antoine Thomas marked the East Sea as "Mare Coreanum" on a map of East Asia that he made in 1690. The Jesuit priest from Flanders, while staying in Beijing from 1686 to 1709, participated in the preparations for the border talks between China and Russia for the Treaty of Nerchinsk and had the opportunity to look into maps on Asia made in Russia. His marking of the East Sea as the "Sea of Korea" on the map that he made within four years after he arrived in China suggests that in all likelihood he referred to the map of Japan attached as an appendix to the book by Arnoldus Montanus, a priest who also came from Flanders. Upon the request of China, Thomas completed "Map of Beijing" in 1705 together with Jean-Baptiste Régis, Joachim Bouvet and Dominique Parrenin. Then, by order of the Kangxi Emperor who was satisfied with the capabilities of missionaries, he helped with the business of making maps of the entire China. The Kangxi Emperor had a special relationship with Manchuria and traveled there to show his appreciation to the missionaries for the survey work that they had been doing for over ten years since 1689 to lend them encouragemet in drafting the maps. Father Thomas accompanied the emperor on the journey and recorded a journal of it. In the quotations from the diary cited in Professor Bernard's 1935 paper, Professor P. Pelletier came upon the passage to the effect that 'When the Kangxi Emperor rose up in the morning, he mentioned the "East Sea" several times in reference to the sea east of Manchuria.' Professor Pelletier argued that Father Thomas transcribed what he heard from the emperor into "Eoum Mare" ("East Sea") in Greek.[7]

7) Philippe Pelletier, "The Role of French Geography in the Naming of

Jean-Baptiste Du Halde, who read Thomas' record of accompaniment, repeated the name, "East Sea," several times in his *Description géographique, historique, chronologique, politique, et physique de l'empire de la Chine et de la Tartarie chinois* (*Geographical, Historical, Chronological, Political and Physical Description of the Empire of China and Chinese Tartary*). But on the map included in the book, he indicated the East Sea as "Mer du Japan." The discrepancy of the notation between the book and the map is likely to suggest that Father Thomas' record did not have much impact on Du Halde. Anyway, Du Halde's *Description* and Jean Baptiste Bourguignon d'Anville's Atlas made for the book as an appendix, are evaluated as one of the greatest historical records compiled in the 18th century by missionaries in Beijing.

The fact that the East Sea was an endonym was recognized by Guillaume Delisle and Nicolas de Fer on their maps. Delisle, the chief royal geographer who learned that the East Sea was an endonym from many sources of information, including missionaries, was obsessed with indicating the East Sea as "Mer Orientale." De Fer directly explained on his map that the East Sea was an endonym.

the Sea between Korea, Japan and Siberia from the 17th to Early 19th Century," The 8th International Seminar on Sea Names, 2002, The Society for East Sea.

In addition to their true duty, the Vatican missionaries also served as a bridge making China, Korea and Japan known to Europe during the 17th and 18th centuries. Their records and their notation of the East Sea are, therefore, very significant for many reasons. Most indicated the sea as either: 1) the Japan Sea, 2) the Small East Sea, 3) the East Sea or 4) the Sea of Korea, or 5) did not leave any indicatoin. To note the various names they used is only to scratch the surface of the matter, however. More important is our gaining of understanding of how these names came into use.

Chapter 4

Old Maps and the Notation of the Name "East Sea" in the German-speaking World

There was not really a period of time when the German-speaking world, including Austria, took the lead in cartography in Europe. However, as the Renaissance was spreading rapidly from Italy to the areas beyond the Alps, the German-speaking world came under its influence and studies on classics became more active there. As a consequence, Ptolemy's *Geography* was republished, accompanied by highly qualified research and revisions by scholars in the German-speaking world. Cartography saw steady development, centering on Nuremberg, one of the cities where the printing business was most brisk in Germany. Due to their politico-geographical locations, Germany and Austria had long maintained close relations with middle and eastern European countries, such as Czechoslovakia, Hungary and Poland.

Although they were influenced first by Italy and the Netherlands, and then by France and Great Britain in the 18th century, Germany and Austria showed their own characteristics in naming what is the East Sea on old maps. While working for a Portuguese company, Martin Behaim acquired geographical information on the world, especially Southeast Asia, which Portugal obtained from all over the world. He labeled "Oceanus Indicus Orientalis" in the Southeast Asian sea areas, including the East Sea, when he made a terrestrial globe in 1492, the year of Columbus' discovery of America. It was a name made by a combination of direction and the name of a country. Later, Laurent Friese used the same name on his map of Southeast Asia that he attached to his re-publication of Ptolemy's *Geography* in 1528. Until then, "Indicus" was included in the name, but thereafter only "Oceanus Orientalis" was used because "Indicus" was considered redundant. In 1596, Andreas of Germany called what is the East Sea "Mare Cin" ("China Sea") on his "Mappa-Mundi" ("World Map"), a name which, later, great cartographers, such as Abraham Ortelius and Gerardus Mercator, favored.

Many European maps of the times did not show Korea

and left what is the East Sea as blank. Still, K. Durant named the East Sea as "Océan Oriental" on a map of Japan in 1679. When publishing *History of Japan* in 1700, he, however, labeled the East Sea as "Mer du Nord du Japan" ("North Sea of Japan") on the map that he made with the assistance of Matthäus Seutter as an attachment to the book. Heinrich Scherer, a professor of mathematics in Munich, published some 200 maps with the aid of Johann Homann. On the map, "Asia," published in 1705, he divided the sea areas from India to the east Pacific into three areas: "Mer d'Arabie," "Gulf de Bengale" and "Mer de Chine." For the East Sea, he used the name "Oceanus Orientalis." However, no solid evidence is found to assert that it is the Latin translation of the endonym, "East Sea." Rather, it seems like a directional name.

Homann, a leading cartographer in 18th century Germany, named the East Sea as "Mare Orientale Minus" ("Small East Sea") on his map, "Asia," which was published in 1707 and republished in 1714. In fact, "Mare Orientale" was already used by Italian and Dutch map-makers in the 16th and early 17th centuries and also by some French cartographers in the late 17th century. To add a diminutive "Minus" was an ingenious idea of the German. However, on the 1720 map, "Asia," Homann gave names favorable to Japan by marking

"Mare Iaponicum Occidentale" ("West Sea of Japan") in the part of the East Sea off the northern coast of Japan and "Mare Iaponicum Orientale" ("East Sea of Japan") in the sea off the south of Japan in smaller print. He did this in spite of the fact that, when it is seen directionally with Japan at the center, the East Sea lies to the north of Japan and the "East Sea of Japan" lies actually to the south of Japan.

Hasius, Homann's pupil and assistant, was deeply influenced by Homann and named the East Sea as "Mare Orientale Minus," just as Homann had previously done, on his "Planiglobii Terrestris" in its first publication in 1739, its second publication in 1741 and its third publication in 1746. The successor of Hasius also labeled the East Sea as "Mare Orientale Minus" on the map, on "Russici, Tartariae Majoris" in 1744 and on "Asia" in 1744 and its re-publication in 1753. August Gottlieb Boehme used the same notation on his map of Asia in 1744 and "Asia Secundum legitimas Projectionis Stereigraphicae" ("Asia according to the Legitimate Stereographic Projection"), made jointly by Hasius and Boehme in the same year shows the same name.

On the 1720 first edition of "Regni Japoniae Nova Mappa Geographica" and its second and third re-publications in 1730 and 1740, respectively, Matthäus Seutter named the East Sea as "Mer nord du Japan" ("North Sea of Japan") and

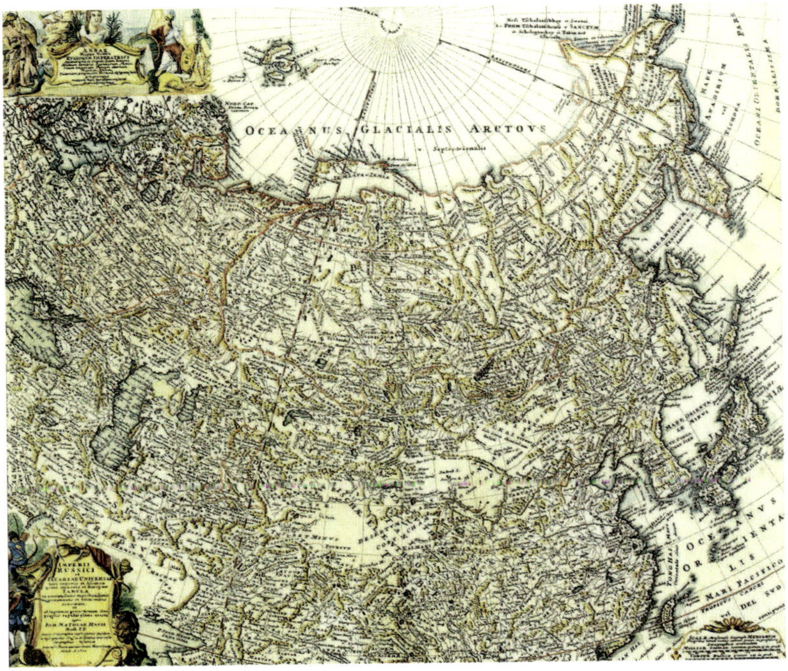

"Imperi Russici et Tartariae Universae" ("Russian Empire and the Whole of Tartary") made in 1730 by Hasius who acquired Homann's business. A map prior to d'Anville's, Korea is depicted in a relatively exact shape. The East Sea is indicated as "Mare Orientale le Minus" ("Small East Sea").

the south of Japan as "Maris Iaponicum Pars" ("Part of the Sea of Japan"). In 1745, he deleted the adjective "North" and simply marked, "Japanisches Meer." On the 1727 map of "Japan," Scherer, in a departure from earlier practice, put "Die Japanische Zee" above the Kamchatka Peninsula. Georg Moritz Lowitz named the East Sea as "Mare Orientale Minus" on his 1746 "Mapp Universalis." Franz Ludwig Güssefeld, using a German diminutive, labeled "Kleine

"Chinesisches Reich" drawn by Mollo from Swiss in Vienna in 1820. The East Sea is marked as "Japanisches Meer" and the East China Sea, "Meer von Corea."

Orientalische Meer" on "Russische Reich" in 1786. On the map of "Imperii Russici" carried in *Berlin Academy* in 1753, the East Sea was named as both "Mare Orientale" and "Corea Sien" supposedly under the influence of French cartographer Delisle. When Mataeus Albrecht named the East Sea as "Mare Orientale" on "Asia" in 1750, he was also likely to have been influenced by Delisle or de Fer.

However, in the 19th century, the notation of German maps tended to shift to the "Sea of Japan" under the influence of La Pérouse. Johann Walch named the East Sea as "Japanisches Meer" on a map of Asia in 1816. Streit also named the East Sea as the "Sea of Japan" on "Karte von Asien" in 1817. Campe made the same notation as Streit on his "Asien" in 1817. On "Chinesisches Reich" in 1820, Tranquillo Mollo named the East Sea as "Japanisches Meer" and the East China Sea as "Meer von Corea."

Overall, French maps tended to use the country name Korea and named the East Sea as "Mer de Corée" in many cases, while German maps generally favored "Mare Orientale." The addition of the diminutive "small" ("Minus" or "Kleine") in consideration of the size of the East Sea, however, can be evaluated as being creative in naming the East Sea on the part of the Germans.

Chapter 5

Old Maps and the Notation of the Name "East Sea" in Portugal

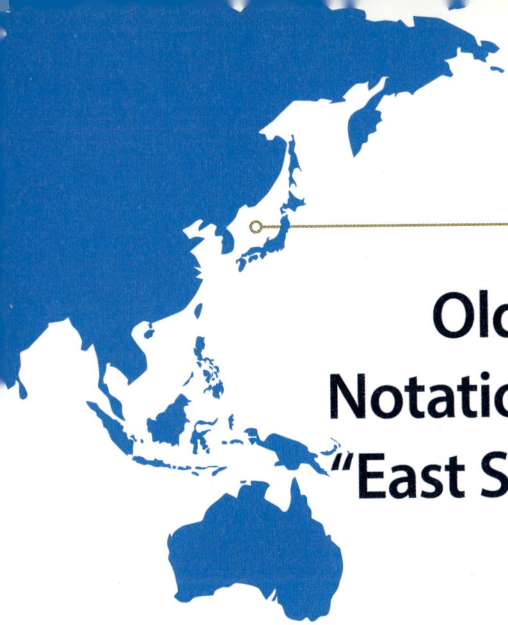

With the commencement of the Age of Discovery in the wake of the discovery of America by Columbus, Spain and Portugal, the two countries of the Iberian Peninsula, embarked on overseas expeditions with a view to "killing three birds with one stone": accumulating wealth, finding colonies, and disseminating Catholicism. This naturally led to frequent conflicts between the two countries, and they petitioned the Vatican for preference and support. Failing to bring them to peace through the first mediation, the Vatican arranged the Treaty of Tordesillas for the two countries, providing for Spain precedence over South America, excluding Brazil; and for Portugal, precedence over the Eastern hemisphere including Brazil.

Both Spain and Portugal commonly resorted to arms first when they advanced overseas, but they had different styles of overseas expansion. Spain deployed its army to conquer foreign lands and acquired gold. To this end, the Spanish waged war with the natives in many places, massacring them extensively. They destroyed local cultural heritages and traditional folk beliefs and forced conversion to Catholicism. They brought back to Spain the gold that they plundered, which led to adverse effects, such as serious inflation.

Portugal, under the commandership of Prince Henry the Navigator, built a strong naval force and concentrated on constructing ships. Making its way to Southeast Asia, passing around the Cape of Good Hope, Portugal established a foothold in East Africa. Portugal secured cheap goods from Southeast Asia, including Indonesia, and exported them to Europe through the bases it had established in the state of Goa in India, Malacca in Malaysia, and Macau in China, in an effort to carve out a major presence in the consumer market of Europe. Unlike Spain, this precluded the need for Portugal to occupy vast swathes of foreign lands, supress the natives, and plunder gold. It only showed a strong desire to monopolize trade with the East. The Portuguese engaged in trade with China and Japan, but gave up on pursuing trade with Korea due to Joseon's closed-door policy.

Portugal, however, encountered a strong obstacle in its advance to the East, as Arab merchants had traded with Silla and Goryeo as well as China and Japan from early on. Armed conflicts were thus inevitable. Arab merchant ships were simply no match for the Portuguese navy. Armed with powerful cannons aboard agile sailing boats, the Portuguese navy easily suppressed the Arab merchant ships, ousting them from the trade with the East and supplanting them.

Spain did not rely much on its naval power as it largely utilized its army to lead its wars, making it not quite necessary to make maps. Portugal, on the other hand, focused on advancing into foreign lands via the seas and thus definitely needed charts and maps of many places in Africa and Northeast Asia. Naturally, cartography came to be considered a very important business in Portugal. It was for this reason that many famous cartographers were produced by Portugal, with some of them handing over their skills to succeeding generations, giving rise to long-standing renowned families of map-makers.

Unfortunately, however, Portugal's dominance of the eastern routes did not last long. Moreover, after the royal line of João III died out, Philippo III of Spain, Portugal's archrival, succeeded to the Portuguese throne in 1580. It brought Portugal under Spain's colonial rule. It is thus only fortunate that old Portuguese maps preserve the traces of Portuguese overseas maritime explorations intact. Of particular note, the Portuguese government published *Portugaliae Monumenta Cartographica* in 1962 to commemorate the 500th anniversary of Prince Henry's demise. It was a great achievement in that it was a comprehensive compilation of the most important old Portuguese maps.

Portuguese explorers landed in Japan in 1543, taking the first steps of mutual exchange. In contrast, no evidence of any Portuguese contact with Joseon can be found in official records. According to other Portuguese materials, however, during the Japanese Invasion of Korea in 1592, some of the Portuguese soldiers who had been in China participated in the war as part of the Ming Dynasty army when it went to Joseon's aid against the invading Japanese.

Among the old Portuguese maps are some depicting a country that is presumed to be Korea according to its shape and location but without giving the country's name. Fernão Vaz Dourado's 1573 map, Lopo Homem's 1554 map, and Bartolomeu Velho's 1560 map are such cartographic examples. Dourado's map, however, does have a country named "Comray," a misnomer of "Coray" with an "m" wrongly inserted into what China and Japan called Korea at the time. This presumption is based on the fact that on a map by Jan Huyghen van Linschoten, Korea is also marked as "Comray." The names of Korea and the East Sea are, however, clearly indicated on a map by Manuel Godinho de Erédia, which is included in Vol. 4 of *Portugaliae Monumenta Cartographica*. Erédia's map of East Asia which he made in Macau in 1615 records "Coria" for Korea and "Mar Coria" for the East Sea.

A map of East Asia drafted in 1571 by Dourado of Portugal when he was living in Southeast Asia. On the seashore of what is supposed to be Korea, the map shows "Costa D. Comrai."

In fact, Korea's current English name has a background story. During the Goryeo Dynasty (918-1392), some Japanese residing in Macau told the Portuguese there about a country with the name "Goryeo," which was somehow transcribed as, among others, "Coray." However, in some Latin-based languages, including the Portuguese, diphthongs are avoided and "ai" and "ay" were transcribed as "e." Hence, Coray became Core. And in the Portuguese and Spanish, "o" and "a" are suffixed to the masculine and feminine nouns, respectively. Hence, "Core," a feminine noun as a country name, became "Corea," a pre-modern spelling of Korea.

Before it was known to the Portuguese, Korea was called "Cori" or "Cory" by Arab merchants who traded with Goryeo. The name was introduced into the Arab-Islam world and even today, Arabs and Middle Eastern people call Korea "Cori" (*or "Cory"*). If it is true, as some Korean language scholars argue, that the Goryeo people at the time of the Goryeo Dynasty pronounced Goryeo as "Gori," then

Linschoten served as the Portuguese Viceroy's secretary in Goa, India. He published *Itinerario* in Dutch in 1596. Depicting China, Japan and Korea, the map was produced on the basis of the information gathered from navigators. It was drawn with the east facing the upper side of the map, according to the Indian tradition. Korea is wrongly portrayed as being composed of a bigger island of "Ilha de Corea" and a smaller island "Corea" above it. In the East Sea off the eastern coast of Korea, "Costa de Comray" is indicated just as on Dourado's map, and there is an inscription "Ilhas dos Ladrões" ("Islands of Thieves") below it.

Arab merchants made quite an exact transcription when they recorded it as "Cori." The traces of this transcription are found more on old Portuguese maps than on old Arab-Islam maps.

On the map of Japan which Luís Teixeira put in Ortelius' atlas *Terrarum* in 1590, Korea is depicted as an island in the shape of a triangle with two long sides and the country name is marked as "Corea." In the south of the island "Corea," a marking "Cory" is found, which is neither the name of a province nor of a city. Now, let us speculate how this notation was made an old Portuguese map.

The first key to this question can be found in the relationship between Portugal and the Arab-Islam world. When the Portuguese fleet ousted Arab merchant ships from the Southeast Asian routes, the Portuguese navy must have obtained needed materials from them, including most likely nautical charts. The charts bore the marking "Cory," but Portuguese cartographers must not have known what that meant. It seems that they just copied down the name on their maps because it was marked on the nautical charts that they had obtained. "Cory" was, in fact, the first notation of Korea on a map of the world at the time. The name also seems to have been derived from Arab merchant ships. Erédia used the marking "Coria" by adding "a," a feminine

Teixeira of Portugal published in 1595 this "Iaponiae Insulae Descriptio" in Latin with the aid of Ortelius of the Netherlands. Korea, as it shows here, is an elongated island, with the name "Island of Thieves" in the south and the same name where Jeju Island might have been. There also is the marking "Cory," which means "Korea" in Arabic.

suffix, to the country name "Cory." From this, some Portuguese referred to Korea as "Coria." It is presumed, however, that more Portuguese called Korea "Corai," which was then transformed into "Corea" before spreading to other countries. Then, why did Eéredia mark Korea as "Coria"? The answer may be found in his life story.

Manuel Godinho de Erédia was born to a Malaysian princess and a Portuguese high official working locally in Malacca, an important base for Portugal's advance to the East. He is known to have received secondary education in Goa, a Portuguese colony in Eastern India, and higher education in Portugal. He excelled in mathematics and was active in that area, but he was also a mythologist who worked on myths of the Asia-Pacific, especially Australia, which had been known as "Terra Australis." While he was perusing materials from Arab merchant ships, it is presumed he came to know about geological shapes of China, Korea and Japan and drew a map of the three countries. Although he is believed to have been the first in history to depict Korea correctly as a peninsula, it is yet to be studied further whether he named the East Sea as "Mar Coria" because he copied down what had been written in the material he referred to, or he concluded that it was the most appropriate name. At any rate, Erédia published the map in Macau, a Portuguese base in China, in 1615.

A map depicting the three Asian countries of China, Korea and Japan, published by Erédia in Macau in 1615. Korea, correctly represented as a peninsula here, is presented as "Coria." "Mar Coria" is indicated at the center of the East Sea.

Erédia's map was made quite early on, only 13 years later

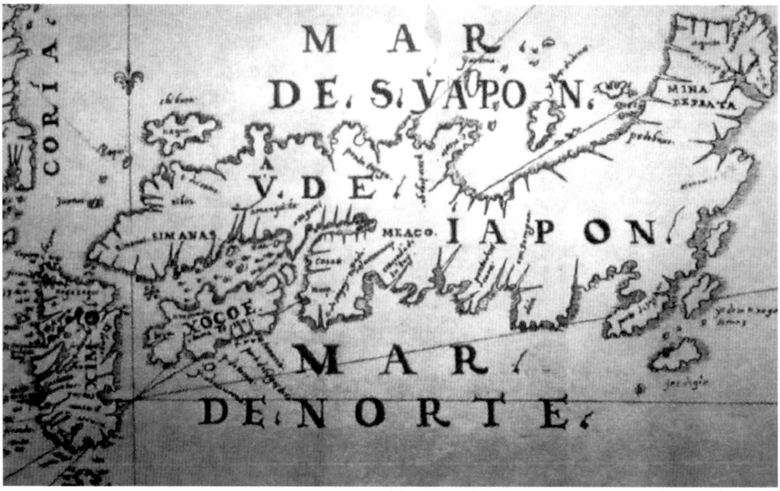

On this 1615 map, Japan is marked as "V. DE IAPON" but the East Sea is identified as "MAR DE S. VAPON."

than Matteo Ricci's map and, for this reason, the Japanese conducted a thorough analysis of the map. As a result, two Japanese scholars, after performing an extensive survey of Erédia's unpublished maps, found another map, which was made in the same year of 1615, and recently made a presentation about it.[8] On that map, Japan is marked as "V. de Iapon" and Korea as "Coria." The sea off southern Japan is marked as "Mar de Norte" probably because it lies north of the Pacific Ocean. However, regarding "Mar de S. Vapon" marked on what is the East Sea, the Japanese cannot explain what it means and just insist that "Sea of Japan" was marked that way without much evidence.

8) Watanabe & Yaji, "Study on the Geographical Name 'Japan Sea.'"

However, on "V. de Iapon," which is marked as the country name of Japan, it is still not known what "V" represents and "Mar De S. Vapon" looks like a far cry from "Iapon" in the first place. Not having a title like "Map of Japan," this map only shows a part of the eastern coastline of Korea and does not even show China. The Japanese claim that this map is similar to Matteo Ricci's map but it is deemed only wishful thinking with no ground to support it. The Japanese think that this map can neutralize the notation of "Mar Coria" by the same cartographer, but they need to provide a reasonable explanation about "S. Vapon" first.

In Portugal, the study of old maps is a discipline in and of itself and is considered very important. The University of Lisbon has an institute for cartography and a huge volume of materials must be stored in its archive of documents on maritime transportation. We are advised to make even more efforts to find valuable information.

Chapter 6

Old Maps and the Notation of the Name "East Sea" in the Netherlands

In the past, with the highest population density in the world living on lands that were below sea level and with insufficient natural resources, the Netherlands was worse off in spite of its people working hard and living thriftily. In order to survive, the country turned its eyes overseas and, though later than Spain and Portugal, set off to find foreign lands to colonize. With the growth of its foreign trade, the Netherlands also emphasized early education in foreign languages, such as English, German and French, in a bid to become a maritime power. While sailing its way to make overseas advances, the Netherlands unavoidably came into conflict with Portugal. Fortunately for the Netherlands, it won several battles it engaged in with Portugal, which gradually lost its passion for overseas ventures. Furthermore, for political reasons, Portugal was annexed by Spain in 1580. Along with Great Britain, the Netherlands then inherited a vested interest in overseas exploration. Afterwards, flying its colors as a new marine power, the Netherlands colonized the Indonesian archipelago. It also increased various exchanges with Japan, triggering the so-called "Dutch studies" phenomenon in Japan.

As the Netherlands was striving to improve the level of astronomy and geography which could be helpful in navigation, cartography also grew as an important industry. The cartography industry in the Netherlands developed rapidly for several reasons: First, the maps satisfied the curiosity of the well-off middle class about foreign countries. Second, with the decline of the cartography industry in Italy, from which the Netherlands had imported maps, the Netherlands promoted its own cartography industry to the point where it exported maps to many European countries and Russia. And third, a considerable number of Dutchmen who worked for Portuguese companies and institutions were quick to convey to their families and relatives back home any new geological information that they acquired. This enabled map-makers in the Netherlands to obtain new information about foreign countries easier and faster and continue to produce more accurate and complete maps.

Gerardus Mercator and Abraham Ortelius, who started cartography in the Netherlands for the first time, were both from Antwerp, Belgium, and thus, strictly speaking, they were Belgians. However, as the Flemish that they spoke is spoken also in the Netherlands, they are recently classified as Dutch. Moreover, Ortelius moved to Amsterdam early on and worked there and, although Mercator made his maps in Duisburg, Germany, the maps of the two cartographers were mostly sold in the Netherlands.

These two cartographers led very different lives. Mercator studied astronomy and mathematics under Gemma Frisius, a renowned scholar of the times, at the prestigious University of Leuven. Afterwards, working with his teacher, he started his career as a manufacturer of terrestrial globes but finally settled in Duisburg where he could work more freely as a Protestant. There he produced *Atlas,* which is considered an important collection of maps. In contrast, Ortelius, 15 years junior to Mercator, studied Latin and mathematics before landing a cartographic job as an illustrator. Quitting the job to conduct business on his own, he became a map seller, importing and selling Italian maps. In his 20s, he started up the business of map-making. Ortelius was very successful in business partly because he started his business relatively early in life and formed relationships with map sellers, but also because he had secrets of his own. At first, he published maps on single sheets of paper, but later he started to collect them into atlases. He revised and supplemented them each year to produce new editions and translated them into many languages, including English, French and German. His atlases became sensationally popular in the contemporary Europe. Ortelius and Mercator were friends. Mercator was older than Ortelius but Ortelius started making maps before him.

Ortelius neither knew about the existence of Korea nor did he have any opportunity to do. That is why Korea does not appear on his 1570 map, "Asiae Nova Descriptio." Ortelius simply marked the Southeast Asian sea area as "Oceanus Eous" on the map. On "Tartariae sive Magni Chami Regni Typus" ("Tartary under the Kingdom of the Great Khan") contained in his 1570 *Theatrum Orbis Terrarum* (*Theater of the World*), there is neither any reference to Korea to be seen nor a name of the East Sea. Instead, "Mare Cin" was marked for the East Sea and the sea areas near China and "Oceanus Orientalis," in the south in a bigger print, in the same meaning as on Italian maps. After a while, Ortelius got acquainted with Teixeira of Portugal and, in his 1595 *Theatrum Orbis Terrarum*, Korea was included in "Iaponia Insula Descriptio," a map by Teixeira. Having been made with reference to Japanese-made maps of Japan, Teixeira's map was more accurate than other previous maps of Japan. Still, as the cartographer did not have sufficient information about Korea, Korea was depicted as an island, cone-like shaped and vertically long, and marked as "Corea Insulae." The map also has a marking "Cory" in the south of what is depicted as Korea, but it is not clear what it exactly is because it does not seem to be the name of a city or a province. The two notations of "Ilhas dos Ladrões" ("Islands of Thieves") in the south of the map look like an expedient marking of hearsay.

Mercator put "Mare Cin" between the West Sea and the East Sea on his "Asia" in 1587. Gerard de Jode, on the 1589 "Mappa Mundo," marked the East Sea as "Oceanus Chinese." However, except that of Teixeira's, these maps do not show Korea. On a double-hemispheric map of 1590, Petrus Plancius marked the East Sea as "Oceanus Chinensis" without Korea. But on a 1594 map, he depicted Korea as a peninsula for the first time in Europe. A Protestant minister, he seems to have obtained the latest information from his relatives working in Portuguese organizations. He was related to Jodocus Hondius by marriage and received help in the making of maps but it seems that he was not influenced by Hondius in terms of geographical information. In addition, apparently Plancius' maps did not have much impact on other map-makers.

The state of Goa, India, was a Portuguese colony from early on which served as a base for Portugal's advance into Southeast Asia. Linschoten, the Portuguese Viceroy's secretary there, compiled geographic information that he had gathered, and published *Itinerario: Voyage ofte schipvaert van Jan Huyghen van Linschoten naer Oost ofte Portugaels Indien, 1579-1592* (*Travel Account of the Voyage of the Sailor Jan Huyghen van Linschoten to the Portuguese East India, 1579-1592*), in 1596. This map does show Korea, but Linschoten did not travel to Korea himself. He simply drew it on the map based on what he heard from his friend Dirck Gerritsz. Pomp who heard about Korea when he visited Japan. According to the information that Pomp acquired, Korea was an island country between Japan and China located within 34-35 degrees north latitude and was called "Core." This map, incidentally, seems to have been influenced by Dourado. Linschoten's map has the marking, "Corta de Comray" ("Comray Coast") on the southeast of the round potato-shaped Korea, and Dourano's 1573 map also has a peninsula country, presumably Korea, with the marking "Corta de Comray" off its eastern coast.

On Linschoten's map are marked with "Ilha dos Ladrões" ("Island of Thieves") and the country name "Ilha de Corea" ("Island of Korea"), but identifying Korea with "Island of Thieves" is absurd and the shrimp-shaped Japan is depicted in the wrong shape.

Jacob Comelisz van Neck's 1600 map of Asia shows Korea as an island country, "Core Insula." Hondius' 1602 "Asiae Recens Summa Accurata" ("The Most Accurate Recent Asia") shows no Korea – only the marking "Oceanus Eous" for the Pacific Ocean. In contrast, another "Asiae," which was published in the same year, indicates "Oceanus Occidentalis" because, after the discovery of the Americas, it was believed that Asia could be reached by continuing in a westward direction. Willem Blaeu marked "Oceanus Chinensis" on what is the East Sea on his maps of 1607 and 1608. Claes Jansz. Visscher made the same marking on the map, "Asiae," in the same year.

Until the mid-17th century, many maps marked Korea as "Corai Insula." On a 1624 map of Asia, P. Cluverius marked the East Sea as "Mare Eoum"; however, it had nothing to do with the endonym "East Sea," but simply meant a "sea in the east." Johannes Janssonius, who was much influenced by Blaeu, left the East Sea as blank on his 1630 map.

The Dutch East India Company's maps, designed for

"Asia Antiqua et Nova," published by Cluverius of the Netherlands in 1624. Unlike maps by great Dutch cartographers, this map depicted Korea as an elongated peninsula and marked the East Sea as "Mare Eoum" in a mixture of a Greek word.

internal use, have markings of "Oceanus Occidentalis" for the northeast of the East Sea and "Oceanus Chinensis" for the sea south of Japan. Probably because this information was known to the outside, "Oceanus Occidentalis," "Oceanus Orientalis" and "Oceanus Chinensis" are found on most maps that Blaeu, Mercator and others made in the 1630s. Joan Blaeu, the son of Willem Blaeu and his successor, marked the East Sea as "Oceanus Occidentalis," as Hondius preferred, in *Atlas Maior* of 1635 and 1662. On the map

“Asiae” in 1650, however, he labeled the East Sea as “Oceanus Chinensis.” Martini, who visited Beijing as a missionary, left the East Sea as unmarked due to disagreement on its name among missionaries on “Japonia Regnum” in *Novus Atlas Sinensis* which he published jointly with Blaeu in 1655.

On 1640 “Asie,” P. Bertius depicted Korea as a long peninsula and marked it “Corea.” He also used a peculiar name of “Mare de Mangi” in smaller print for the part of the East Sea close to Korea. On the same map, he marked the wide body of water in the northeast “l’Océan Occidental” and “l’Océan de China” on the sea off the south of Japan. In

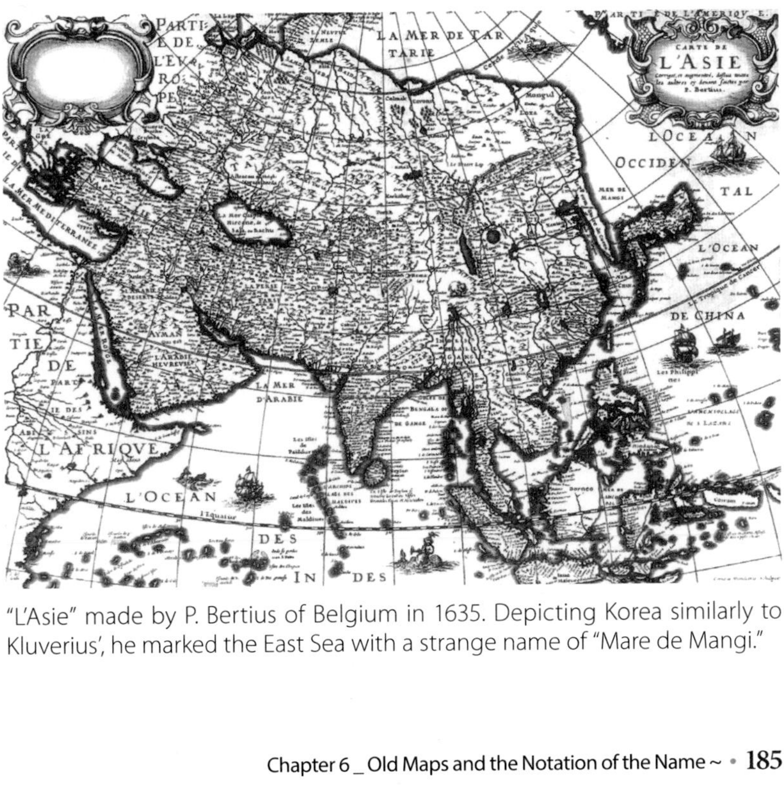

"L'Asie" made by P. Bertius of Belgium in 1635. Depicting Korea similarly to Kluverius', he marked the East Sea with a strange name of "Mare de Mangi."

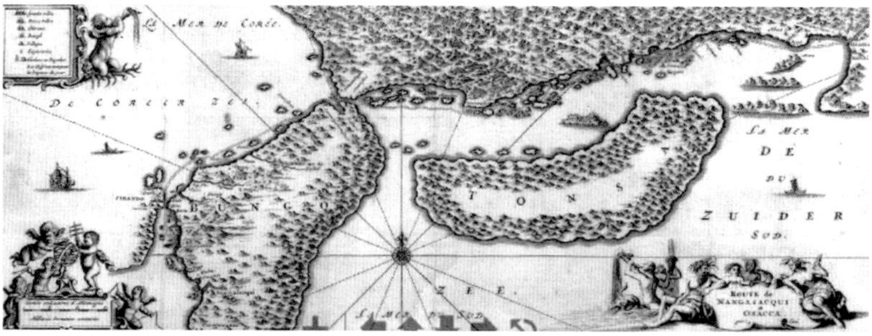

In 1669, Montanus, a Dutch Protestant theologian, identified the East Sea as "Mer de Corée" in his book on Japan. The book became an unprecedented success in Europe.

contrast, Janssonius, who was influenced by Blaeu, marked the East Sea as "Oceanus Chiensis" on a map of East Asia in 1658. Hondius and Visscher II, by using an old name of China, named the East Sea as "Mare Cathaye" on the map "Asia" in 1660. On his solo map of 1670, Visscher II referred to a map by de Vries and labeled the northeast Pacific Ocean as "Oceanus Occidentalis."

In the meantime, a new and important "wind of change" started to blow. Montanus, a Protestant theologian who was well versed in Latin, compiled a book containing all kinds of extraordinary stories of adventures that a party of Dutch experienced when they were traveling from southwestern Japan to Edo on their way to have an audience with the Japanese Emperor. The book, titled *Gedenkwaerdige Gesantschappen der Oost-Indische Maetschappy in't Vereenigde Nederland, aen de Kaisaren van Japan. Getrokken uit de Geschriften en Reiseaentekeninge der zelver Gesanten* (translation published with the title: *Atlas Japannensis being remarkable addresses by way of Embassy from the East India Company of the United Provinces, to the Emperor of Japan*) was an unprecedented success in the history of publishing and many European countries translated it into their own languages. On a map of the entire Japan, an appendix to this book, Montanus named the East Sea as the "Sea of Korea." Afterwards, Jean Baptiste Tavernier of France marked the East Sea as "Océan Oriental" and "Mer de Corée" in 1679 in his book on Japanese history. Nicolaes Witsen labeled the East Sea as "Mare Septentrionale Japonia" on his Asian map of 1687, while Johan Nieuhof, on his "Karte von China," called the East Sea "Mare Coreum."

Toward the 18th century, the monopolistic glory that Dutch maps and the great cartographers of the 17th century enjoyed finally started to subside and cartography was not as active a business as before. On his 1700 map "Asia," Leonard Valk marked the East Sea as "Mare Septentrionale Japoniae." Peter Schenk named East Asia as "Mer Orientale" on his 1708 map "Asie" and Pieter van der Aa, "Mer de Corée" on his 1710 "Imperium Japonicum." However, Halma Francius used "Oceanus Sinensis," which the great cartographers used, on the "Asiae" that he sent to the Royal Academy in 1720.

Witsen, taking interest in the East while he was working at the German Embassy in Moscow, made this map "Asia." He put "Mare Settent Iaponis" ("North Sea of Japan") to the north of the East Sea.

Abraham Maas, on his 1721 "Nieuwe Carte Van de Ootkuste van Groot Tartarie" essentially, "New Map of Northeast Asia," marked the East Sea as "Japanse Zee." Yet, Cornelis Mortier, a Frenchman who published maps in Amsterdam, put "Mer Orientale du Japon" for the East Sea on his "Carte du Monde" in 1720. He seems to have attempted to be eclectic by accommodating both "Mer Orientale," which Guillaume Delisle insisted on, and "Mer du Japon." Although Ferdinand Verbiest, who had been a missionary in Beijing, also used the same name, but, as the East Sea is a body of water lying northwest of Japan, and not part of the Pacific Ocean to the east of Japan, the name is simply a misnomer in that it is in discrepancy with the reality.

Isaak Tirion marked "De Japanische Zee" in the north of the Kamchatka Peninsula in the Pacific Ocean on "Asia" in 1733 and used both "Mer de Corée" and "Mer Septentrionale du Japon" for the East Sea on "Asiae" in 1735. On the map of 1740, he also marked "Mer Septentrionale du Japon" near Japan together with "Mer de Corée." The name "Mer Septentrionale du Japon" ("North Sea of Japan") here is a combination of "North Sea," as the Japanese have called the East Sea, and "Japan" a postmodifier. The name supposedly came from the influence of de Fer because he used it for some time, but it is not certain. His "Mer de Corée" is also presumed to have been made in reference to the French "Mer de Corée," but this conjecture also has no clear rationale. What is important, however, is that Tirion attempted to be fair and not be partial by presenting two contradictory names for the East Sea together. Probably because of this view on the name of what is the East Sea, on "Kartiji van het keiger rych Japan" ("Map of the Empire of Japan") in 1728, 1740, and 1747, Tirion gave the East Sea rather an absurd name, "De Nor Zee van Japan van Coreasegee" ("North Sea of Japan in the Sea of Korea"). This puzzling notation was

In 1740, the famous Dutch map-maker Tirion included Asian countries in his "Nouvelle Carte de la Chine." This map shows some influence of Delisle of France. Making mixed use of French and Dutch, this map marks the East Sea as both "Mer de Corée" and "Mer Septentrionale de Japon."

an outcome of his attempt to reconcile two names into one. However, on his 1749 "Mappemond," he named the East Sea as "Mer Orientale," giving the impression that he now referred to de Fer's map of East Asia of 1703, Delisle's "Map of India and China" of 1700, and maps thereafter. When they made their maps and gave the name "East Sea" for the corresponding sea, de Fer and Delisle were obviously convinced that the "East Sea" was the most appropriate name, which Tirion seemingly took as a trustworthy name. Other than these, the name Tirion used for the East Sea varied greatly according to which map he referred to when he made a map.

Unlike Tirion, Adam Friedrich Zürner, following the conventional notation of European maps of the times, marked the East Sea as "Sin Corean" on his "Planisphaerium Terrestre" in 1741. Following Delisle, Johannes Covens and Cornelis Mortier marked the East Sea as "Mer Orientale" on "L'Asie" which was reported to the Royal Netherlands Academy of Arts and Sciences in 1740. In its cartouche, they unusually emphasized the contribution of Arabic maps. On his 1747 map "Asia," De Lat marked the East Sea as both "Sea of Korea" and "North Sea of Japan" as on Tirion's 1735 "Asiae." Tirion, who said he was influenced by Jacques-Nicolas Bellin, a French marine expert, made the two markings, "Mer de Corée" and "Mer Septentrionale du Japon," on "Nieuwe Kaart van Keissery China" ("New Map of Imperial China") in 1755, as he had done on his 1735 "Asiae."

Emanuel Bowen, who made maps mostly in Great Britain, marked the East Sea as "Zee van Korea" on his 1770 "Wereld" ("World") and 1773 "Asia." Willem Albert Bachiene also used the marking "Sea of Korea" for the East Sea on "Asia" in 1773. Gerrit Brender and Abram labeled the East Sea as "Corease Zee" on their "Kaart van Asia" in 1778.

J. B. Elwe, who seems to have been influenced by Delisle, called the East Sea "Mer Orientale ou Mer de Corée" ("East Sea or Sea of Korea") on his "Inde, Chine et Japon" in 1792, as on Delisle's map of 1705.

In the 19th century, maps were rarely still made in the Netherlands. Philipp Franz von Siebold, a German-born naturalized Dutchman, taught medicine and studied natural history, Japanese history and Japanese geography in Japan for about seven years. He married a Japanese woman there. After returning home, he published a book on natural history and made in 1832 "Nippon," a partly

Siebold was a doctor, natural historian and researcher of Japan's history and geography who was posted to Japan. He published "Nippon" in 1832 on the basis of "Nippon henkai ryakuzu" by Takahashi Kageyasu. On this map, Siebold indicated the part of the East Sea close to Japan as "Japanische See" and the sea area from the Korea Strait to the middle of the East Sea as "Kanal van Korai."

revised map from Takahashi Kageyasu's 1809 "Nippon henkai ryakuzu" (日本邊界略圖, "Simplified Map of Japan's Periphery"), where he marked the East Sea as "Japanische Sea." Along with maps by La Pérouse and Adam Johann von Krusenstern, Siebold's map provided an important opportunity by which the notation of the East Sea on the maps of 19th- century Europe turned toward "Sea of Japan."

The history of Dutch maps shows that even the great cartographers did not know about the existence of Korea until relatively late. Regarding the notation of the East Sea, Dutch maps generally featured a full collection of the name as, unlike those of other countries, they have names for the East Sea that are found only on their maps. Names made with a country's name or a direction do exist on the maps of other countries but Dutch maps have a wider variety: "West Ocean," "Sea of Korea," "North Sea of Japan," and "North Sea of Japan in the Sea of Korea." These names may not seem to be very sensible at first glance, but when the "why" and "how" of their coming into being are considered, they are found to reveal some aspects of Dutch rationality with some rationale of their own, making worthwhile their appreciation.

Professor P. Pelletier, who has made insightful analyses and comments about the name of the East Sea, concluded, "The Dutch cartographers prefer the "Sea of Japan"'s naming. Their sources are coming from Ricci's map and Japan."[9] However, a closer look at the old maps made in the Netherlands reveals that they are hardly found to have been influenced by Matteo Ricci and Japanese maps. Especially, almost none was influenced by Matteo Ricci because his was a large map compiled in Chinese. As for Japanese maps in their shapes and composition, Shiba Kokan marked the East Sea as the "Inland Sea of Japan" on his map for the first time in 1792, a time when almost no maps were made in the Netherlands.

To summarize, the East Sea was called simply "North Sea" in Japan, which some French cartographers, including de Fer, took and marked "North Sea of Japan" on their maps. Tirion and De Lat, partly influenced thereby, used both "Sea of Korea" and "North Sea of Japan" together. Tirion also came up with another name, "North Sea of Japan in the Sea of Korea."

9) Pelletier, "The Role of French Geography in the Naming of the Sea between Korea, Japan and Siberia from 17th to early 19th Century."

Chapter 7

Old Maps and the Notation of the Name "East Sea" in France

What Nicolas Sanson did for the development and flourishing of French cartography can be said to be what Ortelius, Mercator and Blaeu did for the development of Dutch cartography. When the great Dutch cartographers and their successors dominated the European map industry, Sanson was running a small printing business in the French village of Abbeville. Inspired by bigger ambitions, he moved to Paris and entered the wilderness of the cartography industry. Afterwards, his son-in-law learned cartography from him before going independent. Pierre Briet, a French Jesuit priest from the same hometown as Sanson, started making maps on a small scale. Not just competitors but also collaborators, they chose to grow together, maintaining interaction among themselves. Sanson's sons helped their father and ran their father's business together.

At the onset of his business, Sanson made maps on order – mostly maps of French provinces, historical maps, and directional maps. Increasingly, however, he expanded business areas and started to make maps of different regions of the world. It inevitably led to competition with renowned Dutch map-makers. Sanson had been inspired and influenced by them and learned a lot from them, but he needed a strategy of differentiation in order to attract customers and survive in the competition. Convinced that maps should provide more and accurate facts about the areas of consumers' interests, Sanson first removed the drawings of imaginary animals, plants and humans and all the elements intended to arouse exoticism that typically decorated maps of the times. Taking a strategy of highlighting the shapes and visual clarity of maps, he produced maps that reflected the changing tastes and interests of customers. Fortunately, Sanson's strategy paid off, as an increasing number of people wanted to know more about foreign affairs; and France, following Portugal, Spain and the Netherlands, thus started showing greater interest in finding overseas colonies.

According to records, J. de Dieppe marked the East Sea as "Océan de la Chine" on his "Mappe monde" in 1625. Jean

Guérard also used the same name for the ocean beyond India when he made "Mappe monde" in 1634. They did so probably because when they made those maps they referred to the maps that had previously been produced in the Netherlands and Italy. However, Sanson, who started producing maps a step behind, marked the same sea area as Guérard's "Océan Oriental" in large letters on a map of Asia that he made in 1650. On the sea area in the south of China, he marked "Mer de Chine" and on what is the Indian Ocean, "Mer des Indes," both in smaller letters. Sanson, of course, must have referred to maps that were previously published in the Netherlands, but he seems to have adopted a method where he first gave a name to a large ocean according to the bearings and then to smaller seas near the lands based on the name of the major country of the area. For example, on a map of East Asia that he published in the same year, he named the East Sea and the East China Sea together as "Mer de Chine." This was the method Sanson used when he named a faraway ocean.

In the first edition in 1650 and the re-publication in 1658 of his "Royaume du Japon" ("Kingdom of Japan"), Father Briet labeled the limited sea area of the East Sea as "Océan Oriental," in a departure from the practice of other map-makers who used the same name to describe the sea area that covers both the part of the Pacific Ocean in the south of Japan and the East Sea. This was presumably made possible because he was corresponding with other Jesuit priests staying in Beijing and interacting with those who had come home from the Chinese city. Regarding his map of the entire Japan, he revealed that he had referred to Japanese maps that he received from his friends who returned home from Japan. Considering this fact, the name "Océan Oriental" that he used only for the area of the East Sea is believed to be a French translation of the endonym "East Sea," as the locals called the sea. By today's usage, "Océan" refers to a body of water larger than a sea, while "Mer" refers to a sea area smaller than an ocean. However, until the early 18th century, "Océan" and "Mer" were used interchangeably. Briet also is believed to have translated "East Sea" into "Océan Oriental" without regard to the size of the sea area. Jean Baptiste Tavernier also marked the East Sea as "Océan Oriental" and is thought to have used "Océan" and "Mer" interchangeably.

In his first edition of "Les Isles du Japon" in 1652 and its republication in 1662, Sanson referred to the East Sea and the sea area south of Japan collectively as "Océan Oriental." On the 1654 map "Tartarie" and in 1652 *Descriptions des Atlas du Japon*, he made the same mark for the same area. It was a confirmation of his principle that the markings of far-off sea areas would be made primarily in accordance with the bearings. When he was preparing *Cartes Générales de Toutes les Parties du Monde* (*General Maps of All Parts of the World*) in 1658, he asked Briet, who was au fait with world geography, for help to review the atlas. He also received Briet's help when he was making *Cartes Générales de la Géographie Ancienne et Nouvelle* (*General Maps of Old and New Geography*) afterwards. The atlas was published in 1676, nine years after Sanson's death, but it is certain that Briet was already delivering information about the East Sea to Sanson and his successors before 1658 when Sanson was making *Cartes Générales de Toutes les Parties du Monde*. It is because, unlike in the past, Sanson used "Océan Oriental" only for the East Sea area on "L'Asie" which he published in 1667, the year of his demise.

Nonetheless, the successors to Sanson marked the Southeast Asian sea areas, including the East Sea, as "Mer de Chine" on "Carte de Chine," which was published after Sanson died – a notation made with the name of a country as the primary element. On "l'Empire du Japon" published in 1669, the East Sea is marked as "Mer du Japon." Naming a body of water according to the name of a country that is the subject of a map was a convention by map-makers for faraway seas until the mid-17th century. The fact that

Sanson's successors followed this principle in the 1670s is, thus, presumed to be regression to the past. It was then considered to be a careless and irresponsible notation of the Northeast Asian seas. Fortunately, on the last issue of "L'Asie," published by Sanson's successors, the East Sea was marked as "l'Océan ou Mer Orientale" probably because they remembered the information that Briet had brought them. Later, the entire business of Sanson and the copperplates of the maps were turned over to Alexis Hubert Jaillot. However, the reflected glory of the Sanson family continued in the history of French cartography.

Pierre Duval, Sanson's son-in-law, was no exception, in that he made the marking of the East Sea inconsistently. On the 1651 "L'Asie" and 1661 "Les Isles," he marked the East Sea as "Océan Oriental," whereas on the 1662 "L'Asie," he used "Mer du Japon" for the same sea area. Again, on 1667 "Nouvelle description de L'Amerique," he marked a wide sea area that includes what is the East Sea as "Mer du Sud" in larger letters and "Mer Pacifique" in smaller letters. There is no clear evidence as to whether he was influenced by Briet when drafting his early maps. However, he ultimately adopted notation by which the Pacific Ocean was marked in French on the one hand but was somewhat expedient in naming the area of the East Sea on the other. Further, on 1684 “La Chine avec l’Empire du Mogol” (“China with the Mongol Empire”), he gave the East Sea a somewhat ambiguous name of “Mer de Tartares ou Orientale.” The name, though, implies that he knew that the Manchus living in Manchuria called the sea the “East Sea.”

Gaudeville, on his 1650 “Carte de L’Asie,” labeled the Southeast Asia sea areas and the East Sea as “Océan Oriental,” the same name as Sanson’s, as he was presumably influenced by the latter.

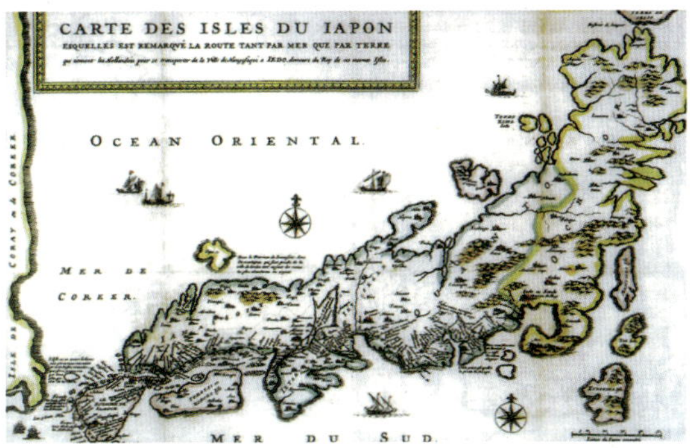

Tavernier was a French traveler who studied history. He labeled the East Sea as “Océan Oriental” in a book on Japan, with another marking of “Mer de Corée” in the south of the East Sea.

The year 1669 marked a turning point in the naming of the East Sea. Arnoldus Montanus, a Protestant Dutch scholar, marked the East Sea as “Mer de Corée” on a map of Japan, an attachment to his book which was a sensation throughout Europe. As this book was translated into many European languages, his naming of the “Sea of Korea” had a great influence. In 1679, a decade later, Jean Baptiste Tavernier marked the East Sea as “Océan Oriental” and the sea area from the Korean

"L'Asie," a map that Delisle, a renowned French royal geographer, produced in 1700 on the basis of the information obtained from missionaries. He marked the East Sea as "Mer Orientale."

Strait to the southwest of the East Sea as "Mer de Corée" in a book on Japan which was quite popular at the time. On his map, "Le Japon" (1683), which is regarded as having referred to the maps of missionaries, including Briet, Alain Manesson Mallet marked the East Sea as "Océan Oriental" just as Briet. The name of the East Sea took another turn when A. de Garel named the East Sea as "Mer Orientale" on his "Carte de la Chine."

As seen above, the tradition of naming the East Sea as "East Ocean" or "East Sea" continued from Briet through Tavernier to Manesson Mallet. Later, Guillaume Delisle, who was most respected in his time as the chief royal geographer, joined the tradition. A geographer-cum-cartographer, Delisle, while he collected new geographic information of the world over, acquired the necessary information from missionaries with whom he had interacted, including the information that the East Sea was called "Mer Orientale"

De Fer, a proprietor of a large map store and producer of over 700 kinds of maps, marked the East Sea as "Mer Orientale" on this map. He drafted the map based on the information that he obtained from China and added to it an explanation that it was the local name that the Manchus used.

as an endonym. This is not a far-fetched assumption but a convincing reasoning in view of the names Delisle used afterwards.

On 1698 "L'Asie" and its re-publication in 1700, Delisle marked the East Sea as "Mer Orientale." This naming was backed up by de Fer. A proprietor of a large map store on the riverside of the Seine River and a cartographer who was passionate enough to publish some 700 kinds of maps during his lifetime, de Fer was very competent in collecting

De Fer, a proprietor of a large map shop who published over 700 kinds of maps and atlases, marked the East Sea as "Mer Orientale" on this map, using the information that he acquired from China. He added a note to the map, explaining that it was the local name used by the Manchus.

a variety of geographic information through a wide human network. From a trader who did business with Yokohama, he learned that the Japanese had no specific name for the East Sea and called it the "North Sea," in the simple sense that it is a "sea in the north." On that account, he marked the East Sea as "Mer Septentrionale de Japon" ("North Sea of Japan") on his 1696 "L'Asie." On "L'Asie en Quatre Feuilles" ("The Asia in Quartet Leaves"), published in the same year, he labeled the East Sea as "Mer Orientale de la Grande Pacifique" ("Oriental Sea of the Great Pacific"), which allows for the interpretation of "Oriental Sea belonging to the Pacific Ocean" – rather than, of course, the Oriental Sea lying in the east of the Pacific Ocean.

At the time, de Fer must have known that the "East Sea" was the legitimate endonym of the sea area. In the upper margin of his 1703 "L'Asie Orientale," he wrote in explanation, "Mer peu ou point connue des Européens. Les Tartares l'appelle [sic] Orientale" ("Sea little or not known to the Europeans. The Tartars [or Manchus] call it [sic] Oriental [Sea]"). It is probable that unlike other map-makers who generally refrained from giving the sea a name, de Fer felt obliged to provide consumers the information and thus came up with the very unusual explanation. However, not long after he did that, he named the East Sea as "Mer Septentrionale du Japon" on "Mappemonde" in 1705. It is unclear whether it was a simple mistake, or if he made the change based on other information, but he did not put any explanation on this name this time. Nevertheless, having shuttled between the two names, de Fer now merged them into "Mer Orientale de la Chine & Septentrionale du Japon" on "L'Asie" in 1713 supposedly in an effort to reflect the two names at the same time.

De Fer was inconsistent in the naming of the East Sea, but thanks to him, the legacy of the "East Sea" was carried on since Briet. In addition, despite Delisle's influence, the name "Sea of Korea" came into wider use beginning in the early 1700s with wider acceptance by the people. Then, in his 1705 *Carte des Indes et de la Chine*, as if to subdue the spread of the "Sea of Korea," Guillaume Delisle remarked in the cartouche for the map title that the Sea of Korea and the East Sea are not two different names but they both refer to the same body of water. Still, probably convinced of the name "East Sea," he named the East Sea only as the "East Sea" on 1708 "L'Asie" and "Hémisphère Septentrional pour voir plus distinctement les Terres Arctique" ("Northern Hemisphere to See the Arctic Lands More Clearly" in 1714.

Probably foreseeing that the "Sea of Korea" would be the general trend and attempting to go with the flow, Delisle marked the East Sea as the "Sea of Korea" on his "Carte d'Asie" in 1723 and "Hémisphère Orientale" in 1724 before he died, indicating that his conviction on the name "East Sea" was wavering. Philippe Buache, his son-in-law who inherited his business, and J. N. Delisle, his brother, followed Guillaume Delisle's naming before they turned to the "Sea of Korea" presumably because they thought it was a more reasonable name.

On his 1696 map of "L'Asie," G. M. Cassini, an astronomer, labeled both the sea off the south of Japan and its north, or the East Sea, as "Oceanus Orientalis." It is speculated that he did so not because he translated the endonym "East Sea" but because, as had been the case in

Observing that other map-makers marked the East Sea as the "Sea of Korea," Delisle made it clear on this 1705 map that "Mer Orientale" and "Mer de Coree" refer to the same sea.

the past, he adopted a bearing-oriented name for the sea area at a location in the east. F. d'Ablancourt used the same marking as Cassini, probably for the same reason, when he made "Carte des Côtes de L'Asie sur L'Océan" ("Map of the Coasts of Asia on the Ocean") in 1700. However, Chambon named the East Sea "Sea of Korea" on his "Mappemonde" in 1700 and on its re-publication in 1723. On the other hand, Janvier marked the East Sea as "Mer du Japon" on his 1794 "L'Asie." Jean Baptiste Nolin also named the East Sea as the

In 1723, Chambon named the East Sea as "Mer de Coree" on this decorative map, "L'Asie."

"Sea of Japan" on his "Carte du Royaume du Japon" ("Map of the Kingdom of Japan") in 1704. He then changed his mind and adopted "East Sea" for the same sea area, probably following Guillaume Delisle, on his "L'Asie" in 1714 and "Mappemonde" in 1720. Then again, on his "Map of the World" in 1720, he seemingly attempted to reconcile both names and came up with "Mer Orientale du Japon." This could not have been the proper name because the East Sea actually lies northwest of Japan, not to its east. Probably because he realized this contradiction, Nolin changed the name of the sea to the "Sea of Korea" on his "L'Asie" in 1730 and then to the "East Sea" on his "Mappemonde" published in the same year. Nolin was completely inconsistent in his notation of the East Sea on nearly all of his maps.

Adriaan Reland, a renowned Orientalist, was in a position to make free use of the materials of the East India Company. On a map of Japan which he made in 1715, he marked the sea off the southern Japan as "Maris Japonici Pars" ("Part of the Sea of Japan"), but on a 1716 map, he labeled the same sea area simply as "Mer du Japon." On both maps, he left the sea area of the East Sea unmarked. It is known that due to his academic achievements, the maps of Reland had a considerable impact. On his "Nouvelle Carte de L'Asie" in 1719 and "Carte des Indes, de la Chine & Isles du Japon, de Sumatra, de Jave" ("Map of India, China & Isles of Japan, Sumatra, Java") in the same year, Henri Abraham Châtelain named the sea "Mer Orientale ou du Japon," as if to embrace them both.

Rigobert Bonne, who was considered as the most faithful student of d'Anville, used "Mare Orientale Minus," a name invented in Germany, on his "Les Isles du Japon. L'Empire

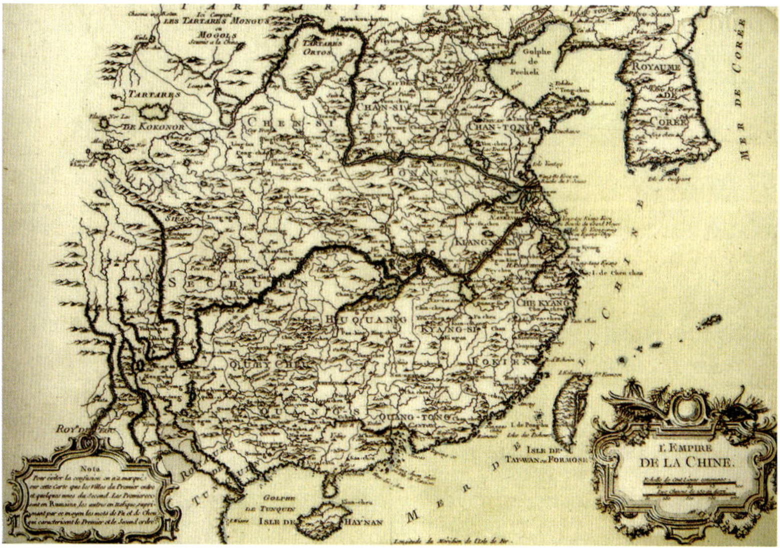

On "L'Empire de la Chine" published in 1748, Bellin, an eminent hydrographer, identified the East Sea as "Mer de Corée."

de la Chine" in 1720 and its re-publication in 1730. And he marked the Pacific Ocean as "Oceanus Orientalis." That is to say, he made a differentiation between the East Sea, which he called the "Small East Sea," and the Pacific Ocean, "Oceanus Orientalis." However, on "L'Empire du Japon," he left the East Sea unmarked as his teacher d'Anville did and, on "L'Asie" in 1762, revised the name to "Mer de Corée."

Clermont marked the East Sea as "Mer de Corée" on "L'Asie" in 1729. Saint Robert replaced "East Sea" with "Mer de Corée" on "L'Asie" when he published in 1729 a revision of Sanson's "L'Asie" of 1650.

As is mentioned in the passages about old maps made by the Vatican, Father Du Halde, who published an encyclopedia on China in 1730 which was recognized as the finest in Europe, used the name "Mer ou Océan Oriental" to represent the East Sea in the main text of pages 6, 9, 33, 37, and 57 in Vol. 4 of the book. He was probably referring to what Father Thomas wrote. He, however, caused confusion by marking the East Sea as "Mer du Japon" on the map in the encyclopedia. Jean Roussel de Missy also marked the East Sea as "Mer du Japon" in his *Nouvel Atlas Géàgraphique, Historique* (*New Geographical and Historical Atlas*) in 1742. However, Jacques-Nicolas Bellin[10] consistently marked the East Sea as "Mer de Corée on a series of his maps, including "La Carte de L'Empire du Japon" in 1735, "L'Asie" in 1748, its re-publication in 1752, "La Carte du Royaume de Kaoli ou de Corée" ("The Map of the Kingdom of Kaoli or Korea") in 1764, and the maps carried in "Das Kaiserthum China, Königreich Korea" ("The Empire of China and the Kingdom of Korea") which was published in German in 1748.

D'Anville, arguably the greatest cartographer in the 18th century, started drawing maps of ancient European history since he was about 15 years old. His "Royaume de

10) Bellin studied hydrography for the first time in France and got paid for it over ten years earlier before the *Académie de Marine* was established. When the *Académie* was launched, he was appointed its first member.

On this hand-drawn map of the late 1720s, a collection of d'Anville's, the East Sea is twice marked as"Mer de Corée."

Corée" ("Kingdom of Korea"), the first of its kind in history, became the prototype of the maps of Korea on maps of many European countries for the next 100 years or so. On the map contained in Du Halde's *Description Géographique, Historique, Chronologique, Politique, et Physique de l'Empire de la Chine et de la Tartarie Chinois* (*Geographical, Historical, Chronological, Political and Physical Description of the Empire of China and Chinese Tartary*), d'Anville named the East Sea as "Mer du Japon." But on a hand-drawn map, which has never been published formally and that is now part of the collection of the National Library of France, he marked the East Sea as "Mer de Corée." In yet another turn, on the map of "Kingdom of Korea" in the atlas, which was published as an appendix to the *Description*, he left the East Sea unmarked. These many variants notwithstanding, an unvarying principle of naming a place that he tried to maintain in his maps was not to make an arbitrary name when he did not know the endonym of the local place. This principle was applied to all place names, on lands or seas. However, most other map-makers who made their maps in imitation of his marked the East Sea what they thought to be most appropriate, with the "Sea of Korea" being what they preferred most.

Robert was also one of those map-makers who followed d'Anville's map of Korea. On his "L'Asie" in 1739 and its

In 1735, d'Anville, the most respected cartographer in the 18th century, published the "Royaume de Corée" ("Kingdom of Korea"), which served as the model of the maps of Korea on European maps for the next 150 years. On this map, he did not make any marking on the sea area of the East Sea according to his principle that he would give no name to a sea whose name he did not know.

reproduction in 1749, he labeled the East Sea as the "Sea of Korea." Also on "An Accurate Map of Asia," which was published in English in 1764, he adopted the "Sea of Korea." Bertrand René Pallu, who left only one map, marked the East Sea as the "Sea of Korea" on his "L'Asie" in 1748. Later, however, on "L'Empire du Japon," Robert divided the sea area into two parts and gave both names: "Mer de Corée" to the Korean side and "Mer du Japon" to the Japanese side. Bellin, a marine expert, marked the East Sea as "Mer de Corée" on "L'Empire de la Chine" in 1748, and Janvier also used "Mer de Corée" for the East Sea on his "L'Asie" in 1759.

Philippe Buache, Guillaume Delisle's grandson who inherited Delisle's map business, was a physical geographer. In "Carte Physique de la Grande Mer" ("Physical Map of

In 1759, celebrated geographer Janvier followed d'Anville on "L'Asie" but, regarding the name of the East Sea, he marked "Mer de Corée" in accordance with his conviction.

the Great Sea") in 1744, he marked the East Sea as the "Sea of Korea." However, when he was requested to draw a map of Japan for Denis Diderot's encyclopedia, he marked the East Sea as the "Sea of Japan." Yet again, when he published "L'Asie" in 1744 and "Mappemonde" and "La Carte Physique du Monde" ("The Physical Map of the World") in 1754, he gave the East Sea when he thought to be the most reasonable name, the "Sea of Korea." On "Map of Northeast Asia" (1750 & 1752), which he re-published jointly with Guillaume's brother Joseph-Nicolas Delisle, and "L'Asie" in 1772, he continued to label the East Sea as the "Sea of Korea." J. N. Delisle also marked the East Sea as the "Sea of Korea" on "L'Asie" which he published solely in 1750. Meanwhile, J. Palairet named the East Sea as the "Gulf of Corea" on "L'Asie" in 1760.

Professor Pelletier assumed that Guillaume, who used to name the East Sea as "Mer Orientale," marked it as the "Sea of Korea" on a map of 1723 in a change of his belief under the influence of his brother Joseph-Nicolas Delisle.[11] However, Professor Pelletier surely must be mistaken because Joseph-Nicolas had never made any maps before Guillaume died in 1726. In addition, Joseph-Nicolas marked the East Sea as the "Sea of Korea" on many maps of his because while he was active in Russia for over 20 years after his brother died, he witnessed some Russian scholars marking the East Sea as the "Sea of Korea." Therefore, in terms of the time sequence, it is very unlikely that Joseph-Nicolas had any influence on his brother Guillaume.

11) Pelletier, "The Role of French Geography in the Naming of the Sea between Korea, Japan and Siberia from the 17th to Early 19th Century."

"Carte pour L'Histoire Generale" ("Map for the General History") of 1763, which was collected by d'Anville and is now in the collection of the National Library of France, was made by Michel Picaud, an obscure local map-maker. He marked the East Sea as "Mer de Coree."

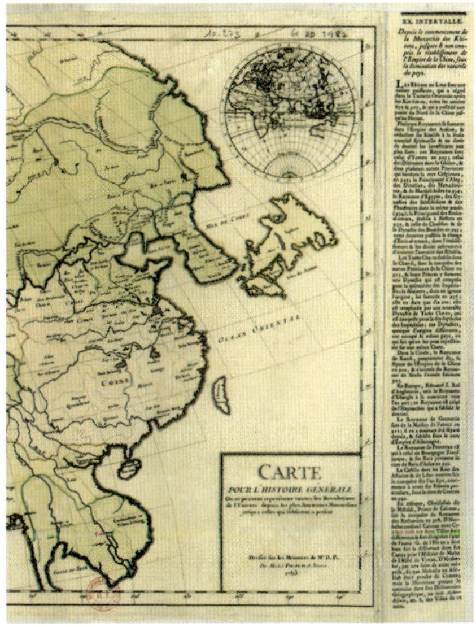

Picaud, who was active locally, marked the East Sea as "Mer de Coree" in the part of the three Asian countries in his "Carte pour L'Histoire Generale," an atlas related to history made in 1763. This atlas was included in d'Anville's collection of maps.

Gilles Robert de Vaugondy[12], who inherited the map business of the Sanson family from Jaillot owing to his blood-ties with the family, formed the most active map-maker family of his own in Europe since the mid-18th century. Robert de Vaugondy and his successors accepted d'Anville's map of Korea as the most trustworthy and followed it. With regard to the notation of the East Sea, however, they did not leave it unmarked as d'Anville, but gave a name they thought appropriate. On "L'Asie" in 1739 and its re-publication in 1750 and 1751, and "Map of the Empire of China," published in English in 1750, Robert de Vaugondy marked the East Sea as "Mer de

12) In French names, Robert is often a given name, but in his case, Gilles is the given name and Robert de Vaugondy is the family name.

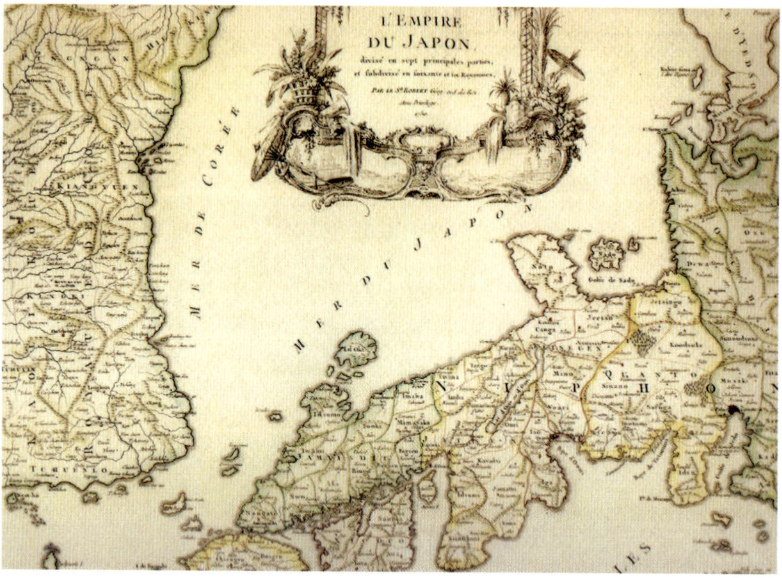

In 1750, Gilles Robert de Vaugondy, who raised the most important map-making family in the mid-18th century, divided the East Sea into two parts and gave the Korean side the name "Mer de Corée" and the Japanese side, "Mer du Japon." However, on other maps, he and his son Didier marked the entire East Sea as the "Sea of Korea."

Corée," or "Sea of Korea." However, on "L'Empire du Japon," also published in 1750, he marked the Korean side of the East Sea as the "Sea of Korea" and the Japanese side, "Sea of Japan."

It is generally known that Robert Dudley was the first map-maker to give the East Sea two different names on the same map, but this is also somewhat mistaken. On "Carta particolare della Grande Isola del'Giapone è di Iezo con il Regno di Corai et altre Isole in torno" ("Detailed Map of the Big Island of Japan and Hokkaido with the Kingdom of Korea and Other Nearby Islands"), contained in the first edition (1647) of his atlas, Dudley placed the notation "Mare di Corai" in the middle of the East Sea. In the second publication in 1661, he placed it closer to Korea and marked "Il Mare Settentrionale di Iappone" ("The North Sea of Japan") in the middle. And he also marked "Il Mare Australe di Iego" ("South Sea of Hokkaido") in the northeast or on the sea off the south of current Hokkaido, using a total of three names. Specifically, "Mere di Corai" is marked in larger letters, while "Il Mare Settentrionale di Iappone" and "Il Mare Australe di Iego" are printed in smaller cursive letters. And, unlike "Mare di Corai," these two names have the definite article "Il" at the front. Therefore, it is understood that "Mare di Corai" was used as the title of a sea, while the remaining two were used as a description of the seas. By the same token, as the marking "Mare Australe di Iappone Ō Giappone" ("South Sea of Japan") on the sea off the south of Japan does not have a definite article, this should be taken as the name of the sea. As such, although they both presented two (or three) different names for the same sea, Robert de Vaugondy and Dudley differed.

On "L'Asie" in 1750, a map that they jointly made, Robert Géor and Saint Robert divided the East Sea into two parts and marked the Korean side as the "Sea of Korea" and the Japanese side, "Sea of Japan," just as Vaugondy did on his 1750 "L'Empire du Japon." However, in consideration of the date of their publication, it is not very likely that Géor and Saint Robert followed Robert de Vaugondy's notation. Still, it is quite interesting to note that on two different maps that were published in the same year, two names were to represent the same sea in a different way from the past.

Didier Robert de Vaugondy, son of Gilles Robert de Vaugondy, produced maps independently under his own name while his father still lived. In 1749, Didier marked the East Sea as the "Sea of Korea" on "L'Asie" in 1749. In 1755, he did the same on "L'Empire du Japon" and "Sibérie ou Russie Asiatique" ("Siberian or Asian Russia"), the latter he produced jointly with Dussy in 1755. In 1772, however, he left the East Sea unmarked on "L'Asie." Then again, he marked the East Sea as the "Sea of Korea" on "L'Asie" in 1775 and "L'Empire du Japon" in 1787. To summarize, like Gilles and Didier, the Vaugondy family used "Sea of Korea" most of the time, with only a few exceptions.

It cannot be definitely said that the Robert de Vaugondy family influenced map-makers of the late 1700s, but they generally used the notation of the "Sea of Korea." Nicolas Antoine Boulanger's "Nouvelle Mappemonde" in 1760

This map, "Mappemonde," was published in 1775 by Didier Robert de Vaugondy who inherited his father's business. The East Sea is marked as "Mer de Coree."

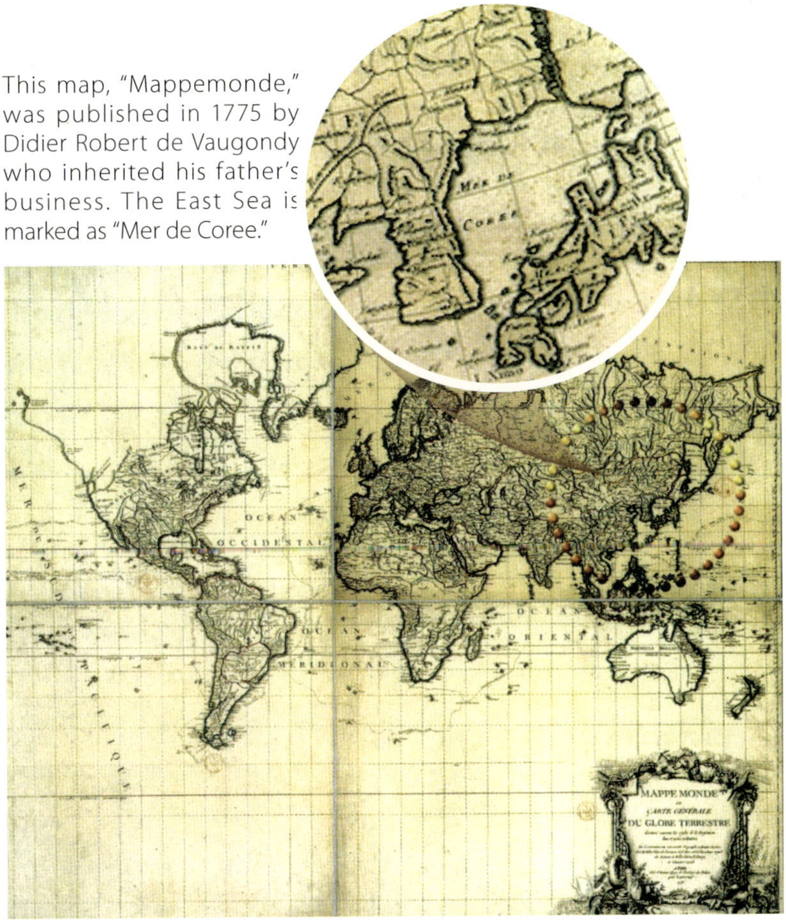

had the "Sea of Korea" for the East Sea. Jean Baptiste Louis Clouet's "Carte d'Asie" in 1764 and its re-publication in 1787 also used the same marking. So did "L'Asie" of 1772 by L. C. Desnos and "L'Asie" of 1776 by Desnos and L. Charles. In addition, Louis Brion de la Tour also marked the East Sea as the "Sea of Korea" on "L'Asie" in 1765. However, probably due to lack of conviction on the name of the East Sea, Nicol marked both "East Sea" and "Sea of Korea" on his "La Chine et le Japon" in 1796.

On French antique maps in the mid-17th century when endonyms of places began to be known, such names as "Océan ou Mer Orientale" and "Sea of Korea" are found. Then, until the early 18th century, the "East Sea" remained in existence together with the "Sea of Korea." Beginning in the mid-18th century, however, the "Sea of Korea" formed the general trend. It is presumed that, when the shape of the maps is taken into account, the name "Sea of Korea" was found most appropriate to the French rationalism that emphasizes logic.

Another reason has something to do with the linguistic habits of the French people. Like other Europeans, they write from left to right, and their sentences are usually arranged in the order of the subject, followed by the verb, and the object or the complement. Therefore, the elements appearing on the right are governed by the elements on the left and should be in agreement with them. For example, a verb on the right should agree with a subject on the left in their gender and number. Accordingly, it is rational that the sea on the right should take its name from the country on its left. Naming the East Sea as the "Sea of Korea" then must have corresponded most accurately with their unconscious linguistic habits.

Toward the 19th century, however, the notation of the "Sea of Korea" began to face a critical change. While many countries in Europe enthusiastically engaged themselves with finding overseas colonies, France was squandering national finances on its extravagant palace and military armaments and lost one battle after another with Great Britain in their colonial wars. Consequently, Louis XVI of France spent national resources in exploring undeveloped areas overseas and uncharted seas as well as keeping an eye on world affairs. As part of these efforts, Louis XVI appointed Count La Pérouse, a national hero who won a battle with the British army in Canada, as captain of a fleet of two ships. Scientists who were handpicked beforehand and sufficient supplies which were prepared over years were aboard the fleet.

Count La Pérouse went around the tip of South America, passed by Alaska, and proceeded north toward Southeast Asia. As he passed the sea near Jeju Island of Korea and the seas off the coast of southern Korea, he measured the depth of the seas and observed the inhabitants' movements. While they sailed north along the east coast, Joseph Lepaute Dagelet, an astronomer, discovered Ulleungdo and named the island after himself. A sudden gust of wind

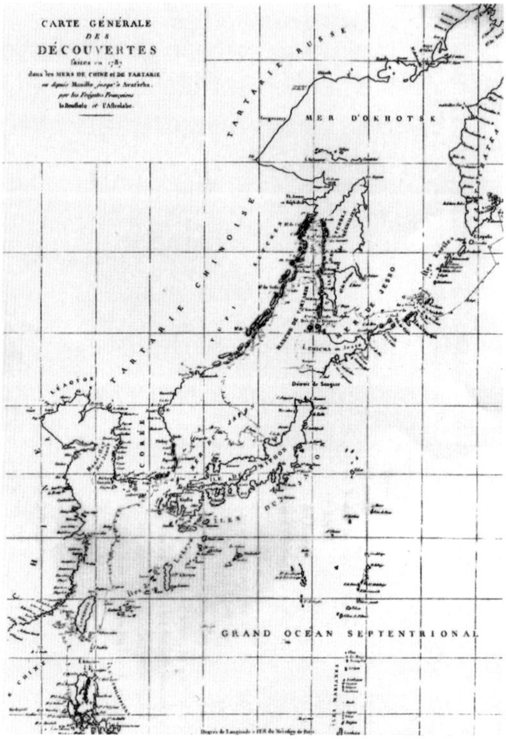

In 1787, La Pérouse passed through the south seas of Korea and explored the East Sea in his voyage. On the map of the East Sea in his voyage atlas, which was published posthumously, the East Sea is marked as "Mer du Japon." However, in his journal, he alternated the use of "Sea of Korea" and "Sea of Japan."

forced them to drop the plan to continue to go northward along the coast and navigate northeast until they reached a small port near the Kamchatka. Enjoying warm hospitality there, the captain sent the ships' logs to Paris with someone. Then on entering the South Pacific, La Pérouse wanted to be restocked with supplies in Australia but things did not turn out as he wanted. There, La Pérouse sent the next logs home before leaving the port but he and his crew all went missing. Some speculate that they were all murdered by natives of the island of Vanikoro but it is more likely that they all drowned in a shipwreck caused by high winds and waves. The French navy made several searches but to no avail. Some articles were discovered but turned out to be meaningless.

The voyage logs and charts that La Pérouse sent home comprised five volumes, which were published in 1798. In the main text of the voyage atlas, an appendix of the book, the East Sea is recorded as the "Sea of Korea," but on the maps Nos. 3 and 5, it is named as "Mauche de Tartarie" ("Tartary Strait"). However, what is important, the marking of "Sea of Japan" on the maps Nos. 39 and 46 had great repercussions on the notation of the "Sea of Korea."

La Pérouse's voyage atlas received great attention from map-makers. Among them, British map-makers were quick to reflect La Pérouse's maps and charts into theirs. Noticing that La Pérouse marked the East Sea as the "Sea of Japan" on some of his maps, British map-makers immediately changed the previous name of the East Sea, the "Sea of Korea" or "Gulf of Korea," to the "Sea of Japan." Some French map-makers, however, adhered to the "Sea of Korea" even after La Pérouse's voyage atlas. It may be because they were late in getting the latest information, but it could be said that the "Sea of Korea" was more in keeping with French rationalism.

In the 19th century, map-making in France declined, most likely due to socio-political changes. Above all, the French Revolution, the seizure of power by Napoleon, and the hard war against Europe deprived France of social and economic

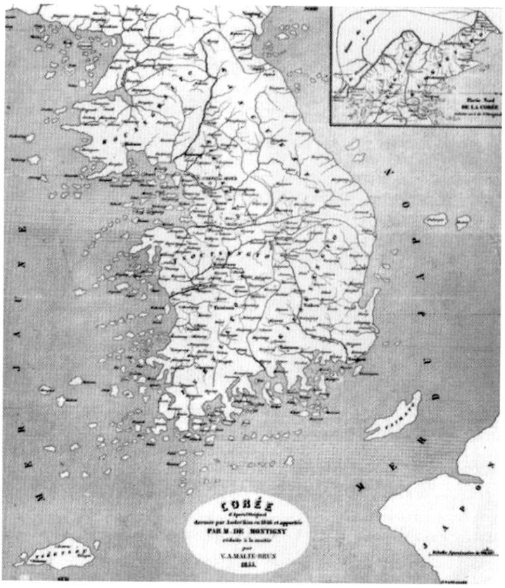

A map of Korea drawn in 1855 by Malte-Brun, secretary-general of the Paris Cartographic Association, based on "Carte de la Corée" which Saint Andrew Kim Taegon sent to France. Malte-Brun marked the East Sea as "Mer du Japon" at his discretion.

stability. A succession of defeats in a war with Great Britain exhausted France's finances, and lessening interest in overseas countries also had a great influence on map-making in France. In the meantime, de Jorsh named the East Sea as the "Sea of Korea" on "Carte de L'Asie" in 1800 and in its re-publication in 1805, he marked "Sea of Korea" in larger letters and "Sea of Japan" in smaller letters. However, Edme Dentelle marked the East Sea as the "Sea of Japan" on "Carte de la Chine" in 1803. Tierry also labeled the East Sea as the "Sea of Japan" on "Carte de L'Empire Chinois" in 1810. On the other hand, Delamarche, who mostly published maps for educational purpose, marked the East Sea as the "Sea of Korea" as he saw fit on "Carte de L'Asie" in 1811. In contrast, Malte-Brun, who immigrated to France and became a geographer, marked the East Sea as the "Sea of Japan" on "China" in 1812, a map he made with reference to the map by Saint Andrew Kim

On "L'Empire Chinois et du Japon" which Lapie of France published in 1832, the East Sea is marked as "Mer du Japon," and the East China Sea to the south of Jeju Island is marked as "Mer de Corée."

Taegon, the first Korean Catholic priest.

Turning from the 18th century to the 19th century, the notation of the "Sea of Japan" increased. In the midst of this change, a strange phenomenon took place. On "De L'Asie" in 1830, Herisson marked the East Sea as the "Sea of Japan" but the sea area of the current East China Sea as "Mer Orientale de Corée" ("East Sea of Korea"). In fact, it lies in the south or southwest of Korea. Nonetheless, it can be assumed that the naming was a kind of compensation for the change of the name "East Sea" to "Sea of Japan." On "Carte de l'Empire Chinois et du Japon," published in 1832, Lapie marked the East Sea as "Mer du Japon" while naming the sea area stretching from Jeju Island to the East China Sea as "Mer de Coree." Instead of marking the East Sea as the "Sea of Japan" on "Carte de L'Asie" in 1836, Guillaume-Henri Dufour made two Korea-related markings on the East China Sea by marking the "East Sea" in large letters and the "Sea of Korea" in small letters. On the map "Océanie" ("Oceania") published in 1847, Victor Levasseur named the East Sea as the "Sea of Japan" and the part of the East China Sea off the south of Jeju Island as the "Sea of Korea." Laurens, an Englishman who made maps in France, marked the East China Sea as "Mer Orientale ou de Corée" on his "Sibérie, Chine, Japon" in 1850. However, Brué marked the East Sea simply as the "Sea of Japan" on "Asie" in 1865. Brué, on the other hand, on "Carte Générale de L'Asie," which he made jointly with C. Piquet in 1867, marked the East Sea as the "Sea of Japan" and the East China Sea as "Mer Orientale ou Mer de Corée" just as Laurens did. In contrast, R. Hausermann marked the East Sea as "Mer du Japon" on an appendix map to a Korean-French dictionary.

As if he referred to Lapie's map, V. Levasseur of France also marked the East Sea as the "Sea of Japan" and the East China Sea as the "Sea of Korea" on his map, "Océanie."

In 1880, R. Hausermann of France named the East Sea as "Mer du Japon" and marked "Détroit de Corée" ("Korea Strait") on "Corée," an appendix map to a Korean-French dictionary which was produced in Yokohama, Japan.

Old French maps played an important role in establishing the names of sea areas during the time when the International Hydrographic Organization (IHO) did not yet exist and a considerable number of their names were later determined as official names. With many twists and turns, the naming of the "East Sea" went through a variety of different phases: From a period when it was called "Oceanus Orientalis" that encompassed the sea areas in Southeast Asia, including the East Sea; to the introduction of the endonym of "Océan ou Mer Orientale;" to the gradual transition to "Mer de Corée" and its peak period from the mid-to-end of the 18th century; to a period when the "Sea of Japan" was the mainstream under the influence of La Pérouse; and, a while later, to the movement of the "Sea of Korea" to cover the East China Sea, rather than the East Sea, in compensation.

The most important fact of all is that it is impossible to find the specific name of the "East Sea" used consistently in old French maps, and even the same map-maker used different names over different times. However, it is also important to remember that no name was given without a reason that was supposedly rational on its own, and understanding it would be the first step in studying the naming of the East Sea.

Chapter 8

Old Maps and the Notation of the Name "East Sea" in Great Britain

The germination of old maps in Great Britain can be traced back to as early as the Middle Ages. However, their maps began to be printed in the early 17th century, about the same time as the French maps. In the early phase of map-making, Great Britain had active human exchanges and cooperation with other European countries, including Italy, Portugal, and the Netherlands. Despite such history, Great Britain did not lead the map-making of Europe during the 17th and 18th centuries. While the Netherlands was the leader in map-making in the 17th century, Great Britain was rather under its influence. In the 18th century, Great Britain still did not produce many maps independently, remaining under the influence of France which was the leading map-maker in

Europe. However, the situation changed in the 19th century. As British maps attracted wider attention, Great Britain accomplished great achievements both in terms of quantity and quality.

There were several reasons behind this change. First of all, Great Britain produced many great explorers and travelers and map-making reflected the results of their explorations and discoveries. It also took the lead in making maps of North America and Australia. The British Royal Navy was recognized as an authority by compiling exact records of the results of both direct and indirect explorations. After all, as a country with a small territory in proportion to its population and the poor soil for agriculture, Great Britain had to find ways to explore overseas territories as a priority. Fortunately, the government's strong overseas drive was successful. Although a latecomer in overseas exploration after Portugal and the Netherlands, Great Britain won consecutive victories in naval battles with Spain and France, colonizing diverse overseas territories and establishing "the empire on which the sun never sets." The supply of resources from the colonies fueled British economic growth, swelling the middle class who had interest in maps. In other words, Great Britain's overseas advancement and expansion of colonies promoted interest in and consumption of maps greatly.

John Speed was a passionate map-maker who produced an atlas for the first time in Great Britain. On "Asia" in 1626, he represented Korea as a peninsula for the first time in the history of Great Britain. The notation of sea areas on the map must have referred to Dutch maps. He marked the East Sea as the "West Ocean," the Indian Ocean as the "East Ocean," and the seas off China as the "Sea of China" in smaller print. According to his logic, in terms of bearings, India was to the east of Great Britain, but the Pacific Ocean was the "West Ocean," because one could reach it by sailing in a westward direction since the discovery of the Americas. The marking of "Sea of China" on the neighboring sea of China is deemed to have been made in consideration of the size of China. Still, another name for the same sea, "Chinian Ocean" on "Map of China" in the same year gives the impression that the naming was made arbitrarily according to circumstances. George Humble, who published a map of East Asia in the same year, also marked the sea off the northeast of Japan as the "West Ocean."

Later, P. Chetwind named the East Sea as "Oceanus Occidentalis" when he published "Asia" in Latin in 1666. It is not clear whether he was influenced by the Netherlands or if he merely followed Speed or Humble. In essence, early

On "L'Empire Chinois et du Japon" which Lapie of France published in 1832, the East Sea is marked as "Mer du Japon," and the East China Sea to the south of Jeju Island is marked as "Mer de Corée."

British maps do not appear to show any particular interest in the East Sea.

On the 1694 map of East Asia by Bichell and Gluer, Korea is depicted in about the same shape as Delisle's, and the East Sea is marked as the "Oriental Sea." K. Durant, a German-born map-maker, marked Korea as "Corea" and the East Sea as the "Ocean Oriental" on "Japan," an English map published in 1679. When he published "A General Map of Asia" in 1669, Richard Blome marked the East Sea and the northern sea of the Pacific Ocean together as the "Oriental Ocean" in larger print and the "Sea of China" in smaller print. Unlike Speed, he seemed to have thought of the Pacific Ocean as a sea that can be reached when one

"China" published by H. Moll, who emigrated from the Netherlands to Great Britain, in 1714. He depicted Korea similarly with Delisle's and marked the East Sea as the "Sea of Corea." He maintained the naming consistently.

sails in an eastward direction. The "Sea of China" printed in smaller letters gives the impression that he referred to Speed and to Dutch maps. In the 18th century, John Thornton left the East Sea unmarked when he made a map of Asia in 1704 probably because he had no firm conviction about its name.

Herman Moll, who originated from the Netherlands, moved to London to seek a bigger market and entered the map business there. In 1710, he marked the East Sea as the "Sea of Corea" on "A New Map of Asia." It is evaluated that

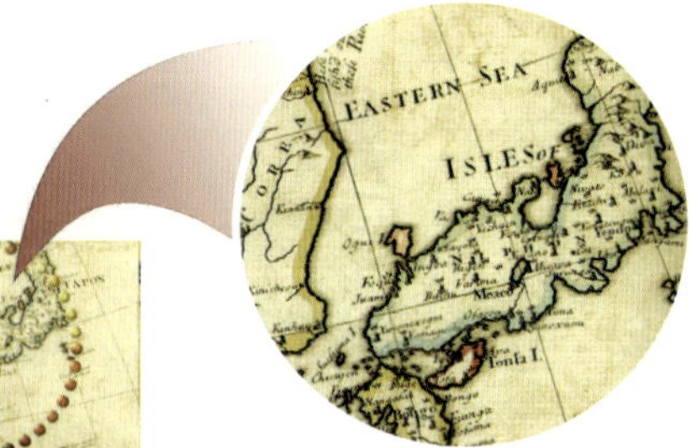

"New Map of India and China" published by Senex of Great Britain in 1721. He followed Moll on Korea and marked the East Sea as the "Eastern Sea," like Delisle did.

he did not follow the nomenclature of his Dutch and British predecessors, but translated the French name "Mer de Corée" into English. Later, he maintained consistency and belief in the name by still naming the East Sea as the "Sea of Corea," as on "China" in 1714, "Whole World" in 1719, and "The Empire of China" in 1720. In contrast, John Senex, a geographer to the British royal court, named the East Sea as "The Eastern or Corea Sea" on "Asia Corrected" and "A New and Correct Map of the World" in 1711. Later, in 1721, he produced two maps of "Asia," with the marking "The Corea Sea" on one of them and "The Eastern Sea" on the other. He was still wavering in the naming when he returned to "The Eastern or Corea Sea" on "Asia" in 1725 and "Asia Corrected" in 1740 but "The Eastern Sea" on another "Asia Corrected"

Babut of Great Britain published "The Kingdom of Korea" in 1740, which was similar to d'Anville's map. He was among the first to start with a "K" rather than a "C" when he marked "Korea." He marked the Yellow Sea as "Hwang Hay" but did not make any marking on the East Sea.

in the same year of 1740. Both "Eastern" and "Oriental" refer to east, but Senex used "Eastern" with the definite article "the" and the rest, without it. Sometimes he made the markings which seemed to have been influenced by Delisle and at other times he made markings that reflected the perceptions of the French general public. Though it may not be an ingenious naming, the names that Senex gave to the East Sea are still noteworthy because all of them were related to Korea. On "The Kingdom of Korea" in 1740, Babut marked Korea with a "K" as the first letter, rather than a "C."

T. Bakewell named the East Sea as "Oceanus Sinensis" on "Asia" in 1729 presumably because he referred to great Dutch cartographers. On the other hand, Bolton marked the East Sea as the "Gulf of Corea" on "Asia" in 1740, while Overton left it unmarked on his map of the same year. Emanuel Bowen, who established the Bowen family known for active map-making, marked the East Sea as the "Eastern Sea" on "Marco Polo's Voyage & Travels in 13C" in 1744. Later, on "Asia" in 1747 and its re-publication in 1752, he marked Korea as "Corea" while marking the East Sea as the "Sea of Korea." Thomas Kitchin also labeled the East Sea as the "Sea of Korea" on "A Map of Quan-Tong or Lea-Tonge and Kingdom of Kau-li or Corea" ("A Map of Kwantung or Liaodong and Kingdom of Korea") in 1745. It is unclear

On this 1747 map, "A New & Accurate Map of Asia," Bowen, who raised a thriving map-making family, marked Korea as "Corea" and the East Sea as the "Sea of Korea."

why they made such a mixed use of the name, but Babut, Bowen and Kitchin were the first to write "Korea" with a "K," signaling the first use of the current nation's name, "Korea." The alteration from "C" to "K" can be explained linguistically. In Latin-based languages, when C combines with the vowel of "a," "o" or "u," it has the phonetic value of /k/, hence Corea. In English-Germanic languages, the /k/ sound is made basically by the letter K, hence Korea. Anyway, Bowen wrote "Sea of Corea" again on "An Accurate Map of Asia" in 1766 and then "Sea of Korea" on the map,

"The Empire of Japan" in the same year. His confused, mixed use of "C" and "K" is deemed to have originated from an unconscious and intuitive mistake. On "Asia," which he published jointly with W. A. Bachiene in Dutch in 1773, the East Sea is marked as "Zee van Korea." On "A Map of Asia" in 1777, the East Sea is also marked as the "Sea of Korea." Thomas Bowen, the son of Emanuel Bowen, marked the East Sea as the "Sea of Korea" on "Russian Empire" in 1778, but he followed the German-style marking and used the

In 1773, Bowen and Bachiene used "Korea" for the name of both the country and the sea area, that is, "Korea," and "Zee van Korea," on a map of Asia which was produced in Dutch.

name “Kleine Orientalische Meer” (“Small East Sea”) on its German edition in 1786.

Green marked the “Sea of Korea” on the East Sea on “Asia” in 1746. John Harris marked the East Sea as the “Eastern Sea” in 1748 as Bowen did on his “Marco Polo’s Voyage & Travels in 13C.” However, Bennett marked the East Sea as the “Sea of Korea” according to the general trend on “Asia” in 1759. Gibson marked Korea “Corea” and the East Sea as the “Sea of Korea” on “A New & Accurate Map of the Empire of China” in 1750.

Thomas Jefferys, one of the most important figures of British map-making in the 18th century, marked the East Sea as the “Sea of Korea” on “The World Agreeable” in 1758, but used “Sea of Corea” on “Asia” in 1769, exhibiting the same confusion as Bowen. John Bennett and Robert Sayer marked the East Sea as the “Gulf of Korea” on a map of Asia that they jointly published. However, the map published by Bennett by himself used “Sea of Corea,” and it suggests that the “Gulf of Korea” was Sayer’s idea. The name “Gulf of Korea” also seems to have been derived from the same way of thinking as the “Small East Sea” on German maps. J. Hinton also marked the East Sea as the “Gulf of Korea” on “An Improved Map of Asia” in 1762.

Salmon named the East Sea as the “Sea of Corea” on “Asia”

In 1750, Gibson gave Korea and the East Sea the name "Corea" and the "Sea of Corea" on his "A New & Accurate Map of the Empire of China."

in 1767 and its re-publication in 1781. G. Rollos marked the East Sea as the "Sea of Korea" on "An Accurate Map of the World" in 1770. And from around this time, an increasing number of maps used the English name of Korea with a "K."

J. Palairet named the East Sea "Gulf of Korea" on "Asia" in 1752 and 1753. On "Map of Asia" which was attached to the 1771 Encyclopedia Britannica as an appendix, he marked the East Sea as the "Sea of Korea." However, on the maps that followed, the East Sea was marked as the "Sea of Japan." Kitchin labeled the East Sea as the "Sea of Korea" on "A Map of Quan-Tong or Lea-Tonge and Kingdom of Kau-li or Corea" but marked it as the "Gulf of Korea" on

"Asia According to the Sieur d'Anville" from a different perspective from d'Anville's. On "Asia" in 1774 and 1781, he again marked the East Sea as the "Sea of Korea," going back and forth between "Gulf" and "Sea" and "Corea" and "Korea."

Kitchin marked Korea as "Corea" and the East Sea as the "Sea of Korea" on "A Map of Quan-Tong or Lea-Tonge and Kingdom of Kau-li or Corea" in 1745.

Samuel Dunn used "Corean" as an adjective when he labeled the East Sea as the "Corean Sea" on "A Map of Chinese Tartary with Corea" in 1774. But he marked the East Sea as the "Gulf of Corea" on "The Map of the World" in the same year and maintained the same marking in its re-publication.

Duke and Orleans labeled the East Sea as the "Corean Gulf" on the map, "Northeast Asia" in 1780. C. Dilly also used "Gulf of Corea" on "An Accurate Map of Russian Empire" in 1785. C. Bowles made the same marking on "Bowles New Four Sheet Map of Asia" in 1789.

Laurie and Whittle called the East Sea the "Corean Sea"

when they made "Empire of Japan" in 1789 with reference to Kaempher's maps and old Portuguese maps. They, however, turned to the use of "Sea of Japan" on "Asia" in 1799, presumably because they referred to La Pérouse's charts. Sayer marked the East Sea as the "Sea of Corea" on "Asia" in 1790 but marked it as the "Gulf of Corea" on "Asia" in 1794.

J. Palairet and Bowles marked the East Sea as the "Sea of Korea" on "Asia" in 1786, while Andreuss labeld it as the "Sea of Corea" on "Asia" in 1793. Wilkinson called the East Sea the "Gulf of Corea" on "New Map of Empires, States, Provinces of Asia" which was published in 1794 and 1798.

Thomas Conder marked the East Sea as the "Sea of Corea" on "Bowles New Pocket Map of the World" in 1792. Palairet also called the East Sea as the "Sea of Corea" on yet another "Bowles New Pocket Map of the World" in 1792. The two map-makers used the same name for the East Sea on two different maps of the same name produced in the same year. De la Rochette called the East Sea the "Gulf of Corea" on "Asia" in 1793, a map revised from Palairet's. On the other hand, Dalaiset & Bowles marked the East Sea as the "Sea of Korea" on "A New-Sheet Map of Asia" in 1791, a map made on the basis of Palairet's. S. Dunn used an adjective form to name the East Sea as the "Corean Sea" in *A Universal Atlas* in 1794. On "The World According to

Dalaiset & Bowles marked Korea as "Korea" and the East Sea as the "Sea of Korea" on "A New Sheet Map of Asia" in 1791.

the Latest Discoveries" in 1794, A. Keith identified the East Sea as the "Korean Sea" but on "Asia" in the same year, he marked it as the "Gulf of Corea." Then again, he marked the East Sea as the "Corean Sea" on "Map of the World According to the Latest Discoveries" in the same year, failing to maintain consistency of the name even on the maps made in the same year. R. Wilkinson applied the same mixed use

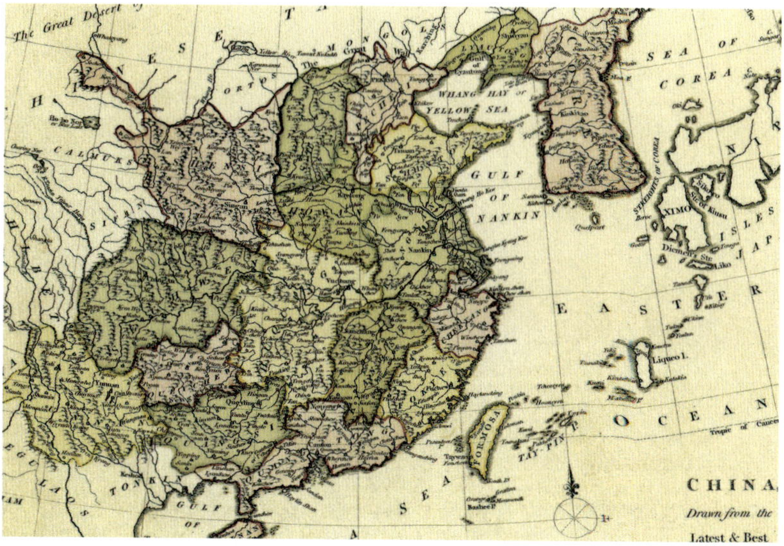

Wilkinson marked Korea and the East Sea "Corea" and the "Sea of Corea" on a map of China in 1794.

of the name when he marked the East Sea as the "Gulf of Corea" on "A New Map of Asia from the Latest Discoveries" in 1794 and then the "Sea of Corea" on "China Drawn from the Latest & Best Discoveries" in the same year.

John Russell labeled the East Sea as the "Gulf of Corea" on "Asia" in 1795 and then used the same name on "Russian Empire" which he produced together with Robinson in 1799.

John Arrowsmith, who came from a well-known British map-making family from the late 18th to early 19th centuries, marked the East Sea as the "East Sea" on "Asia" in 1794, 1798

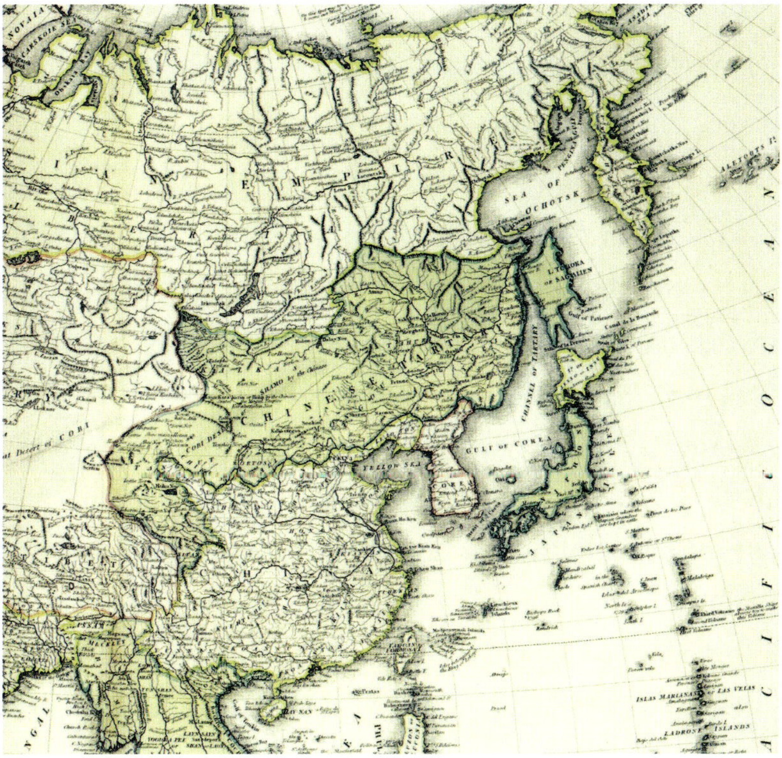

Faden made a map "Asia" in 1808. Faden, who was a student of eminent cartographer Thomas Jefferys, succeeded his teacher's business and became a royal geographer after the latter's death. On a map he made based on d'Anville's map with some revisions, he marked Korea as "Corea" and the East Sea as the "Gulf of Corea."

and 1809. Baker named the East Sea as the "Sea of Korea" on "Asia" in 1795. William Faden, a renowned British royal geographer, labeled the East Sea as the "Gulf of Corea" on "Asia" in 1808. In contrast, T. Coldwell and Davis labeled the East Sea as the "Sea of Japan" on "Japan" in 1802.

G. Tomas marked the East Sea as the "Gulf of Corea" on "A New Map of Asia" in 1799, but used "Sea of Japan" on "Corea and Japan" in 1815 and "Tartary" in 1817.

The notation of the "Sea of Japan" appearing in the voyage atlas of La Pérouse of which, after its publication, an English edition was published, had a rapid impact on British maps. John Pinkerton marked the East Sea as the "Sea of Japan" on "Asia" in 1814. Aaron Arrowsmith, who represented cartography from the late 17th to the early 18th century, also used "Sea of Japan" on "Empire of Japan" in 1835. However, Thomas Illman marked the East Sea as the "Gulf of Corea" on "Asia" in 1835. James Wyld, who took over Faden's business, also marked the East Sea as the "Gulf of Korea" on "Asia" in 1846. In contrast, John Tallis named the East Sea as the "Sea of Japan" on "Japan and Corea" in 1851 and William Hughes also used the same marking, "Sea of Japan," on "Asia" in 1859. Later, E. Welles used "Gulf of Corea" on "Asia" in 1872, but changed it to the "Sea of Japan" on "Chinese Empire" in 1888.

It is observed that the sea names on old British maps largely underwent three stages of change. Until the mid-17th century, at the dawn of the era of antique maps, the sea names assigned by great Dutch cartographers were generally accepted. From the late-17th to mid-18th centuries, they came

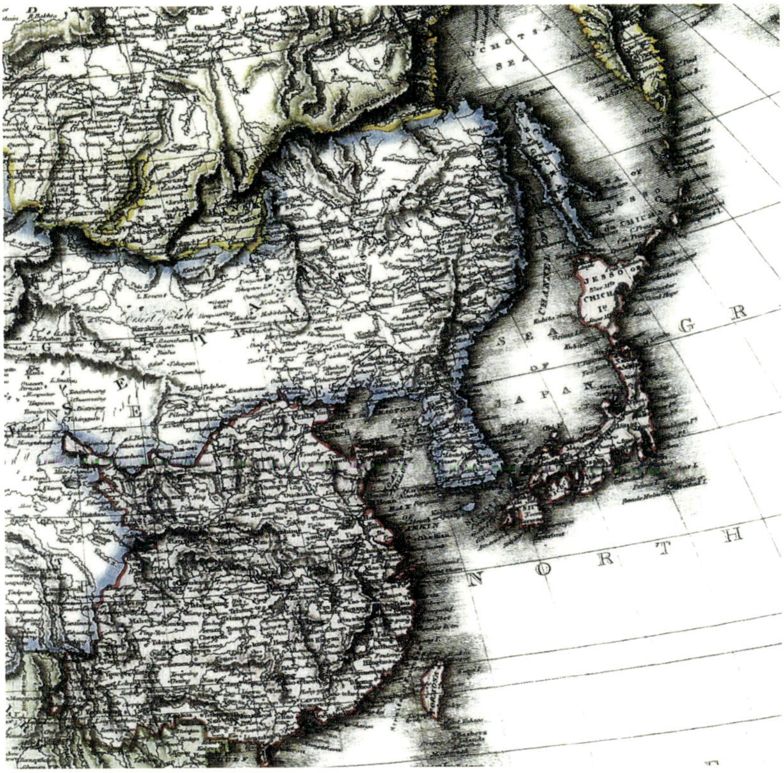

J. Wyld inherited Faden's business and published "Asia" in 1846. Korea was depicted differently in shape from d'Anville and Faden but, like Faden, he marked Korea as "Corea" and the East Sea as the "Gulf of Corea."

under the influence of old French maps and their English translations were used. However, from the late-18th century, the old British maps showed independent originality in establishing sea names.

From the late-17th to the mid-18th centuries, French geographers and cartographers quickly applied to maps of

J. Wyld, who inherited Faden's business after he died, published "Asia" in 1846. Korea was depicted differently in shape from d'Anville and Faden but, following Faden in names, he marked Korea as "Corea" and the East Sea as the "Gulf of Corea."

their times the latest information and discoveries that they acquired mostly from missionaries. During this period, influenced by them, the notation of the East Sea in Great Britain was mainly the "Sea of Corea." At the time, the name "Sea of Japan" was hardly to be found. Since that time, however, British maps started to add a new dimension by reflecting the exploration records of brave British captains who crisscrossed the entire globe. They adopted the record of La Pérouse's exploration of the East Sea at the end of the

18th century sooner than France, triggering the shift of many maps from using the Korea-centered name of "East Sea" toward the use of "Sea of Japan." In the end, Great Britain became the first to accept and reflect the marking of "Sea of Japan" in La Pérouse's atlas. In the midst of this transition, some major map-makers adhered to the use of "Sea of Korea (or Corea)" or "Gulf of Korea (or Corea)" until the mid-19th century. The use of "Sea of Korea" instead of "Sea of Corea" on British maps in the mid-18th century sparked wider use of the current country name, Korea. They also attempted to show that the East Sea was, unlike other large seas, a "gulf" around the present Gulf of Wonsan in North Korea.

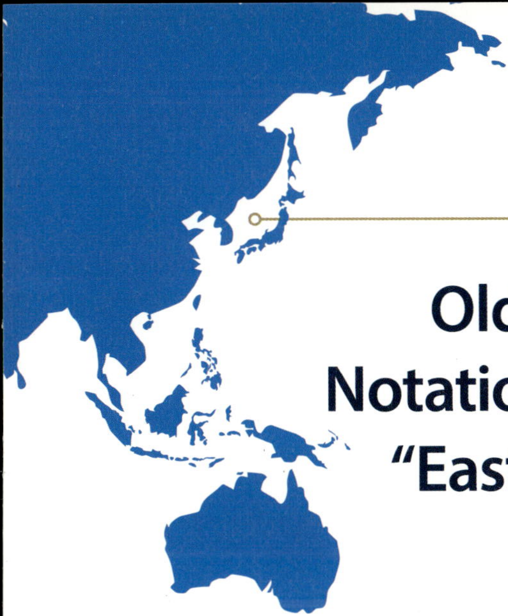

Chapter 9

Old Maps and the Notation of the Name "East Sea" in Russia

Russia is especially noteworthy as it borders on the East Sea. In the past, it incorporated Noktundo, then part of the Korean territory, into its lands and is still in a territorial dispute with Japan over the Kuril Islands. These factors add to what attracts our attention to how the East Sea has been marked on old Russian maps. This chapter is largely based on the research of Russian and European scholars who have studied the markings of the East Sea on Russian maps.

In Russia, not many old maps have survived. Those few which have been discovered include some from the 12th century and some others from the mid-16th century with the depictions of private lands. Although they were produced for administrative purposes, these maps were made mostly by non-professionals as raw data. In the early 17th century, the Russian government decided that it needed more professional maps and started to collect maps made in the Netherlands. In the meantime, Michael I, the first Russian Tsar of the House of Romanov who came to power in 1613, speeded up the territorial expansion to Siberia, finally reaching the Pacific coast. In the late 17th century, maps of Siberia were made, with that of Semyon U. Remezov in 1682 being the most representative.[13]

Unlike maps made for commercial purposes in Europe, the maps made in Russia in those days were mostly made by the administrative authority for administrative purposes to meet some practical needs. Although territory-related, they were not made based on exact cartographic principles. In recognition of this problem, the Russian government built infrastructure for cartography by building territory survey schools, mathematics-navigation schools, and geodetic survey institutes from the end of the 17th to the early 18th centuries.

When it was proposed that Russia invite expert cartographers from advanced European countries, Russia's Czar Peter the Great invited Joseph-Nicolas Delisle, a famous

13) Valerie Kivelson, *Cartographies of Tsardom: The Land and Its Meanings in Seventeenth-Century Russia*, Cornell University Press, 2006.

astronomer and cartographer from France and appointed him head of the St. Petersburg Observatory. The Russian czar also put him in charge of training cartographers and directly managing map-making in Russia. However, as maps were related to national security, Delisle was not granted full authority, which he had to share with V. Kirilov in making maps. Meanwhile, other than U. Remezov and V. Kirilov, such competent Russian cartographers as Afanasy Shestakov and Spanberg, were engaged in map-making. But it failed to grow into a full-fledged industry as it did in Europe because, in spite of the state and administrative agencies encouraging map-making, there was an insufficient middle class formed who could take interest in and buy maps. It was also partly because the state and administrative agencies were interested primarily in Siberia and Alaska, which were claimed as part of Russia.

Korea first appeared on a 1682 map of Siberia by Remezov but it is not clear what source he referred to. However, as it was known that some of the maps made in Russia were introduced into France through Delisle, it became clear that copies of the maps done by Jesuit priests who had been sent to China were introduced into Russia beginning in the early 18th century. Eventually, Delisle and Kirilov turned out to have referred to the materials of Jesuit priests as d'Anville did. Kirilov made the different markings for the East Sea on two maps that he published in 1734. On "Eastern Hemisphere," he left the East Sea blank but on "Asiae recentissa Deliniatio," unlike d'Anville, he marked the East Sea as the "Sea of Korea." According to S. Ganzei and P. Baklanov, on "A General Map of Russia," yet another map of 1734 along with the two maps above, Kirilov marked what is currently Sea of Okhotsk as the "Kamchatka Sea" and the East Sea on its southeast as the "Eastern Sea."14)

It is not clear what influence the maps of Delisle and Kirilov had on maps made afterwards, but it is certain that, at least until the mid-19th century, most maps produced in Russia marked the East Sea as the "Sea of Korea" except for some where it was left blank and a few where it was marked the "Sea of Japan."15) Some cartographers regarded Delisle with jealousy for his role that they thought was larger than what he deserved, but most wanted to solidify their footing by helping him. It seems that Delisle had conviction in naming the East Sea as the "Sea of Korea."

---

14) S. Ganzei & P. Baklanov, "Russian Geographical Investigations of Seas of North-Eastern Asia in XVII-XVIII Centuries," The 2nd International Seminar on Sea Names, 1996, The Society for East Sea.

15) Alexei Postnikov & Evgenii Pospelov, "The History of Russian Names for Seas, with the Special Reference on the Development of the Korean (Japanese) Sea Presentation on Maps (Seventeenth through Nineteenth Centuries)," The 1st International Seminar on Sea Names, 1995, The Society for East Sea.

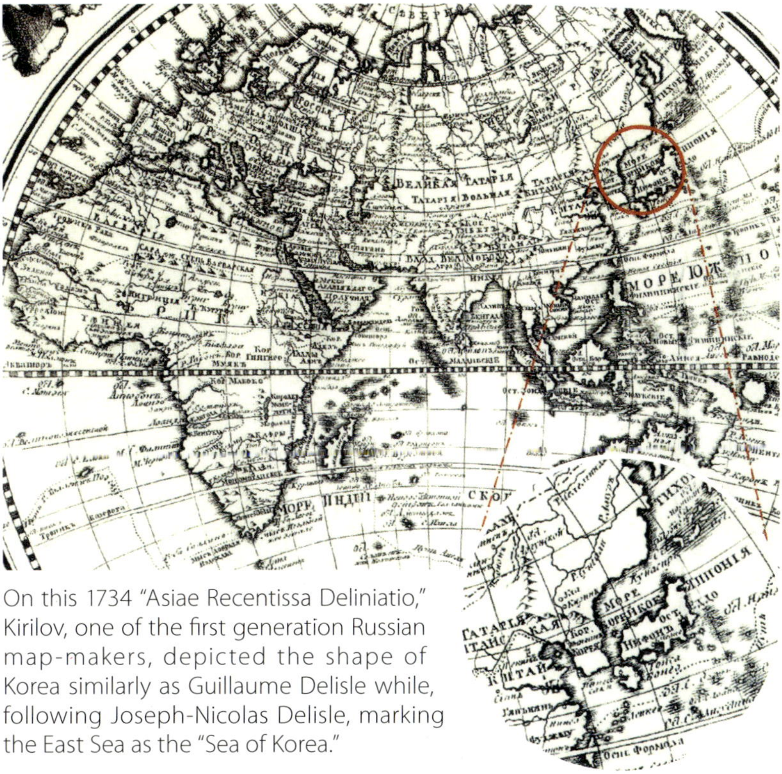

On this 1734 "Asiae Recentissa Deliniatio," Kirilov, one of the first generation Russian map-makers, depicted the shape of Korea similarly as Guillaume Delisle while, following Joseph-Nicolas Delisle, marking the East Sea as the "Sea of Korea."

Perhaps because of national pride, most Russian cartographers are often very sparing in recognizing his contribution. For example, V. Kivelson, who left an important book on the history of Russian cartography, mentioned Delisle three times in his book: The first mention is that he made an atlas of Russia together with Kirilov; the second is made regarding the map of the East Russia which is part of the atlas; and the third is that Delisle sent to France the materials that he treated on Russian salary and even made a presentation at the French Academy of Sciences. Leo Breitfuss took issue especially with this third matter and hurled criticism at him, alleging that what Delisle did was tantamount to an act of treason. However, Albert Isnard advocated Delisle on the ground that the contract Delisle signed with the Russian government clearly stated that he had the freedom to make a presentation on Russian maps overseas.[16]

From the perspective of a third party, although on his contract Delisle was guaranteed his right to make a presentation overseas, it is deemed that he should have been more prudent when he made a presentation at the French Academy and even published it after receiving a salary from Russia for over 20 years. On the other hand, Russia did not treat him well enough relative to his contribution. In particular, it is quite regrettable that he did not receive as much recognition as he deserved. Russian cartographers might well have complaints over excessive rights that they thought Delisle, a foreigner, was exercising, but it would be more appropriate to assume that Delisle exerted authority granted to him for the sake of Russia, not for a third country or for his personal interest. Now, let us take a look at how today's Russian scholars view the name of the East Sea.

16) Kivelson, *Cartographies of Tsardom: The Land and Its Meanings in Seventeenth-Century Russia.*

Shortly before Delisle arrived in Russia, Afanasy Shestakov left the East Sea blank and so did a German-Russian named Müller. Spanberg also left the East Sea unmarked on a map of Russia in 1739.[17] Most scholars marked the East Sea as the "Sea of Korea" until the 1850s after Delisle arrived.

Alexei Postnikov confirms that most Russian maps after Kirilov labeled the East Sea as the "Korean Sea" or "East Sea." On the map of Asia in the *Russian Atlas*, which the Russian Academy of Sciences at St. Petersburg published for the education of youth in 1745, the East Sea is marked as the "Sea of Korea." This atlas had great influence on the later generations, as evidenced by many maps that followed it. Some examples include: First, Kurnakov's "Map of Siberia" in 1778; second, "The General Map" which Golikov published in 1787 to promote trade; and third, "Carte des Nouvelles Decouvertes au Nord de la Mer Sud, Tout à I'Est de la Sibéria et du Kamtchatka Qu'àl'Ouest de la Nouvelle France" ("Map of New Discoveries in the North of the South Sea, All Eastern Siberia and Kamchatka in the West of New France"), which scholars from Russia and France (probably Delisle) jointly produced in French in the 1750s. It is certain that "Bowles' New One-sheet Map of Asia" of 1791 by the British cartographer, which marked

17) Philippe Pelletier, "The French Geographers and the "Sea of Korea"," The 11th International Seminar on Sea Names, 2005, The Society for East Sea.

the East Sea as the "Sea of Korea," was influenced by Russian maps. Postnikov explains that this is because Korea is close to Russia.[18] Objectively, however, this does not appear to be a very rational explanation. Delisle was not mentioned, though it was clear that he co-authored the map made by the Russian-French collaboration in the 1750s. However, it seems that Delisle's place names were used on other maps.

La Pérouse's notation of the East Sea as "Mer du Japon" on some of his maps of 1797 does not seem to have had much influence on Russian maps. Rather, the maps and books of Krusenstern, who traveled around the world aboard the *Nadezhda* from 1803 to 1806, obviously had more influence. On "World Map" in 1800, he marked the East Sea as the "Sea of Japan" and added the "Sea of Korea." On the 1826 map, he marked the south of the East Sea as the "Korean Straits" and its north as the "Sea of Japan," which the Japanese interpret as referring to the entire East Sea area. The last official Russian map that indicated the East Sea as the "Sea of Korea" was the 1844 "Map of the Polar Sea and the Eastern Ocean" which was compiled on the basis of the surveys by the Hydrographical Department of the Russian Navy Ministry. Until the publication of this map, the Russian Navy Ministry

18) Postnikov & Pospelov, "The History of Russian Names for Seas, with the Special Reference on the Development of the Korean (Japanese) Sea Presentation on Maps (Seventeenth through Nineteenth Centuries).

Admiral Krusenstern, who led the first Russian circumnavigation of the globe in 1808, produced a travelogue in three volumes and two atlases, to which he attached this map of East Asia. In the map, the shape of Korea suggests d'Anville's influence, but he explained that he marked the East Sea as the "Sea of Japan" because the Korean coastline was shorter than Japan's. He also added that some called the sea, "Sea of Korea."

was in a position to regard the East Sea as the "Sea of Korea," but after its publication, it started to describe the sea as the "Sea of Japan," as on other European maps at the time.

On his "Nova Tabula Imperii Russici" in 1687, I. Ides of the Netherlands marked the East Sea as "Oceanus Orientalis," as in other Dutch maps. N. Goman marked the East Sea to the southeast of Sakhalin as the "Eastern Ocean" in *Atlas* in 1725. Later, in 1759, he indicated the East Sea as the "Eastern Sea of Japan" on "The Newest Outline of Asia." However, this

"General depiction of the terrestrial and aquatic globe," a map of 1737, reveals that the naming regarding three Asian countries of Korea, China and Japan has seemingly been influenced by Delisle's maps. The East Sea is marked as "The Eastern Sea" according to Delisle.

naming invites speculation as to its source since the East Sea lies to the northwest sea of Japan, not its east.

Some important maps that are related to the East Sea among the Russian-made maps provide new names for the East Sea in the 18th century, such as the "Pacific Sea," "East Sea" and "Korean Sea." However, some earlier maps left it

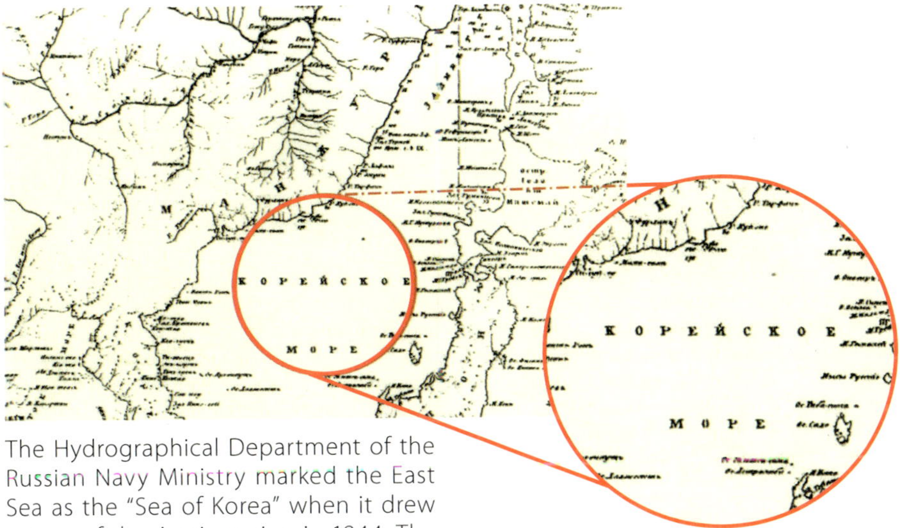

The Hydrographical Department of the Russian Navy Ministry marked the East Sea as the "Sea of Korea" when it drew a map of the Arctic region in 1844. The Russian maps do not seem to have been influenced by La Pérouse and Krusenstern.

blank. One example is "Imperii Russici Tabula generalis" made by Kirilov in 1734. On this map, the East Sea is marked as the "Pacific Sea," a name assumably derived from the perception that the sea is part of the Pacific Ocean.

The name "East Sea" also appears on "General depiction of the terrestrial and aquatic globe," a map included in an atlas for the education of young people in 1737. The notation is presumably not something that came from the use of the term in the Netherlands in the early 17th century but from the influence of the maps by Guillaume Delisle or de Fer of France.

On "Astronomical and geographical map" of 1810, which is in the collection of the Russian State Library, the East Sea is marked as the "Strait of Korea." As Kirilov was, along with Delisle, one of the most prominent cartographers in Russia, his notation of "Bay (Sea) of Korea" and his identification of the East Sea as the "Sea of Korea" on Russian maps until about 1944 was like a result of the influence of Delisle who had had a strong conviction in use of the name. This suggests that something important was missing as J. N. Delisle was not even mentioned.

The Society for East Sea and the Korean Culture and Information Service in Korea published *East Sea in Old Western Maps* in 2004. For the Russian part, the Korean Embassy in Moscow made a survey of Russian maps in 2000 in places like the Russian State Archive of Ancient Acts and the Russian State Naval Archives in St. Petersburg. The results of the survey were as follows:

Korea-related Names				Japan-related Names	Others			Total
Sea of Korea	East Sea	Eastern Ocean	Gulf of Korea	Sea of Japan	Un-marked	Gulf of Korea Sea of Japan	Sea of Pacific	19 (100%)
7	1	1	1	3	3	2	1	
10 (52.6%)				3 (15.8%)	6 (31.6%)			

Western Maps in 2004. For the Russian part, the Korean Embassy in Moscow made a survey of Russian maps in 2000 in places like the Russian State Archive of Ancient Acts and the Russian State Navy Archive in St. Petersburg. The results of the survey were as follows:

No.	Year	Map	Notation	Location
1	1737	Map of China, Korea and Japan	Sea of Korea	Russian State Archive of Ancient Acts
2	1793	Complete Map of Asia Sea of Korea	Sea of Korea	Russian State Archive of Ancient Acts
3	1818	Complete Map of the Korean Peninsula (Geographical review of three parts of Asia, Africa and America, picked out from latest geographers for their Academy named after Alexander Nevski)	Eastern Ocean & Territorial Sea of Korea	Russian State Archive of Ancient Acts
4	Late 19th C.	The Korean Peninsula and Appended Maps	Gulf of Korea & Sea of Japan	Russian State Archive of Ancient Acts
5	1904	Map of the Far East	Sea of Japan	Russian State Archive of Ancient Acts
6	1737	Map of the Far East Region	The Eastern Sea	Russian State Library, Department of Cartographical Editions
7	1790s	Map of China, Korea, Japan (Atlas, composed for readers, bulletins and historical books)	Sea of Korea	Russian State Library, Department of Cartographical Editions

8	1793	Map of Asia divided into main territories	Sea of Korea	Russian State Library, Department of Cartographical Editions
9	1770-1790	Planisphere of the Globe (Sketch of the terrestrial globe)	Sea of Korea	Russian State Library, Department of Cartographical Editions
10	1810-1812	Map of Asia (Historical, genealogical, chronological & geographic Atlas)	Gulf of Korea	Russian State Library, Department of Cartographical Editions
11	Early 19th C.	Kruzenstein's Journal of World Travel	Sea of Japan	Russian State Library, Department of Cartographical Editions
12	Early 18th C.	Complete Map of Russian Far East	Pacific Sea	Russian State Naval Archives
13	1811	Complete Map of the Korean Peninsula (Marine Map including The Korean Sea and Coast)	Sea of Korea	Russian State Naval Archives
14	1740	Complete Map of Japan	No name of the sea	Russian State Naval Archives
15	Mid-18th C.	Complete Map of Alaska	No name of the sea	Russian State Naval Archives
16	1802	Map of the Korean Peninsula	No name of the sea	Russian State Naval Archives
17	1805	Complete Map of Japan by Kruzenstein	Sea of Japan	Russian State Naval Archives
18	1811	Complete Map of the Korean Peninsula	Sea of Korea	Russian State Naval Archives
19	Late 19th C.	Sea Map of East Asia	Gulf of Korea & Sea of Japan	Russian State Naval Archives

A total of 19 maps were related to the notation of East Sea. The specifics are:

Afterwards, the Press Relations Office of the Korean Embassy in Moscow discovered two additions and provided the following table:

	Un-marked	East Sea	Sea of Korea	Sea of Japan	Pacific Ocean	Sea of Korea & Sea of Japan	Total
18th C.	1	1	6	3	1	-	12
19th C.	2	1	2	2	-	2	9
Total	3	2	8	5	1	2	21

As Russia has a relatively short history of its territory expanded up to Siberia and the Pacific coast and Korea is so far away from Russia's political and cultural life, which is centered around Moscow, few Russian historical documents are found with regard to the notation of the East Sea. Again, Russia has a short history of cartography and the map-making did not develop into a full-blown industry. As a consequence, only around 20 maps are known to have anything to do with the East Sea. Aspiring to advance to the Pacific coast from early on, Russia was interested in the East Sea area and sent exploration vessels there several times from the late 18th to the end of the 19th centuries. As the country, however, was not interested in the notation of the

East Sea, Krusenstern had an impact on the naming of the East Sea on Russian maps when he marked the East Sea as the "Sea of Japan."

From the time when Kirilov named the East Sea as the "Sea of Korea" for the first time in Russia until the Russian Navy's "Map of the Polar Sea and the Eastern Ocean," the name "Sea of Korea" has a history of 110 years. By contrast, the "Sea of Japan" has a history of only 50 years on old Russian maps as it came into use around 1805 under the influence of Krusenstern and European maps. It is estimated that the "Sea of Korea" was the mainstream on the Russian maps from the 18th to the mid-19th centuries because of the influence of J. N. Delisle.

Nonetheless, as an important maritime nation and superpower which has attempted to enhance its national standing in the Far East, the time is now ripe for Russia to raise its own voice independently in the issue of the notation of the East Sea.

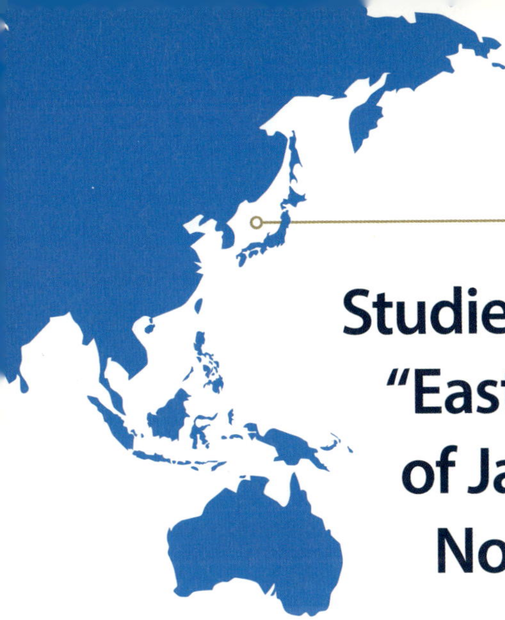

Chapter 10

Studies of the Names "East Sea" and "Sea of Japan" and their Notation in Japan

The study on the "East Sea/Sea of Japan" in Japan was set in motion when Korea began to make the request internationally in the 1990s to use the "East Sea," along with the "Sea of Japan," for the body of water between Korea and Japan. For Korea, it had first something to do with the settling of past affairs with Japan. More than anything else, however, it was a request for fairness and rightfulness based on the historical truth. In contrast, for Japan, it was a request that could undermine an established authority that they possessed and they thus went all out to defend the justification of that name. Japan's Ministry of Foreign Affairs was the first to move against Korea's request. The Ministry organized a task force in anticipation of Korea's request to the international community and checked Korea's moves. It then started to translate articles and papers related to the issue and distribute them to the press and related organizations. Afterward, though it is not certain if the Ministry exercised any influence, institutes for the study of the Sea of Japan were established at more than 10 universities along the east coast of Japan. Among them, the one at Niigata University has been most active, hosting a seminar twice a month and publishing a collection of papers. In addition, an association of institutes studying the Sea of Japan was also formed to present seminars on the issue by experts on a regular basis.

Japan's defensive moves on its Sea of Japan have called for Korea's responses in an endless tit-for-tat. The Korean government instructed the sections responsible for cultural affairs at Korean embassies in foreign countries to survey the notation of the East Sea on old maps in the libraries of their respective countries. The results showed that until the 18th century, the notation of the East Sea/Sea of Korea was the usage in the absolute majority, but in the 19th century, the notation of the Sea of Japan began to increase to finally become the majority usage. They also reported that, while Korea was under Japanese colonial rule, the international hydrographic established the name of the sea as "Sea of

Japan" and it became an internationally recognized name. In response to Korea's such results, Japan's Ministry of Foreign Affairs immediately sent a technical panel to countries and conducted an extensive survey. It then announced internationally that Korea's survey results were unreliable and full of errors. However, when we examined the results of the surveys by the two countries, they had different investigation items to begin with. For example, the Koreans regarded the "Oriental Ocean," "Oriental Sea," "Eastern Sea," "Sea of Korea," and "Gulf of Korea" as all related to the East Sea and counted them as referring to the East Sea. However, the Japanese denied that any of them had anything to do with the East Sea of Korea, except the "Sea of Korea," which they recognized as supportive of the Koreans' argument. The truth is that both countries have problems in the way they performed the surveys. The notation, "Oriental Ocean," appearing on Dutch maps in the early 17th century and the maps by Sanson of France before the 1650s was made in reference to not a specific ocean but "a certain ocean in the east." By contrast, the "East Sea" appearing on the map of 1650 by Briet, the map of 1683 by Manesson Mallet, the maps since 1869 by Guillaume Delisle, and the maps since 1703 by de Fer refer to the East Sea as a translation of the local endonym.

Another problem is that the statistics of both countries were largely influenced by the subjectivism of the surveyors in their selection of the survey items. More specifically, it is estimated that there are 15,000 to 20,000 old maps available in Europe and the statistics could vary according to which library they chose and what maps of which cartographers they surveyed. The statistics can be subject to variability as the maps of the same author can have different markings depending on when they were produced, and even the maps of the same year by the same author can still have different notations. Moreover, the surveyors for the statistics tend to see only what they want to see. In our opinion, in order to insure the reliability of the statistics, the two countries concerned should ask a professional agency of a third country to conduct an objective survey on their behalf. No country has made such a move yet.

More recently, each of the two countries argued that its notation was made first.[19] The "Isolario" of 1528 by Bordone, which Korea presented at the 16th Seminar on Sea Names by the Society for East Sea, has "Mare Orientale" in the sea off the southern end of Korea, but it cannot be verified as referring to the East Sea of Korea. Likewise, it is hard to tell whether "Océan Oriental" marked on the 1552

19) The 16th International Seminar on Sea Names, 2010, The Society for East Sea.

map of Japan by Sanson and the1661 map of Japan by Duval refers only to the East Sea.

Recent arguments of Japanese scholars on the East Sea/Sea of Japan are treated in Part III of this book. Of particular note is that when Western ccartographers began to use "Sea of Japan" intead of "East Sea," or "Sea of Korea," under La Pérouse's influence from the early 19th century, a considerable number of maps by the Japanese themselves appeared in the 19th century showing the East Sea as the "Joseon Sea." The most important of them all are "Nippon henkai ryakuzu"(日本邊界略圖, "Simplified Map of Japan's Periphery") of 1809 and "Shintei bankoku zenzu" (新訂萬國全圖, "New and Revised World Map") of 1810, both by Takahashi Kageyasu.

Takahashi Kageyasu (1785-1829) was a well-known astronomer as was his father, Yoshitoki, and cartographer in charge of the Tenmongata (天文方, Astronomy Institute) of the Shogunate, the ruling body of Japan at the time. On both maps that he made on the instructions of the Shogunate, he marked the East Sea as "朝鮮海" ("Josen kai" in Japanese, or "Joseon Sea"). But the two maps were a bit different in the marking of the sea name. On "Nippon henkai ryakuzu," "Joseon Sea" is marked in the immediate east of the Korean Peninsula, with no name marked on the Pacific Ocean side. In contrast, on "Shintei bankoku zenzu," the name, "Joseon Sea," is marked in the middle of the East Sea, with the marking "大日本海" ("Dainihon kai" or "Great Japan Sea") on the Pacific Ocean side. Taking the author's status into account, these appellations should be interpreted as representing the Shogunate's position. It is also possible that, because the Korean Peninsula on "Nippon henkai ryakuzu" looks like those on maps after d'Anville and the larger part of the 18th-century maps in the West marked the East Sea as the "Sea of Korea," the author used the name "Joseon Sea" according to such circumstances. With regard to "Shintei bankoku zenzu," it is interpreted that the author used "Joseon Sea" because, when the name "Great Japan Sea" was already used for the Pacific Ocean side, the author could not make the same marking for the East Sea nor could he call it "Small Japan Sea." Anyway, due to the authority he held, Takahashi influenced other map-makers who followed him. According to Dr. Lee Sang-Tae's survey, 24 maps from 1794 to 1894 had the marking "Joseon Sea," some of them having both the "Joseon Sea" and the "Japan Sea" written together, and still some of them being republished after the 1930s with the same markings. In addition, the notation of the "Joseon Sea" also appears on the eight official documents of Japan.[20]

---

20) Lee Sang-Tae, "Sea of Chosun Appeared in Old Japanese Maps," The 16th International Seminar on Sea Names, 2010, The Society for East Sea/

In 1994, Takehide Hishiyama and Masatoshi Nagaoka tallied up and classified the notation of the East Sea by name and period and came up with the following table:[21]

Sea Name / Period	1601-1650	1651-1700	1701-1750	1751-1800	1801-1850
Sea of Japan / Sea of Japan	4	11	3	10	32
North Sea / North Sea of Japan	3	3	9	1	0
Oriental Ocean / East Sea	2	10	7	0	0
China Sea / China Ocean	16	4	3	0	0
West Ocean	1	3	0	0	0
Joseon Sea	3	4	15	18	5
West Sea of Japan / Others	0	0	4	0	0
Unmarked	19	18	20	5	2
Total No. of Maps	36	48	58	30	37

As surveyed by these authors, the notation of the East Sea is divided into four categories by nation.

First, the Netherlands began to make maps in the late-16th century. Great Dutch cartographers, including Ortelius and Mercator, marked the East Sea as "Mar Cin" ("China

Northeast Asian History Foundation.

21) Hishiyama and Nagaoka, "Changing the Name of the "Japan Sea," quoted in Shim, "Research Trends in Japan on the Place Name 'Sea of Japan.'"

Sea"), which was handed down and changed to "Oceanus Chinensis" and "Mare della China." In the mid-17th century, Janssonius made the marking of "Mer du Japon" and in the early 18th century, Witsen used both "Mer Orientale" and "Mer du Japon." Later, maps of Tirion and others used "Mer du Nord du Japon" ("North Sea of Japan") and "Mare Iaponicum Occidentale" ("West Sea of Japan"). One map marked both the "Sea of Korea" and the "Sea of Japan" in the 17th century.

Second, In France where map-making began in the late 16th century, Briet, Sanson, and Duval mostly preferred "Océan Oriental" until the end of 17th century, while Sanson and Mallet also used "Mer de Chine." The notation of the "East Sea" and the "Sea of Korea" were used in the early 18th century but beginning in the mid-18th century, maps that marked both the "Sea of Korea" and the "Sea of Japan" appeared. Then, after La Pérouse used "Mer du Japon" following his exploration in 1787, the notation "Sea of Japan" came into predominant use.

Third, the British maps started to mark the notation of the East Sea in the mid-18th century. Moll, Bowen, and Sayer labeled the East Sea as the "Sea of Korea" and the trend continued until the end of the 18th century. However, Arrowsmith and others made a mixed use of "Sea of Korea" and "Sea of Japan" depending on different maps in the late-18th century. Then, in the 19th century, the naming was used in uniformity as the "Sea of Japan."

Fourth, on German maps, Gabriel Buccelinius used the name "Japanisches Meer" in the mid-17th century and since then no other name was seen. In the early-17th century Italy, Blancus and Dudley used "Mer du Japon," but in the late-17th century, Coronelli named the East Sea as "Mer de Chine" and also used "Ocean Oriental" as well on the same map. On Dudley's maps, the notation of "Mer de Corée" is observed along the Korean Peninsula. Finally in Russia, the "Sea of Japan" was marked since Krusenstern in the early-19th century.

Dr. Shim pays attention to the maps where the East Sea is marked as the "North Sea" or "North Sea of Japan." Ginnaro marked "Oceano Boreale" on a map of Japan in 1641. On the "Map of Korea and Japan" in Volume 2 of *Secrets of the Sea* in 1646, Dudley marked the East Sea as the "North Sea of Japan" along with the "Sea of Korea." He also made the same markings on the republished map in 1661. Our investigation showed that de Fer, who was informed of latest geographical news, marked the East Sea as "Mer du Nord du Japon" on "L'Asie" in 1696, and other cartographers also used the name.

In the same *Journal of the Korean Cartographic*

Association, Dr. Shim surveyed the use of "North Sea" in geography textbooks at Japanese schools of different levels. According to him, in the introduction to the revised edition of *Nihon chishiryaku* (日本地誌略, *Digest of Japanese Geography*), which was edited by Shihan Gakkō, or the Normal School, in 1874, the name "Japan Sea" appears only once. In place of the name, the terms "Sea," "Ocean" and "Open Ocean" were used and "North Sea" was used 13 times. On the "Map of the Entire Japan" in *Keitei heiyō Nihon chishi* (改訂兵要日本地誌, *Revised Japanese Military Geography*) by Nakane Shuku, a military textbook of 1874, "Japan Sea" was never used, while on "Hokurikudō chido" (北陸道地圖, "Map of Hokurikudō") in Volume 2 and "Indou chido" (陰道地圖, "Map of the Side Streets") in Volume 3, "Japan Sea" appears. The military textbook contains the name "Japan Sea" a total of four times, "North Sea" eight times, and "Sea," instead of "Japan Sea," 49 times. The same author made a mixed use of "Japan Sea" and other names and used "North Sea" twice more frequently than "Japan Sea," suggesting that in Japan, "North Sea" was more commonly used and more familiar to the Japanese. In *Shōgakkō chishi* (小學校地誌, *Geography for Elementary School*) of 1879 by Nanma Kouki, "North Sea" was used twice but "Japan Sea" was never used. In *Kōtei saikoku shōgaku Nihon chishi* (校定再刻小學日本地誌, *Revised & Reprinted Edition of the Geography of Japan for Elementary School),* edited by Yoshinori Kobayashi in 1880, "Japan Sea" was used four times and "North Sea" was used twice. However, it was taking time for the use of "Sea of Japan" to be in place in regions.

The 1886 Chiri shōgaku (地理小學, *Geography for Elementary School*), edited by Wakayabashi Satosaburo made dominant use of "Japan Sea," 15 times, but "North Sea" only once. However, *Shinsan chishi* (新纂地誌, *New Geography*), edited by Okamura Soutarou, had eight references to "Japan Sea" and four to "North Sea," suggesting that the notation of "North Sea" had not become extinct. Having said that, the 1893 *Nihon chiri shoho* (日本地理初步, *Elementary Japanese Geography*), edited by Gakkai Shishinsha (學海指針社) used "Japan Sea" six times but "North Sea" three times and *Shōgakkōyō Nihon chiri* (小學校用日本地理, *Geography of Japan for Elementary School*), published by the Kinkodo Publishing Co. (金港堂) in 1893, used "Japan Sea" 24 times and "North Sea" only twice. In *Chūgaku Nihon chishi* (中學日本地誌, *Geography of Japan for Middle School*) of 1895 by Yazu Shoei, "Japan Sea" was used 32 times, while "North Sea" was used only once, and in the meaning of "an adjacent sea of Hokkaido."

These examples show that the notation of "North Sea" was used in many school textbooks until the late 19th century because the Japanese had used it for a long time and that the use of "Sea of Japan" was established in Japan after the late 19th century.

Additionally, the use of "Sea of Japan" in general, non-textbook documents in Japan was also surveyed. The historical documents of 1877 and 1885 contained in *Kindai Nihon kaiun seisei shiryō* (近代日本海運生成史料, *Historical Materials of Modern Japanese Sea Transport*) of 1988 used the terms "Sea Routes for Northern Countries" and "North Sea" frequently but not at all "Japan Sea." *Ooyashima yūki* (大八洲遊記, *Travel Accounts of Japan*) of 1888 by Aoyama Enju also shows "North Sea" but no "Sea of Japan." In *Chirigaku kōza* (地理學講座, *Lectures on Geography*) of 1889 by Siga, "North Sea" appears first and "Sea of Japan" and "Northern Coast" come in later parts. Asano Shimbun carried a series of eight articles titled "Hokuriku jijou" (北陸事情, "Situations of Hokuriku") from January through December 1893 where "Sea of Japan" was used only once, while "North Sea" was used six times.

The general documents reveal that the use of the notation, "Sea of Japan" was rapidly established from the end of the 19th to the early 20th century. However, the notation took firm root when Japan won the battle with the Russian Navy on East Sea in 1905. When the Imperial Headquarters of the Japanese Army announced the victory, it called the naval battle the "Battle on the Japan Sea," and all the news media reported it nationwide.

There are some mysteries that come up when we review the studies on the "Sea of Japan" by Japanese scholars and experts in Japan:

First, as an island country surrounded by the sea on all its sides, Japan must have had more than sufficient information on the sea, with a large proportion of the population engaged in fishing, related to ships and living by the seaside. How, then, could they have been able to live their lives without a proper name for a sea for such a long time?

Second, Mateo Ricci marked the East Sea as the "Sea of Japan" in 1602 and his map was imported to Japan and copied. It became very influential in Japan so as to open the eyes of the Japanese to the world and provided an opportunity for old Japanese maps to develop. Then, why did his notation of "Sea of Japan" appear on Japan maps as late as 200 years afterwards since then? Why did many Japanese maps mark the East Sea as the "Joseon Sea" from 1800 to 1870? And why did Japanese textbooks use "Sea" or "Ocean," or especially "North Sea," instead of "Japan Sea" until around the end of the 1890s after the notation of "Japan Sea" was established on Japanese maps about 1870?

Third, missionaries who came back home after staying in Japan, and Dudley, named the East Sea as the "North Sea of Japan" – and "North Sea" was favored above "Sea of Japan" until the end of the 19th century. These circumstances suggest that the "North Sea" was the endonym of the sea in Japan; so why do Japanese experts on place names never recognize or mention the existence of the "North Sea"?

In conclusion, the studies on the name of the East Sea in Japan have been all about justifying the name, "Sea of Japan," in order to keep it in place as is now used internationally. Instead of making every effort to defend the 100-year-old name of the Sea of Japan, the Japanese academia and experts are advised to acknowledge the truth and choose a more rational way to promote friendship between the two countries concerned.

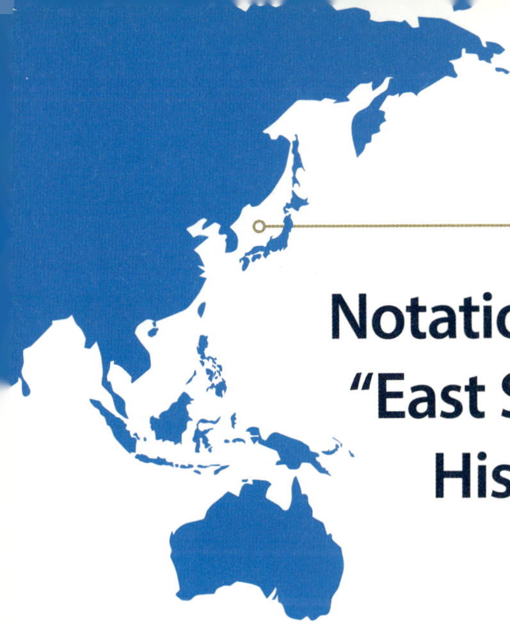

Chapter 11

Notation of the Name "East Sea" in Chinese Historical Records

China has the longest history of archival culture in East Asia. Until the Xianfeng Emperor of the Qing Dynasty ceded the land along the Amur River to Russia in 1858 to 1860, it was also a coastal country with its land in Manchu touching the East Sea. These are why it is imperatively necessary to look up the notation of the East Sea in the historical materials of China. Although it is impossible to search through the enormous amount of Chinese historical materials, Chinese scholars have fortunately made presentations of their studies on this issue since some 20 years ago. An overview of the results of their studies will tell what the East Sea was called in China in the past.

The Babylonian clay tablet maps, the oldest extant maps in history, the Arab-Islam maps, and the so-called *orbis terrarium*, or "T-O maps," of the medieval West have one thing in common: the description of the world surrounded by the sea. This, after all, was an image that people of ancient times had about a mysterious world. The same can be said about China. In the image of ancient Chinese, Gu Renhe[22] and Deng Hui[23] explain that four seas surrounding the periphery of the world are the North Sea, East Sea, South Sea and West Sea. The four seas refer to the same as what Tianxia (literally, "under heaven") denotes – namely, the entire world, rather than the actual names of the particular sea areas. They also were the pronouns for the four cardinal directions. For example, when Mencius said, "[He] occupied the four seas and became the king of Tianxia," he meant the whole world by the four seas in the same meaning as the Tianxia. Later, when it was recorded in "Qin shi huang benji" (秦始皇本紀, "Basic Annals of Qin Shi Huang") in *Shiji* (史記, *Records of the Grand Historian*), "The virtues of the Emperor have stabilized up to the remote and faraway

22) Gu Renhe, "Eastern Sea Area of Korea Peninsula should resume the Original Name: Donghai, Orient Sea," The 7th International Seminar on Sea Names, 2001, The Society for East Sea.

23) Deng Hui, "From the four seas to the four oceans: Changes of Chinese ocean views since the 10th century," The 15th International Seminar on Sea Names, 2009, The Society for East Sea.

countries in the extremities in the four directions to make everything within the six coordinates Emperor's land. They cross Liusha to the West, reach the South Sea to the South, possess the East Sea to the East, and pass the Great River to the North. There is no one but your subjects wherever human traces reach." In this ancient way of thinking, the "East Sea" is an ancient concept referring to a remote, faraway and extensive space. Dong Zhongshu, a scholar of the Western Han Dynasty, said in his *Chunqi fanlu* (春秋繁露, *Luxuriant Dew of the Spring and Autumn Annals*) that: "Therefore, [I] patrolled the entire nation upon [his] orders, it was like all sorts of stars facing the North Star and rivers with all tributaries flowing into the Canghai (滄海, "Deep-blue Sea")." Here, "Cang" (滄) refers to the East in the Five Elements as blue does, so the "Canghai" was the epithet of "Donghai" (East Sea). When Cao Cao, who was a man of letters as well, wrote, "On a towering stone in the East, I look at the Canghai," he was also calling the East Sea by that name. Su Shi, one of the Eight Great Prose Masters of the Tang and Song, wrote, "The waters of the Yangze River flowing to the East are discharged into the Canghai, sweeping everything on its way." He also called the sea to the east "Canghai," but he did not disclose where it was.[24]

---

24) Gu, "Eastern Sea Area of Korea Peninsula should resume the Original Name: Donghai, Orient Sea."

In the traditional literature, the East Sea was an ideational name and was conceived as very extensive and magnificent. As it were, in the hearts of the ancient Chinese, the East Sea was the vast expanse of the ocean and where the sun rises. The sun signifies brightness and hope. As it receives the sun from under the horizon and the sun brings warmth and vitality, the East Sea symbolized something peaceful, beautiful, good and auspicious. That was why the East Sea transcended the boundary of a name of a sea area in folk and oral literature. It was an object of praise that has many implications. Gu Renhe cited some examples:

Xun Kuang wrote "He is so stupid that I cannot plan anything with him. [He is] a man of such limited outlook that I cannot tell the pleasure of the East Sea." *Chunqiu zuoshi zhuan* (春秋左氏傳, *Spring and Autumn Annals*) has a passage "Endlessly blowing wind! The one who reveals the East Sea is called 'Grand Duke.'" Mei Cheng, a Han Dynasty poet, wrote, "When I long for the South Mountain and look at the East Sea, the deep and far-off sky and the narrow cliffs look so worrisome." Du Fu, great Tang Dynasty poet, wrote, "As the faraway North Star has been presented to the thief, I want to pour the waters of the East Sea to wash the world." Guan Hanqing of the Yuan Dynasty wrote, "When I came, it was a time when the moon was rising from the

East Sea; when I go, it is time when the crescent moon is hung over the Western mountain." Cao Xueqin of the Qing Dynasty wrote, "As the East Sea lacks a little bit of elegance of white jade, King of Jinling is invited." Among people, they used to give well-wishing remarks, such as "Be blessed with good luck like the East Sea and live long like the South Mountain!"[25]

Wu Songdi said that there was no specific name for the East Sea from the Eastern Han through the Western and Eastern Jin to the Southern and Northern Dynasties. He cited examples, such as the phrase, "What the Wei army met in the east was the great sea," in Volume 30 of *Sanguozhi* (三國志, *Records of the Three Kingdoms*) during the two Jin and the Southern and Northern Dynasties and the parts in Volume 97 of *Jinshu* (晉書, *Book of Jin*) and Volume 100 of *Weishu* (魏書, *Book of Wei*) where the East Sea was referred to as the "great sea" or "sea." He also presents further examples: Volume 199 of *Jiu Tangshu* (舊唐書, *Old Book of Tang*) and Volumes 219 and 220 of *Xin Tangshu* (新唐書, *New Book of Tang*) where the East Sea is called the "great sea" or "sea;" Volume 219 of *Xin Tangshu* where the East Sea is called the "south sea;" and Volumes 96 and 99 of *Tang Huiyao* where the northern part of the East Sea is described

25) Gu, "Eastern Sea Area of Korea Peninsula should resume the Original Name: Donghai, Orient Sea."

as the "small sea" and its southern part, the "large sea." On the other hand, Wu reveals that the name "East Sea" was used around the time to which Korea's *Samguk sagi* (三國史記, *History of the Three Kingdoms*) makes reference by mentioning the name of the sea in a story it relates, citing such sources as: Volume 85 of *Hou Hanshu* (後漢書, *Book of the Later Han*) as well as the phrase "The inhabitants in proximity of the East Sea are called "Donghai Nuzhen" (東海女眞, "East Sea Jurchens") in *Sanchao beimeng huibian* (三朝北盟會編, *Compilation of Documents Concerning Alliances with the North during the Three Reigns*); the ritual prayer "Ji Donghai zhuwen" (祭東海祝文, "Written Prayer at the East Sea Ritual") contained in the book *Da Jin ji li* (大金集禮, *Collection of State Rituals of the Jurchen Jin Dynasty*); and the phrase, "Yilou was Sushen in the ancient times and lay some 1,000 *li* northeast of Fuyu [夫餘, ancient Korean kingdom Buyeo] with its east adjoining the East Sea" in "Dongyi liezhuan" (東夷列傳, "Treatise on the Dongyi") in *Hou Hanshu*.

Gu Renhe also reveals that although it is generally known that the East Sea had no name before the Sui and Tang Dynasties, it was only a hiatus in the use of the name; in fact, the notation of the "East Sea" already existed 2,000 years ago. As grounds for his argument, he cites phrases from "Hai nei jing" (海內經, "Classic of Regions within the Sea") in *Shan hai jing* (山海經, *Classic of Mountains and Seas*).[26] The quotes are: "The country at the corner of the North Sea on the East coast is called Chaoxian (朝鮮, Joseon)." "Chaoxian is to the north of the East Sea and south of Mount Changbai; and Lieyang belongs to Yan" and "Chaoxian is embraced in the bosom of the East Sea."[27] Zhu Shiguang and Jing Tian also pointed out that the East Sea was mentioned in *Shan hai jing*.[28] What should not be neglected here is that even during the period of time when the name of the East Sea did not appear in historical materials until the Western Han and Eastern Han Dynasties, it was still being used by the Jurchens.

Most scholars agree that the Canghai, which was used during the time of Emperor Wu of Han, referred to the East Sea and the name, "East Sea," was used also in the Liao and Jin Dynasties. Based on such materials as *Ming Taizu shilu* (明太祖實錄, *Veritable Records of Ming Taizu*), *Yuan yi tong zhi*

26) Gu, "Eastern Sea Area of Korea Peninsula should resume the Original Name: Donghai, Orient Sea."

27) Gu, "Eastern Sea Area of Korea Peninsula should resume the Original Name: Donghai, Orient Sea."

28) Zhu Shiguang, "On the Transformation of the Geographical Name in the Area of the Sea of Japan (The East Sea) from a Perspective of Historical Documents," The 3rd International Seminar on Sea Names, 1997, The Society for East Sea; Jing, "Recent Research Progress on a Study of the Sea Name on East Sea and Japan Sea in China."

(元一統志, *Total Annals of the Yuan Dynasty*), *Huan yu tong zhi* (寰宇通志, *Comprehensive Gazetteer of All the Regions*), *Yuandai Manzhou Jiangyu* (元代滿洲疆域, *Manchurian Territory during the Yuan Dynasty*), *Zhongguo lishi dituji* (中國歷史地圖集, *Atlas of Chinese History*) and *Zhongguo gudaishi ditu* (中國古代史地圖, *Atlas of Chinese Ancient History*), some scholars argue that the East Sea was called the "Sea of Whales" because whales were caught in the East Sea during the Yuan and Ming Dynasties, especially in the early Ming Dynasty. Even during these times, the name "East Sea" continued in use by the Jurchens. Still, the East Sea was called by another name, "Sea of Whales," during the Yuan and Ming Dynasties for a reason: According to Cheng Long, the Yuan Dynasty, which the nomadic Mongols built in northern China, had little interest in the East Sea and called it the "Sea of Whales" simply because it was known to them that whales were caught there. On the other hand, to the Ming Dynasty, which the Han Chinese built in Zhongyuan in an uprising of the peasants, the East Sea was too far-off a sea and they just continued to use the same name as given by the Yuan Dynasty; hence "Sea of Whales" during the Ming Dynasty.[29] Wu Songdi reckons that the name East Sea was in continuous use from the 10th to

29) Cheng Long, "Research on Relationship between the Name of 'East Sea' and the Local Non-Han Government of Northeast China after Tang Dynasty," The 11th International Seminar on Sea Names, 2005, The Society for East Sea.

the 16th centuries; in other words, during the Liao, Jin, Yuan and Ming Dynasties. Gu Renhe agrees with this view. Citing "Ji Donghai zhuwen," Cheng Long and Han Maoli emphasize that the name "East Sea" continued to be used from the Liao and Jin Dynasties to the end of the Qing Dynasty.

As such, most Chinese scholars agree that the name, "East Sea" was used without a hiatus from the early Qing Dynasty to the end of the 19th century. The materials proposed as evidence, though, vary according to different scholars, as do the periods that they claim the name was in use. For example, Chen Cai and An Hu Sen argued that what was called the East Sea in ancient times was limited to part of the current East Sea, stating that the Sea of Okhotsk referred to the North Sea and that "East Sea" referred to the northern part of what is now the East Sea while its south was called the South Sea.[30]

However, many historical materials show that the name East Sea was used as a proper geographical name without such distinction as described above. For example, in the records of the 1609 in Volume 3 of *Qing Taizu Wuhuangdi shilu* (淸太祖武皇帝實錄, Veritable Records *of Emperor Taizu of the Qing Dynasty, Emperor Wu*), it is written, "Nurhaci

30) Chen Cai & An Hu Sen, "Our View on the Origin of the Geographical Name of the Sea of Japan (East Sea)," The 1st International Seminar on Sea Names, 1995, The Society for East Sea.

sent an army and reclaimed the area of the Woji Tribe of the East Sea," and in Volume 5, it is recorded as an event of 1609, "Accepted people who were living here and there on the coast of the East Sea [as the people of the Qing Dynasty]." *Liu bian ji lue* (柳邊紀略, *Description of Lands Within and Without the Willow Palisade*) of the mid-Qing period has a sentence, "General Ning Guta's range [of governance] reaches the East Sea to the east."

Yuan Shuren and Huang Yangun assert that the name "East Sea" was used in Qing from the 17th to the end of 19th century, citing such materials as *Kai guo long xing ji* (開國龍興記, *Stories of Building up the Country*), *Shengjing tongzhi* (盛京通志, *Shengjing Gazetteer*), *San xing zhi* (三姓志, *Records of Three Surnames*), *Xiao fang hu zhai yu di cong chao* (小方壺齋輿地叢鈔, *Collection of Texts on Geography from the Xiao-fang-hu Studio*), *Chaoxian yu di shuo* (朝鮮輿地說, *Report of the Korean Geography*), *Dongguo mingseng ji* (東國名勝記, *Famous Sites in the East State*), *Haiguo tuzhi* (海國圖志, *Illustrated Records of Maritime Nations*), *Qu Xibi'er shimoji* (取悉畢爾始末記, *Full Account of the Coverage of Xibi'er*), *Jilin wai ji* (吉林外紀, *A Travel Note on Jilin*), *Zhongguo lishi ditutie* (中國歷史地圖帖, *Atlas of Chinese History*) and *Zhongguo gudaishi ditutie* (中國古代史地圖帖, *Atlas of Chinese Ancient History*), where the northern part is referred to as the "East Sea" and the southern part, "South Sea," but they left out more specific sources than that.[31] On the other hand, the East Sea is marked as the "Sea of Japan" in some late-19th century materials such as *Zhong wai di yu tu shuo ji cheng* (中外地與圖說集成, *Collection of Chinese and Foreign Maps*), *Kuyedao zhi lue* (庫頁島志略, *Abridged Gazetteer of Kuye Island* [Sakhalin]), *Zhonghuaminguo xin ditu* (中華民國新地圖, *New Atlas of the Republic of China*), *Dong nan hai dao tu jing* (東南海島圖經, *Maps of Seas and Islands in the Southeast Sea*), *Eluosi shuidao kao* (俄羅斯水道考, *Study of Russian Sea Routes*) and *Riben guozhi* (日本國志, *History of Japan*).

Xi Guo Jin explains, when *Shengjing tongzhi* says that "General Ning Guta's realm of governance is up to the Southern Sea," the Southern Sea refers to the southern part of the East Sea.[32] He adds that it is written in Volume 68 of *Yi tong zhi* (一統志, *Complete Gazetteer*) that "General Ning Guta's realm of governance is 3,000 *li* of East Sea to the East." It is also recorded in *Qing Taizu Wuhuangdi shilu*: "500 soldiers were sent to subjugate every division of the East

31) Yuan Shuren & Huang Yangun, "Our Opinion on the Geographical Name of the Sea of Japan," The 2nd International Seminar on Sea Names, 1996, The Society for East Sea.

32) Xi Guo Jin, "Nationalities in the Eastern Part of Northeast China in History and Changes in the Name of the Sea of Japan," The 1st International Seminar on Sea Names, 1995, The Society for East Sea.

Sea." It is a description, he explains, of how they combined local tribes in Manchu before the establishment of the Qing Dynasty and a circumstantial evidence that the Jurchens lived in places near the East Sea for a long time.

On the other hand, Huang Zunxian marked the East Sea as the "Sea of Japan" in his *Riben guozhi* at the end of the Qing Dynasty. Wang Xianqian also mentioned the Sea of Japan in Volume 1 of *Yazhou dili zhi lue* (亞洲地理志略, *Abridged Gazetteer of Asia*) in the 2nd year of Xuantong. In addition, Wang Guowei used the expression "Narrow Sea of Japan." As seen here, the name "Sea of Japan" tended to come into general use around the end of the 19th and the beginning of the 20th century.

Zhu Shiguang reminds us that, although the name "East Sea" was the mainstream during the Qing Dynasty, some materials from the Xianfeng to Xuantong Emperors recorded the East Sea as the "Pacific Ocean" or "East Joseon Bay." Zhu further shows that General Ji Lin's memorial to the throne of 1854 (4th year of the Xianfeng Emperor) mentioned the East Sea twice and Jing Chun's memorial on the same year also mentioned the East Sea, with the Emperor's reply too indicating the East Sea. In the 17th year of the Guangxu Emperor or 1891, the name "East Sea" was used in the memorial to the emperor by Xu Jingcheng, envoy to Russia for the Qing imperial court. Zhu also commented that an official document which the Chinese Ministry of Foreign Affairs received during the first year of the Xuantong Emperor's reign contained the phrase, "Entered the Pacific Ocean" where the "East Sea" should supposedly have been used. Two other government documents mentioned the "East Joseon Bay" and "Pacific Ocean." But Zhu could not identify exactly what those place names referred to.[33]

In Cao Tingjie's 1887 *Riben guozhi*, "Sea of Japan" was used instead of "East Sea" but in the same book, the author mixed the use of both names probably due to old habits. In Volume 10 of *Riben guozhi,* which he compiled in 1887, Huang Zunxian also used "Sea of Japan" but in the opinion of Zhu Shiguang and some other scholars it is "something that has to do with the theme of the book and the author's personal usage." The Russian diplomatic offices also used the name "East Sea" frequently but at the turn of the century, from the 19th to 20th century, an increase in the use of "Sea of Japan" is observed, according to the scholars.

Cheng Long took note of the fact that the residents in the northeastern part of China are most closely related to the East Sea and observed that the name East Sea was widely

33) Zhu, "On the Transformation of the Geographical Name in the Area of the Sea of Japan (The East Sea) from a Perspective of Historical Documents."

used in many historical materials since the establishment of the Qing Dynasty, which was built mostly by the Jurchens. For example, he points out that *Kai guo long xing ji* (開國龍興記, *Stories of Building up the Country*), a collection of stories related to the establishment of the Qing Dynasty, shows that the name East Sea had something to do with Nuzhen and the Jurchens used the name for a long time historically.[34] Citing the phrase, "Huntong River in Manchu … flows into East Sea," in Volume 1 of *Shuo fang bei cheng* (朔方備乘, *Peregrinations in the North*), he made clear the relationship between Huntong River and the East Sea. In *Dongbei bian fang ji yao* (東北邊防輯要, *Essentials of Border Defense in the Northeast*), he revealed that Kuye Island, today's Sakhalin, was originally called "East Sea Islands." Taking note of the achievements of Wei Yuan, Cheng shows through the map in Wei's *Haiguo tuzhi* (海國圖志, *Illustrated Treatise on the Maritime Kingdoms*) that the East Sea refers to a sea existing to the northeast of Joseon. Tracing Wei's life, Cheng emphasizes that Wei was a scholar who left great achievements in Chinese history and geography although he entered officialdom at a later age and remained a low-level official without much to hope for in a local region.

34) Cheng, "Research on Relationship between the Name of 'East Sea' and the Local Non-Han Government of Northeast China after Tang Dynasty"; "Yuan Wei (1794-1857), His Research and Maps about East Sea."

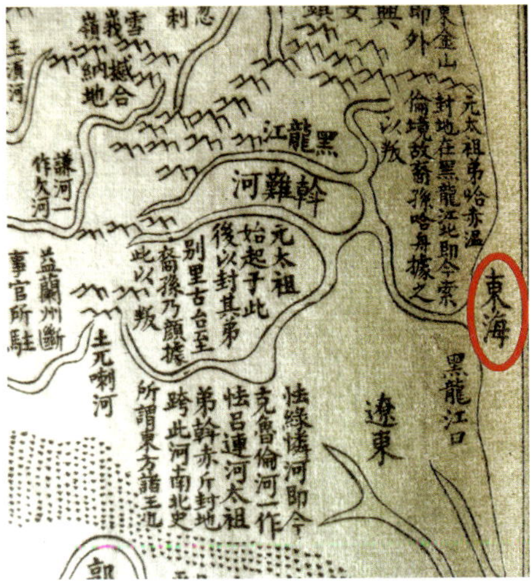

Wei Yuan, who studied modern Chinese history and geography, included a map of Manchuria and related comments in his book *Sheng wu zhi* (聖武志, *Treatise on Military Achievements*) in ca. 1850.

For example, Wei's *Sheng wu zhi* (聖武志, *Treatise on Military Achievements*) is a study of the tribes in Manchuria and, according to this book, important tribes there included "Manchu tribe," "East Sea tribe" and "Mount Changbai tribe." When the tribe of Jurchen-origin became stronger and finally established the Qing Dynasty, an unexpected incident took place. The Warka tribe which was living in the same region fled to Joseon and asked the Ming Dynasty in Zhongyuan for help. When Joseon helped them, Qing was enraged and mobilized a great army to invade Joseon in 1627 (the first Manchu invasion of Korea). The author of *Sheng wu zhi* wrote the book in order to remind readers of the fact that Qing was a powerful country and revive its tradition, Cheng Long explains.[35]

Han Maoli agrees that, after it was widely used from the

35) Cheng, "Yuan Wei (1794-1857), His Research and Maps about East Sea."

Wei Yuan identified the East Sea as "東海" ("East Sea") on his historical map "Chaoxian guo bei jie tu" (朝鮮國北界圖, "Map of the Northern Boundaries of Joseon") in ca. 1850.

Liao and Song Dynasties, the name "East Sea" then rarely appeared in official documents as it was often called "Sea of Whales" during the Yuan Dynasty. However, "East Sea" was originally a name used by the Jurchens, he argues, and as the Manchu people are descendants of the Jurchens, so the name East Sea should be deemed to have been continuously used from the Song and Liao Dynasties through the Jin, Yuan, Ming, and Qing Dynasties. Some argue that during the Balhae period "East Sea" was called "Balhae." But Han Maoli counters that it referred not to the East Sea, but to today's Bohai Bay – and he agrees with those who claim the

Balhae people called the East Sea "South Sea." Paying strong attention to "Ji Donghai zhuwen" in the book *Da Jin ji li*, Han emphasized the linkage between the East Sea and the Jurchens. He also states that Wang Zaijin made the linkage between the East Sea and Korea clearer when he marked the East Sea as the "East Sea of Joseon" in his *Hai fang zuan yao* (海防纂要, *Overview of Coastal Defense*), a book describing the development and progress of the Japanese Invasion of Korea in 1592, as well as *Wanli san dai zheng* (萬曆三大征, *Three Great Campaigns of the Wanli Emperor*).[36]

Jing Tian points out that, since it was mentioned twice in *Shan hai jing* some 2,200 years ago, the name "East Sea" has been used continuously from the Spring and Autumn period and the Warring States period to the end of the Qing Dynasty, whereas the name "Sea of Japan" is a recent name with a history of only about 100 years as it went into common use after the signing of the Treaty of Portsmouth between Russia and Japan in 1905. The name East Sea is not only a name with a far longer history than the Sea of Japan but it also has, in traditional Chinese literature, embodied abundant senses of broadness, generosity, happiness and selflessness. By contrast, "Sea of Japan" is a name given not to an inland sea

36) Han Maoli, "The Naming of the Sea Area to the East of the Korean Peninsula according to the Ancient Chinese Literatures," The 14th International Seminar on Sea Names, The Society for East Sea, 2008.

but a sea area shared by several countries and was a product of imperialism. Therefore, the term "East Sea" should regain its rightful place. Regarding the unjustness of the use of Sea of Japan, he reminds us of the movement against the use of the name in China in the 1940s.[37]

While studying ancient historical documents extensively, Wu Songdi delved deeply into what some scholars treated only briefly and made new findings. A good example of this is his study of *Hou Hanshu*. A reading of this 2,000-year old book reveals that, at the time, a sea was called merely "the sea" without a specific name. Wu showed that the proximity of Yilou and the East Sea was mentioned in Volume 85, "Treatise on the Dongyi," of *Hou Hanshu*. He also found mentions of the East Sea in such ancient Chinese documents as Volume 97, "Si yi" (四夷, "Four Barbarian Tribes") in *Jinshu* (晉書, *Book of Jin*), Section of "Doumolou" (豆莫婁) in Volume 88 of *Weishu* (魏書, *Book of Wei*) and Volume 94 of *Beishi* (北史, *History of the Northern Dynasties*).

However, in Xiboli dong pian jiyao (西伯利東偏紀要, *Notes on the Trip to the Eastern Region of Russian Siberia*), which was published in 1885, the 11th year of the Guangxu Emperor, Cao Tingjie used "Sea of Japan" instead of the

---

37) Jing, "Recent Research Progress on a Study of the Sea Name on East Sea and Japan Sea in China."

"East Sea." Specifically, he wrote, "As the steamboat entered the Huntong River from the Sea of Japan." He then showed inconsistency when he referred to the "East Sea" in his writing about peoples in the Northeast. In contrast, Sheng Lin, Cao's superior, used the name "East Sea" consistently throughout *Tan Zhong E jiaojie tu* (談中俄交界圖, *On the Sino-Russian Border Map*), which he published in the same year. However, the name "Sea of Japan" was used in place of the "East Sea" on "Zhong E jiaojie quantu" (中俄交界全圖, "Sino-Russian Border Map") which Jong Jun made in 1890, the 16th year of the Guangxu Emperor; *Er shi shi ji Zhong wai da di tu* (二十世紀中外大地圖, *20th Century Atlas of China and Foreign Countries*) authored by Zhou Shitang and Sun Haihuan in 1906, the 32th year of the Guangxu Emperor; and "Zhongguo xin yu ditu" (中國新輿地圖, "New Map of China") which was made in 1913, the 2nd year of the Republic of China.

Sun Dong-hu studied the movement to rename the Sea of Japan in China in the 1940s. From the end of the Qing Dynasty afterwards, the Chinese and the government started to use "Sea of Japan" in place of "East Sea," which they had commonly used previously. The outbreak of the Second World War and Japan's invasion of China triggered a movement in China to change the usage. The first one to raise the issue was Yu Youren, an elder member of the Kuomintang in China and a prominent calligrapher and scholar. He was also a politician and was appointed in 1930 as the president of the Control Yuan of the Kuomintang government. On March 15, 1943, he proposed to "Cancel the Sea of Japan, Name the Pacific Sea, Start Peace Eternally" (取消 日本海, 正名 太平海, 爲萬世開太平) through Zhōngyāng Rìbào (中央日报, Central Daily News) and Ta Kung Pao (大公報) in Chungching. His maintenance spread widely and was accepted positively in the academia. As a result, over 300 representatives from the Scientific Society of China, Botanical Society of China, Geographical Society of China, China Zoological Society, Mathematical Society of China and Meteorological Society of China met in Chongqing from July 18 to 21, 1943 to discuss the issue. The Central Daily News reported on July 20, "The six organizations agreed that the name of Sea of Japan should be corrected." Part of the report is as follows:

> The Geographic Society of China discussed the matter of renaming "Sea of Japan" to "Pacific Sea" which President [of the Control Yuan] Yu Youren proposed. All the participants agreed to propose that the government set up an organization to raise this issue. The speakers were very enthusiastic and said

that, in addition to the name "Sea of Japan," other names should also be dealt with. Some proposed that "Sea of Japan" be renamed "Peace Sea" or "Leping Sea" (樂平海, "Pleasant Peace Sea"). They all agreed that the renaming would be certainly meaningful because it would not be overstating that the name "Sea of Japan" was a source of World War II.

Yu Youren wrote an article "South China Peninsula and Taiping Sea: A Study in Geographical Nomenclature" in English, which was published in No.2, vol.14. of Journal of the Geological Society. To quote a passage:

> The name [Sea of Japan] ... is most misleading for only a part of the sea is bordered by Japan. ... this inappropriate name had directly or indirectly seconded Japanese imperialist claims which aimed at converting the sea into an inland lake of Japan. It is proposed that in the interest of world peace the name Sea of Japan be eliminated forever from the publication of all peace loving countries.

The movement to rename Sea of Japan and Yu's article represented the Chinese people's aspirations for peace. Confucius said, "If the name is not right, then speech will not be in order" (名不正則言不順). *Zuixin Zhongwai diming cidian* (最新中外地名辭典, The *Latest World Geographic Dictionary*), published by Zhonghua Book Company in 1948, records that the Sea of Japan was renamed "Pacific Sea."

With regard to the reason why the movement to replace the name did not come to fruition, Sun Dong Hu says that it was because the political situation in China was so unstable at the time that the Chinese government had no leeway to legislate on the matter after the academic discussions. But the renaming movement left a very important lesson, in his view.

The conclusions by the Chinese scholars are worth noting. Wu Songdi emphasized that "Sea of Japan" has a very short history when compared with "East Sea," which has over 2,000 years of history, saying, "The name 'Sea of Japan' was not used until around the 10th year of the Guangxu Emperor (1884) of the Qing Dynasty. Therefore, the period during which the name appeared in China has been only about 110 years."

Chen Cai and An Hu Sen said, "The use of the name 'Sea of Japan' was due to a foreign invasion. In other words, when China closed its doors to the world and was reduced to be half-colonized, the name 'Sea of Japan,' which began to be used internationally at the time, went into use [in China] and has been used until now. Therefore, regarding to the question of what name should be used in place of "Sea of Japan" in the future, the two authors make it clear that the internationally acknowledged principles should basically be respected."

Yuan Shuren and Huang Yangun pointed out that it is very absurd to give a sea shared by plural countries a name of any one country, saying, "If the concerned countries give the sea a name with their own, respectively, in many places of the world, a series of seas would have to be renamed."[38]

In the same vein, Zhu Shiguang said, "If a body of water is not an inland sea of a country, the name of any one country should not be used for the name of the sea lest international discords and disputes arise out of the apparent disrespect for the other countries that share the sea. Therefore, when a sea bordered by a plurality of countries is named, the peoples' sentiments and interests of the concerned countries must be taken into account. Only then can the designated name be approved by the neighboring countries of the sea."[39]

In a brief article, Zhang Lansheng expressed his aspiration for the restoration of peace from disputes, saying,

---

38) Yuan & Huang, "Our Opinion on the Geographical Name of the Sea of Japan."

39) Zhu, "On the Transformation of the Geographical Name in the Area of the Sea of Japan (The East Sea) from a Perspective of Historical Documents."

"Disputes, or potential disputes occur incessantly around the East Sea, and Northeast Asia is an area with the most heated tension. We wish the disputes to be resolved and that we have the wisdom to achieve a peaceful region as in the past." Cheng Long emphasized the legitimacy of the name "East Sea," saying, "The East Sea area has been called by many names, but the records at present suggest that it is most appropriate to call it the East Sea."[40] He also said, "Naming the sea area east of the Korean Peninsula should be done by the countries bordered by the sea and historical records should be carefully considered."[41]

Concerning the renaming of the Sea of Japan, Liu Xin Jun asserted that the Sea of Japan should legitimately be renamed in respect of the historical facts since the name has a history of only over 100 years. "It is not right to name a body of international waters anything with a country's name...... It is desirable to rename it in deference to the sentiments of the neighboring countries of "Sea of Japan," he concludes.[42] In other words, a body of international waters should be named based on historicity and consultation

40) Cheng, "Research on Relationship between the Name of 'East Sea' and the Local Non-Han Government of Northeast China after Tang Dynasty."
41) Cheng, "Research on Relationship between the Name of 'East Sea' and the Local Non-Han Government of Northeast China after Tang Dynasty."
42) Liu Xin Jun, "Ancient Books of China Records and Narrate about East Sea/Japanese Sea," The 12th International Seminar on Sea Names," 2006, The Society for East Sea.

among the neighboring countries. Han Maoli echoed, "The name "Sea of Japan" has no historical grounds as its use came from Western colonialists in the late modern history. Names, including the East Sea, recorded in China and Korea would be a better choice."[43]

43) Han Maoli, "'East Sea' and 'Korean East Sea': Records about the Sea Area to the East of Korean Peninsula on Chinese Literatures during the Last 1000 Years," The 13th International Seminar on Sea Names, 2007, The Society for East Sea.

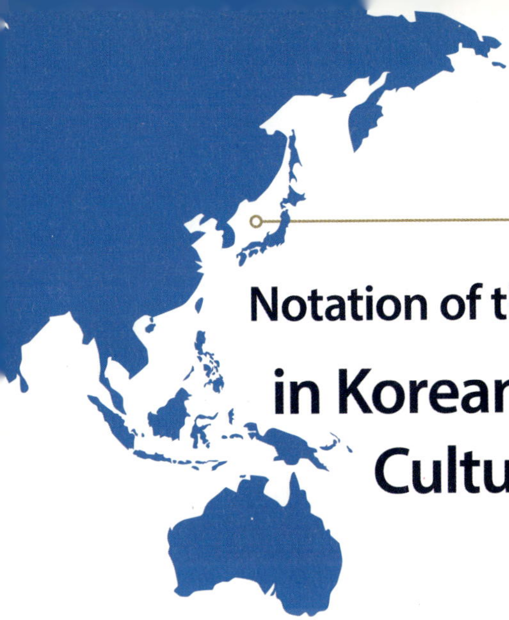

Chapter 12

Notation of the Name "East Sea" in Korean Historical and Cultural Documents and Old Maps

The three Asian countries of Korea, China and Japan have considerable differences in marking the names of seas. Researchers of place names, including Hiru Aoyama of Japan, say that from ancient times, Japanese people did not give a particular name to seas and simply called them the "sea." The same can be said about other Asian countries, they say. Deng Hui of China explains that for ancient Chinese people, the North Sea, South Sea, East Sea and West Sea were used not as the names of particular seas but as an indication of the bearings and areas, such as the sea in the north, south, etc.[44] However, in the case of the East Sea, deeper researches have

44) Deng, "From the Four Seas to the Four Oceans: Changes of Chinese Ocean Views Since the 10th Century."

produced different observations. For example, Wu Songdi said that "East Sea" appeared in Volume 85, "Treatise on the Dongyi," of *Hou Hanshu* some 2,000 years ago referred to Korea's East Sea in relation to the Jurchens.

It has not been reported yet that a name was used for a sea in ancient Japan, and only markings of bearings appear on old maps. But according to the findings of Dr. Lee Sang-tae, in a letter of appreciation by Japan for Korea's sending the *Tripitaka* to them, the Japanese said, "How can we thank you enough even if we scoop out all the waters of the East Sea and blacken all the bamboos on Mt. Namsan?"[45] This can be taken as evidence that the Japanese knew what sea the name "East Sea" referred to. The name could also have been known to the Japanese through the Koreans abducted by the Japanese to Japan.

Korea suffered from many foreign invasions, including that of the Khitan people at the end of the 10th and the early 11th century, the Yuan Dynasty in the 13th century, the Japanese at the end of the 16th century, and the Qing Dynasty twice in the early 17th century. As a result, most extant old maps are those made after the 17th century because maps before the mid-17th century were mostly

45) Yee [Lee] Sang-tae, "A Study on the Understanding the East Sea (Donghae) in the Chosun Dynasty (14th C – 20th C)," The 8th International Seminar on Sea Names, 2002, The Society for East Sea.

destroyed in the whirlwind of the wars. However, the name, "East Sea" remains in other historical and cultural materials from a long time ago. That is why we need to examine the markings of the "East Sea" in those historical and cultural materials in advance of old maps.

In Korea, the history of the marking of the East Sea had not been studied seriously until the 1990s with only a few of scholars tackling the problem. Dr. Lee Sang-tae is one of them and the following are mostly indebted to his study:

1. Notation of the Name of the East Sea in Historical and Cultural Documents

A. The East Sea during the Three-Kingdoms Period and the Unified Silla

The part of King Dongmyeong in Volume 13 of *Samguk sagi* (三國史記, *History of the Three Kingdoms*), one of the 10 volumes that comprise the section "Goguryeo's Records," tells that Aran, daughter of the prime minister of the Bukbuyeo Kingdom, had a dream in which the son of Heaven appeared and gave her a divine message that the Kingdom should move its capital to Gaseopwon near the coast of the East Sea. It was 59 B.C. This means that the Koreans have used the name "East Sea" for more than

2,000 years. In addition, the Gwanggaeto Stele, which was erected in 414 to commemorate the achievements of King Gwanggaeto of Goguryeo, has an epitaph containing the place name “Donghaego” (東海賈, or “Donghaega”). A village presumably near Donghae (East Sea), the name is shown in the inscription along with the number of the grave keepers. *Samguk sagi* mentions the East Sea 15 times in total and *Samguk yusa* (三國遺事, *Memorabilia of the Three Kingdoms*), 14 times, which together means that the name East Sea was used quite frequently during the Three Kingdoms period. The East Sea was mentioned mostly in relation to the spirit for the protection of the country and natural disasters.

As it suffered from the plundering and invasions of Japanese pirates from the earliest days of its foundation, Silla took the defense of the coast of the East Sea seriously as an important national agenda. King Munmu, who unified the three kingdoms into Unified Silla, left a will stipulating that he wanted to be buried in the East Sea to protect the homeland. The subjects buried him under the rock called “Rock of Great King” on the edge of the East Sea. Afterwards, the East Sea became a sea deeply associated with the national spirit of the state-protection. Other Silla kings also left a will where they wanted to be cremated after death and the ash to be sprinkled over the East Sea in a show of their willingness to protect the nation and the East Sea even after death.

King Sinmun, who succeeded King Munmu, is recorded to have made a pipe from a bamboo which was taken from a floating island on the East Sea. When he played the pipe, he could expel the invading enemy, cause rain during times of drought, and stop heavy rain in the monsoon: hence the pipe named "Manpasikjeok" ("Pipe that Calms Ten Thousand Billows"). It is recorded that the pipe was preserved at the warehouse of Cheonjongo.

The East Sea was also a stage where strange natural phenomena occurred. For example, in the 10th year of Cheomhae Isageum (256), the 12th ruler of Silla, a fish measuring 30 *cheok* (approx. 6 meters) long and 12 *cheok* (2.4 meters) high appeared in the East Sea. In the 15th year of Silseong Isageum (416), the 18th ruler, a gigantic fish with a horn was caught in the East Sea. A big surprise to those who witnessed them, those fish are believed to have been a whale, or a fish similar to a whale.

And then there was a natural disaster in the 8th year of Queen Seondeok (639) and the 8th year of King Hyoso (699) where the waters of the East Sea turned bloody red. These phenomena awed the Silla people regarding the power of nature and provided the monarchs with an opportunity to reflect on the way of their governing the state. It is speculated that the reddening of the waters of the East Sea was a temporary red tide.

B. The Goryeo Kingdom and the East Sea

After it moved its capital to Songak (now Kaesong), Goryeo took greater interest in the West Sea which was closer to the new capital than the East Sea. But it still inherited the way of thinking of Silla which held the East Sea sacred and in awe. During the Goryeo period, the state observed a sacrificial ritual dedicated to the sea in the spring and fall. In a reply letter of King Taejo, Goryeo's founder and first monarch, to Gyeon Hwon, founder and king of Hubaekje (Later Baekje), he recommended, "Politely honoring the foreboding … let the broken royal line of the East Sea be continued." Here, the East Sea was used as a metonym in reference to Korea just as were words such as Samhan ("Three Han") and Haedong ("East of the Sea").

In a letter to the Tang Dynasty by King Sinjong of Goryeo in the beginning year of the King's reign (1197), the king said, "I dare … become a model on the shore of the East Sea." In this case, the "East Sea" may be interpreted as "West Sea" from the viewpoint of China, but nonetheless, the name "East Sea" was certainly used in metonymy to refer to

Goryeo.

During the Goryeo period, the idea was firmly established that preventing and effectively coping with possible natural disasters was the top priority agenda for the promotion of national interests and public welfare. In such understanding, it was institutionalized to hold a sacrificial ritual dedicated to mountains and rivers. A shrine was built for the East Sea, West Sea and South Sea and the Geography section of *Goryeo sa* (高麗史, *History of Goryeo*) says that the shrine for the East Sea was built in today's Yangyang. *Dongguk yeoji seungnam* (東國輿地勝覽, *Augmented Survey of the Geography of Korea*), *Yeo jido seo* (輿地圖書, *Collection of County Gazetteers*), and *Daedong jiji* (大東地志, *Geography of Korea*) also record that there was a shrine for the East Sea in the Yangyang military command.

C. The Joseon Dynasty and the East Sea

Also during the Joseon period, the East Sea was discussed in relation to natural disasters and the safety of fishermen. The sea was also mentioned in connection with the protection of the territorial rights over Ulleungdo as Japan visibly showed its intention to gain control over the island and became a diplomatic agenda. Most people believed at the time that the success of farming and overcoming drought in their everyday lives depended on the East Sea, which became the object of folk belief and awe. For these reasons, the sacrificial rituals continued to be held for the East Sea. According to "Orye" ("Five Rites") of *Sejong sillok* (世宗實錄, *Annals of King Sejong*), the shrine for the South Sea was in Naju, Jeolla Province; the shrine for the West Sea was in Pungcheon, Hwanghae Province; and the shrine for the East Sea, the most important of all, was in Yangyang, Gangwon Province.

When they occurred, unusual climate changes and natural disasters affecting the East Sea were recorded in historical documents in Korea. In the 5th year of King Taejong (1405), the seashores of the East Sea were inundated. In the 20th year of King Myeongjong (1565), the East Sea was frozen in the spring. In the 38th year of King Seonjo (1605), the waters of the East Sea turned red, while the Yalu River turned purple. In the 25th year of King Injo (1647), the waters of the East Sea flowed backward to the rivers, and in the 6th year of King Hyojong (1655), the East Sea was frozen again. In the 28th year of King Sukjong (1702), the currents of the East Sea changed and schools of fish moved to the West Sea. In the 13th year of King Yeongjo (1737), the red tide was found again in the East Sea to make the government nervous.[46]

46) Yee [Lee], "A Study on the Understanding the East Sea (Donghae) in the Chosun Dynasty (14th C – 20th C)."

Yang Tae Jin, president of the Misu Literature Society, studied the way in which the East Sea had been represented in Korean oral literature, folk songs and poetry, the very sources of the Koreans' basic emotions. He wrote 803 entries related to the East Sea for *Hanguk gubi munhak daegye* (韓國口碑文學大系, *Compendium of Korean Oral Literature*) published by the Academy of Korean Studies in 1980. He also included in another book in 1995 more than 130 folktales about the East Sea, which were collected by the Kwandong Folklore Society at Catholic Kwandong University. If folktales in North Korea could have also been collected, the number would have been much higher. What is important here is that the folktales testify the awe and dread felt toward the East Sea by people from a wide spectrum of society, from the uppermost bracket, including King Taejo, down to the lowest social class.[47]

The folklore that Yang collected includes East Sea boatmen's songs, which have many different tunes according to different regions and types of work, and the street shamanistic rites along the East Sea coasts, including "East Sea Byeolsingut" among other things.

The East Sea was also a frequent motif in *sijo*, traditional three-line Korean poems, and *gasa*, vernacular narrative

47) Yang Tae Jin, "A Study on the Meaning of 'East Sea', especially based on the National Emotion," The 8th International Seminar on Sea Names, 2002, The Society for East Sea.

verses. According to Professor Kim Heung-kyu, over 150 among the *sijo* of old times are related to the sea, including the East Sea.[48] Dr. Lee Sang-tae introduces a few poems exalting the East Sea, where the sea was mentioned in relation to peace and the source of blessing, while Mt. Namsan was related to longevity.

D. The East Sea Inscribed on Epitaphs

Dr. Lee also studied how the East Sea appeared in many epitaphs which can be taken as a witness to the history of Korea. Among the thousands of them, Dr. Lee discovered 122 epitaphs that mention the East Sea. He examined 43 of them and dealt with the result in his presentation.

Chronologically, some important epitaphs related to the East Sea are as follows:

Gwanggaeto Stele This huge, 7 meter-high stele located in the Chinese province of Jilin, was erected in 414 by King Jangsu of Gogoryeo, son of King Gwanggaeto. The stele is covered with 1,775 Chinese characters in clerical script. The inscription breaks down to three parts: Part 1 introduces the establishment of Goguryeo and King Gwanggaeto. Part 2 deals with the territorial expansion and achievements of

48) Kim Heung-kyu, "The Seas as Shown in Korean Old Sijo," The "Floating Seminar" on the Sea of Dokdo Island, 1997, The Dokdo Institute.

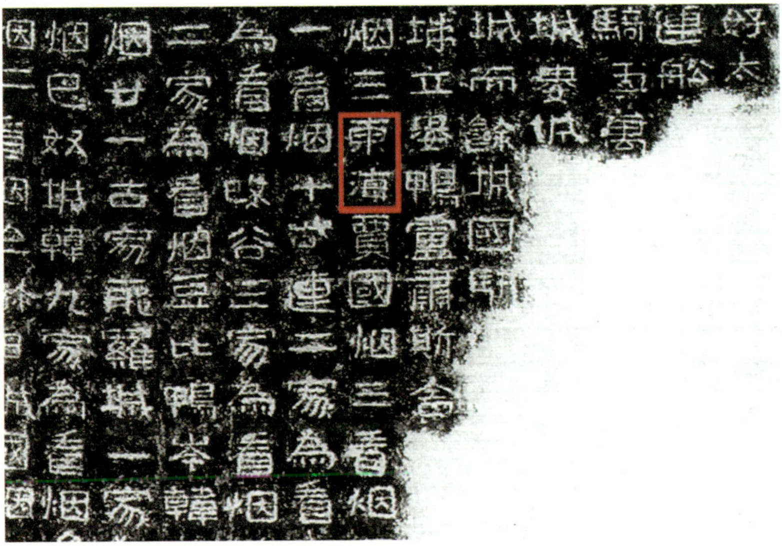

The inscription of Part 3 of the Gwanggaeto Stele, erected in 414, mentions "East Sea."

King Gwanggaeto. And part 3 provides the regulations that grave keepers should observe. The East Sea is mentioned in Part 3. The stele is one of the most important historical materials for the study of the relation that the 5th century Goguryeo had with Silla, Baekje and Japan as well as the ancient history of Korea.

Bell of King Seongdeok

It is also known as the "Bell of Bongdeok Temple" after the place where it was first housed and as the "Emile Bell" after a legend about its casting. This bell was made in the 8th century to commemorate the achievements of King

Seongdeok. A masterpiece of Silla in the artistic form and the quality of the sound, the best of its kind during the Silla period, the bell is Korea's National Treasure No. 29. Standing 3.3 meters high and 2.27 meters in diameter, it is inscribed in relief with 630 characters in the introduction and 200 characters in the main body. The main body clearly describes the East Sea as a sacred site of Silla.

Standing Image of Stone Maytreya Bodhisattva at Gamsansa Temple

This image of Bodhisattva made of granite was built at Gamsansa Temple by Kim Jiseong of Silla, together with the temple itself, to pray for the longevity of the king and the blessings of his family. Through inscription, Kim says that he sprinkled the ashes of the cremated body of his mother on the East Sea. The statue was retrieved from the remains of the temple in 1915 and is now kept at the National Museum of Korea.

Stele for Buddhist Monk Nanghye at Seongjusa Temple Site

Located in Boryeong, South Chungcheong Province, the stele stands 2.51 meters high and 1.81 meters wide. Composed of 5,120 characters, the inscription records that Buddhist Monk Nanghye, who was a prince of the royal family of Silla, entered Buddhism after the competition for the throne and became a great priest with great influence on many of his students. In the inscription of the stele, Korea's National Treasure No.8, the East Sea was used as a metonym of Silla.

Stele for Buddhist Monk Jijeung at Bongamsa Temple

This stele is located at Bongamsa Temple, Mungyeong, North Gyeongsang Province, one of the Nine Mountain Monasteries of the Silla Zen Buddhism. Made in the 9th century and is designated as Korea's National Treasure No. 315, it stands 2.73 meters high and 1.64 meters wide. The inscription is evaluated as valuable in studying the history of the Silla Zen Buddhism. In the inscription, the East Sea is described as a sea on the east of Silla.

Stele for Master Jajeok at Myeongbongsa Temple

Built in the 10th century to remember the life of priest Jajeok who made great contribution to the development of the Zen Buddhism, the stele has inscription composed of three lines with 59 characters each. The inscription explains how Master Jigyeong, teacher of Jajeok, taught students in the East Sea region after he returned home from the Tang China.

Stele for Great Master Bogwang from Bogwangsa Temple Site

This stele was erected in the 14th century and the

inscription tells the life of National Preceptor Wonmyeong and the reconstruction of the temple. The inscription gives detailcd description of how he amazed at what he saw as a miracle of the Buddhism which had been introduced all the way from the Western Regions to the seashores of the East Sea.

Stele for Monk Yuseok

The inscription of this 14th century stele describes the life of priest Yuseok, who helped King Gongmin at the end of Goeyro in reforming the state administration. It also tells what he saw and felt while he was traveling in Mt. Geumgangsan and along the East Sea.

Tombstone of Mok Seo-heum

Mok was a 17th century official who distinguished himself during the course of the 2nd Manchu invasion in 1636 and was appointed magistrate of Yangyang. The inscription praises what Mok achieved as magistrate in this remote county on the seashore of the East Sea.

Tombstone of Yi Bang-beon

King Taejo's seventh son, Yi Bang-beon was slain by his brother Yi Bang-won in the "Stripe of Princes" in 1308. He was restored to his status as prince posthumously and granted the title "Prince of Muan." The inscription says that if he had lived, he would have enjoyed the same honor and wealth as the king of the East Sea.

Other tombstones that relate to the East Sea include the following two:

Stele for the Chronicle of the Repair of the East Sea Shrine

Surrounded by the sea on the three sides, Korea held a sacrificial rite to the seas since the Goryeo Dynasty. Two shrines were built for the East Sea, one in Pungcheon, North Gyeongsang Province, and the other in Yangyang, Gangwon Province. The shrine in Yangyang was promoted with the title, Donghaesinmyo Shrine, and the East Sea was granted a title "King Gwangdeok the Great." The government sent the shrines supplies for the rites twice a year, in the spring and fall. The inscription prays to the god of the East Sea for a good catch and bumper crops.

Stele to the East Sea in Samcheok

The 18th century stele stands 1.75 meters high and 0.76 meters wide. At the time, the residents of Samcheok were greatly suffering from the tidal waves of the East Sea. When Heo Mok, magistrate of Samcheok, erected this stele in praise of the East Sea, it is said that the high waves were calmed, and there was no further damage.

These historical materials provide evidence that the name "East Sea" can be traced back to over 2,000 years ago on the Korean Peninsula. They also show that the sea has been deeply rooted in the lives and hearts of the Korean people from a long time ago; even to the point where they made shrines for regular rituals for it.

2. Notation of the Name of East Sea in Antique Maps

The notation of the East Sea in old maps is outnumbered by those in the historical materials because most of the maps were destroyed when many Korean cultural heritages were damaged during the wars with the Jurchens, Yuan Dynasty, Qing Dynasty, and the Japanese. However, in recognition of the importance of maps, the royal court instructed the making of maps and private efforts were also made to make maps.

We would like to deal with the marking of the East Sea on the maps of the Joseon Dynasty through the research of Professor Yang Bo Kyung who made a deep study of this issue.[49] Yang classified the naming of the East Sea into eight types, including the unmarked one. We, however, simplified them into three types, namely, (1) Unmarked, (2) Naming

49) Yang Bo Kyung, "The Names of the East Sea in Old Korean Maps, 17th to 19th Centuries," Academic Seminar on the Naming of East Sea, 2002, The Chosun Ilbo & Kyung Hee Univ.

according to bearing and (3) Naming "East Sea." We excluded such other markings as "Sea of Korea" and "Sea of Japan" since the maps with those names were deemed to not fit into the category of the traditional old maps.

A. Unmarked

As on Western maps, the East Sea was left unmarked on many of the Korean maps – but for a different reason. In the West, the sea was left unmarked because it was too faraway or they did not know the name. By contrast, on Korean maps, the East Sea was simply marked as the "Sea" or "Ocean" because everybody knew the name.

B. Naming according to bearing

Excluding those maps with the sea name unmarked, on many maps the East Sea was often marked with an indication of bearing, such as "dong," (東) meaning East and "myo," (卯) which also means East in the theory of Yin-Yang and the Five Elements. Such markings for the East Sea as "Dongjeo daehae," (東抵大海) "Dongdaehae" (東大海) and "Dongdaeyang" (東大洋) all infer the meaning, "reaching a big sea to the east."

The most important map that represents the development of cartography in the late Joseon Dynasty is "Dongguk jido" (東國地圖, "Map of Korea," presumed to be of the 18th

century), made by Jeong Sang-gi, a descendant of Jeong In-ji who was a great scholar in the early Joseon. A large-scale map that preceded Kim Jeong-ho's by over a century, this map is a hand-copy of "Dongnamdo" (東覽圖, "Map of Korea"), a woodblock map. The Map's provincial maps are evaluated as superbly elaborate, up to the level that a woodblock map cannot achieve. His Map developed even further as his descendents continued amended and supplemented it, generation after generation. This Map was copied by many people, resulting in scores of different copied versions. Some other provincial maps made in the style of Jeong's mark the East Sea as "Dongjeo daehae" (東抵大海), "Dongnamjeo daehae" (東南抵大海) or "Namjeo daehae" (南抵大海).

C. Marking of the "East Sea"

Since the "Map of Korea" in the "Dongnamdo" (1531), a highly reliable map among those with the marking of the East Sea is "Yeongnam jido" (嶺南地圖, "Map of Gyeongsang Province;" presumably from 1747 to 1750; a collection of Seoul National Univ.), a state-made map published by the Border Defense Council. The Council, which was also responsible for the defense of each province, kept the most exact maps of the regions "classified" and, "Yeongnam jido" was one of them. Presenting the scale in grids, this map is

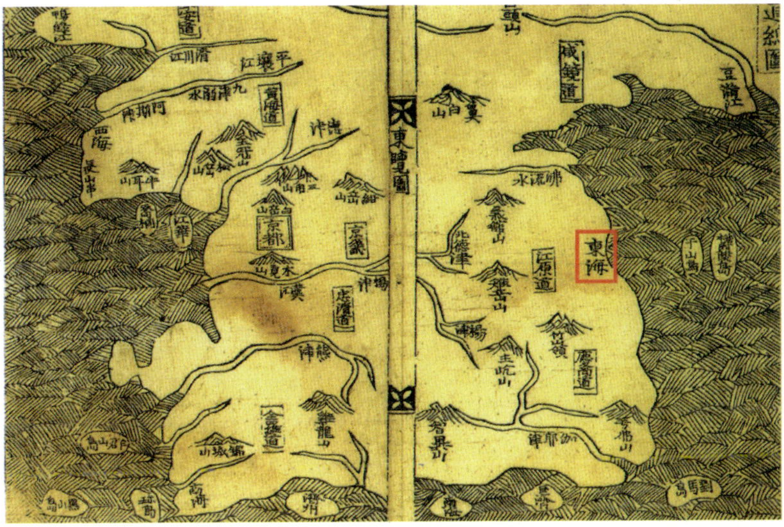

"Paldo chongdo" (八道總圖, "Map of the Eight Provinces of Korea"), a part of "Dongnamdo" (東覽圖, "Map of Korea") made in 1530, marked "East Sea" for the shrine for the East Sea on the coastline of Gangwon Province.

a large-scale map of about 1:53,000 to 1:64,000 and marked the "East Sea" in the sea to the east in the subsection of the "Ulsan Map". *Yeo jido* (輿地圖, *General Map*), a collection of county maps made in the middle of the 18th century, contain those county maps where the East Sea is marked. One, for example, marks the East Sea in the sea to the east of Heunghae County, South Gyeongsang Province. The "Map of Ulsan City" in *Gwangyeodo* (廣輿圖, *Enlarged Terrestrial Atlas*) also marks the East Sea in the east. In addition, a number of county and district maps also have the marking of the East Sea, including "Map of Heunghae County" in *Haedong jido* (海東地圖, *Map of Korea*), which was made

The "East Sea" is marked on "Yeongnam jido" (嶺南地圖, "Map of Gyeongsang Province"), published by the Border Defense Council.

in about 1750; Map of Heunghae in *Gyeongju dohoe jwatong jido* (慶州都會左通地圖, *Map of Gyeongju City*); Map of Tongcheon in *Gwandong seungnam* (關東勝覽, *Map of Gangwon Province*); and another "Map of Ulsan City" in *Yeongnam jido* (嶺南地圖, *Map of Gyeongsang Provinces*; a collection of Yeungnam Univ.).

The marking of the East Sea is also made on "Seobukgye do" (西北界圖, "Map of the Northwestern Frontier of Korea"), presumably made in the mid-18th century; "Aguk chongdo" (我國總圖, "General Map of Korea"); "Map of Korea, Japan and Ryukyu Islands"; and the respective maps of the eight provinces of Korea in *Yeo jido*. On "Cheonha dojido" (天下都地圖, "Map of the World"), the East Sea is marked as "Sodonghae" ("Small East Sea"), probably because the East Sea was thought to be smaller than most other seas in the world.

"Aguk chongdo" (我國總圖, "General Map of Korea"), contained in the 18th-century atlas *Yeo jido* (輿地圖, *General Map*), marks the "East Sea."

Following a series of foreign invasions, the Korean government ordered all counties and districts to make a map of their respective regions and submit them between 1789 and 1793. As a result, more than 460 maps were collected by the Royal Library and "East Sea" was found to have been marked on "Map of Dancheon City" and "Map of Musan" in the maps of Hamgyeong Province, "Map of Samcheok City" and "Map of Pyeonghae County" in the maps of Gangwon Province, and "Map of Ulsan" in the maps of Gyeongsang Province. The marking also appears on maps of the end of the 19th to the early 20th century. For example, "Map of Gyeongsang Province" in the "Dae Joseon jeondo" (大朝鮮全圖, "Grand General Map of Korea") records, "Outside the East Sea are many islands of Japan." As it is known to have been compiled by the Ministry of Education, the map is believed to have been used for educational purposes. Additionally, the map of North Gyeongsang Province in "Daehan sinjiji bu jido" (大韓新地志附地圖, "Map Attached to the New Gazetteer of Korea") has the marking of "Donghaean," meaning "the shore of the East Sea."[50)]

What should be kept in mind with regard to the notation of the East Sea is that the name was not just used for the sea area in hand. On the "Paldo chongdo" (八道總圖, "Map of

50) Yang, "The Names of the East Sea in Old Korean Maps, 17th to 19th Centuries."

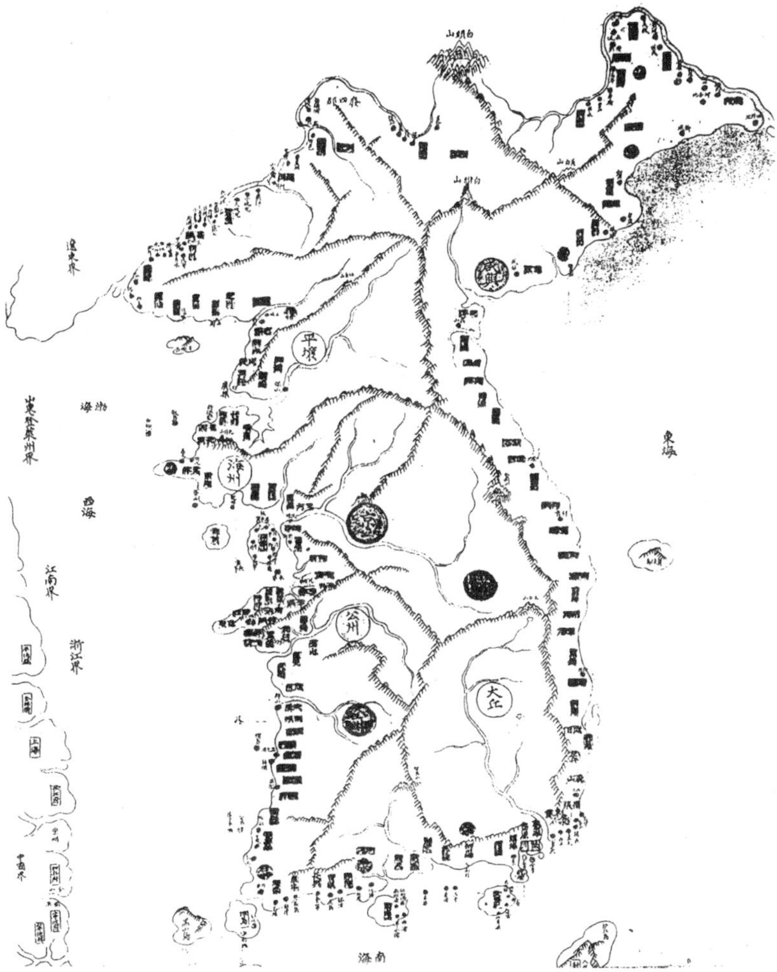

"Map of Korea, Japan and Ryukyu Islands" in *Yeo jido* (輿地圖, *General Map*). The sea to the east of the Korean peninsula is marked as the "East Sea."

the Eight Provinces of Korea") in *Sinjeung Dongguk yeoji seungnam* (新增東國輿地勝覽, *Newly Expanded Edition of Augmented Survey of the Geography of Korea*), the "East

Sea" is marked on the land near Yangyang in reference to the shrine dedicated to the god of the East Sea from the Silla period, or, probably even before that time. It would be more appropriate to regard the marking made on the land as an indirect, supplementary evidence suggesting the sea nearby is the East Sea.

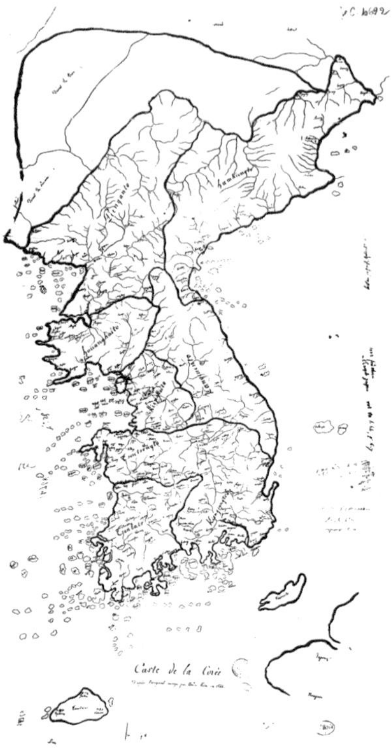

"Map of Korea" by Saint Andrew Kim Taegon in 1846. Although it lacks the name of the "East Sea," it clearly marked the islands of Ulleungdo and Usando. It is thus an important material for the study of the northern territory of Korea.

As seen above, the marking of the East Sea can be found through many extant ancient maps of Korea, from the "Dongnamdo" in the early 16th century through those of the early- to mid-18th century down to those of the end of the 19th century. Most of the maps, whether they were maps of the entire Korea or of counties and districts, are the state-made ones or their hand-copies, proving that the name, "East Sea" was in fact an official name, as well as an endonym, which was used in everyday life. Toward the late 19th century, the number of maps marked with the name "East Sea" increased – presumably in recognition of the importance of marking it, even though most Korean people knew it as a household name. The fact that long time before it appeared on such old maps of Korea as mentioned above, the name "East Sea" is found in historical records as a name deeply rooted in the hearts of the Korean people, makes it all the more necessary and important for it to regain its rightful place.

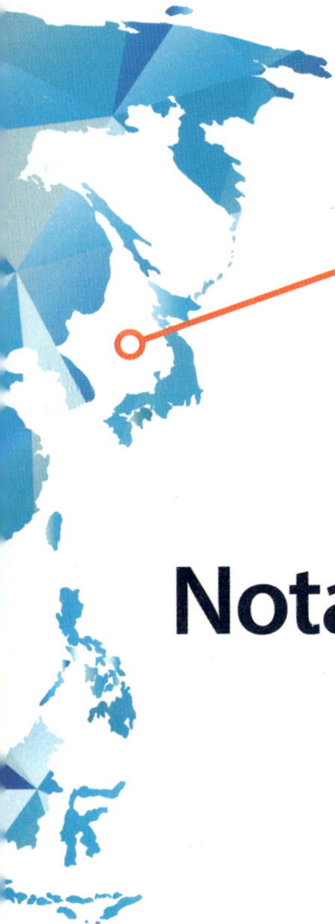

Part III

Papers on the Notation of the Name "East Sea"

Chapter 1

Japanese Studies of Old Western Maps and Their Problems with Focus on the "Origin and Functions of Geographical Names"

Soh Jeong-Cheol
Professor Emeritus, Hankuk Univ. of Foreign Studies

1. Introduction

The four scholars, Hiroshi Tanabe, Masataka Yaji, Yumiko Takizawa and Kohei Watanabe – (hereinafter the "Co-authors" or "Commentators") of the Teikyo University Research Group on Geographical Names, a society composed of graduates from Kyoto Imperial University – published in 2010 a book for the defense of the name, "Sea of Japan," titled *Origin and Functions of Geographical Names – Study on the Geographical Name "Japan Sea"* (hereinafter, the "*Origin*"). Among them, Professors Masataka Yaji and Kohei Watanabe have made several presentations that they delivered together at the seminar of the Society for East Sea.

It is not clear who did what part, but given their ages and scholastic statuses, Professor Yaji seems to have taken care of the preface and the overall organization of the *Origin*. The *Origin*, by the renowned scholars, is the study and summary of what other Japanese scholars has done regarding the the "Sea of Japan" issue so far. Published both in Japanese and English at a sensitive time for determining the sea name, the *Origin* is thought to have been targeted toward publicizing Japan's arguments among geographical experts, especially those at the IHO and relevant UN organizations.

In the preface, the Co-authors present a brief but fundamental academic attitude with emphasis. The study of geographical names, they say, should be done in such as way as to to "remove any political bias in the process" and approach it geographically. We are impressed that they state a noble ideal that ultimately it also should contribute to promoting peace – not only between Korea and Japan, but also for the world.

The *Origin* comprises three chapters: Chapter 1 provides a general discussion on geographical names; Chapter 2, the heart of this book, describes the history and the acceptance of the name, "Japan Sea"; and Chapter 3 compares the notations of the East Sea and the Sea of Japan, emphasizing the importance of the name "Sea of Japan" and geographical education, which is why this paper excludes it from the analysis.

Through a closely constructed structure, the writers start with a strategy to disseminate what they believe is an unshakable justification of the name, "Sea of Japan." In the general discussion of place names, they argue, referring to a thing with a common noun cannot achieve an exact reference. This argument hints at possible problems that can arise when a common noun is used as a place name and thereby suggesting the advantage of a geographical name using a purely proper name. It is presumably a basis for arguing that the name "East Sea," using a common name, can cause confusion, whereas the name, "Sea of Japan" can be used beyond different times and areas. This argument, however, is not linguistically logical in many ways.

The discussions on the language and the name began with the debate over Phusei or Thusei during the times of Socrates. The language is, it is explained, presented to humans as a continuum and a name comes into being when the continuum is articulated into discontinuums. For example, when we see the Taebaek Mountains, the nature is presented to us as a whole. But when we divide them into discontinuums in smaller units, the mountain range is divided into many mountains, including Mt. Taebaek, which, in turn, brings into being the names of valleys, streams and rocks. The principle is like, in natural science, the cells divided into molecules, which are then articulated and named atoms, electrons and protons.

The common noun and the proper noun are closely interrelated and the relationship is dealt with on the semasiological and onomastic levels. Most nouns are elevated onto the onomastic level when they are combined with a modifier on the semasiological level and constitute a proper noun. On the contrary, proper nouns are degraded to the semasiological level when they are reduced to common nouns and their modifiers. For example, when those living in the north point to a mountain in the south and call it "Namsan" ("South Mountain"), it remains as "Namsan" if it becomes a proper noun. But once it becomes a proper noun, it is called by that name whether those calling it are in whatever directions they may be. If a mountain which is called "Namsan" exists in Seoul, Busan, Pyongyang and Gyeongju, then we can avoid confusion by specifying it "Namsan in Seoul (or Busan, etc.)" depending on the context of the dialogue or the text. The same can be said about the "East Sea." If the name exists not only for the sea in the east of Korea but China or Vietnam, thus creating confusion, the name "East Sea of Korea" can always refer to the sea in the east of the Korean Peninsula.

To explain it semiotically, a sign is composed of the signifier, signified, and referent.

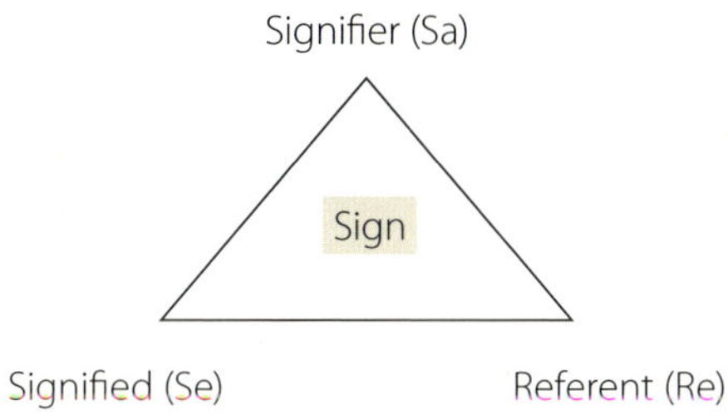

On the semasiological level, when a sign is constituted by the signifier combined with the signified, it automatically refers to the referent. On the onomastic level, the combination of the signifier and the referent makes a sign, with the signified being reduced to something meaningless. However, that is only the case of common nouns; things take a different turn if a name functioning as a modifier on the semasiological level becomes a proper noun. If the "Sea of Japan" on the semasiological level becomes the "Sea of Japan" on the onomastic level, then "Japan" retains the qualities of the signified of the semasiological level still on the onomastic level, thereby making the sea referred to by that name belonging to Japan, or having a special relationship with Japan. However, the East Sea, in fact, faces not just Japan but also South Korea, North Korea and Russia and has a close relationship with China. How then can it be Japan's? Without regard to these facts, the *Origin* portrays the name "East Sea" as inappropriate as a proper noun in Chapter 1 "General Discussion" and makes a caricature of it in [Plate 1] of Chapter 2 "The History of Places for Japan Sea, and the Acceptance of the Name, "Japan Sea."" This is deemed really a far cry from the noble ideal that is pledged in the Preface of the *Origin*.

2. Discussion on the East Sea in Ancient Maps

Beginning with its title, Chapter 2 of the Japanese book attempts to justify that there were various names for what they call "Sea of Japan," which were gradually converged to the name, "Sea of Japan." So the name has undergone a natural and inevitable process before being accepted, it says.

In subsection 2.1.1 of Chapter 2, which corresponds to the introduction to the chapter, the Co-authors argue that traditionally there were no names for the seas in the East and the four seas of East Sea, West Sea, South Sea and North Sea as they were called in China, which considered it as the center of the world referred to the lands in the four directions. They further argue that especially "East Sea" referred to what now is known as the "East China Sea" in the southeast of China. Their argument is partially true.

In China, the names of the four seas referred to the border areas in each direction. However, they conceal the fact that the Japanese themselves called the East Sea "North Sea" for a long time in the meaning of "the sea that is in the north of Japan." Above all, they do not know at all that Chinese classics made it clear that the "East Sea" referred to "the sea in the east of the Korean peninsula." For example, at the seminars of the Society for East Sea, such Chinese scholars as Wu Songdi, Gu Renhe and Cheng Long asserted that the Chinese classics of 2,000 years ago, *Hou Hanshu* (後漢書, *Book of the Later Han*) and *Shan hai jing* (山海經, *Classic of Mountains and Seas*), recorded that the Jurchens referred to the East Sea as the sea in the east of the Korean peninsula and

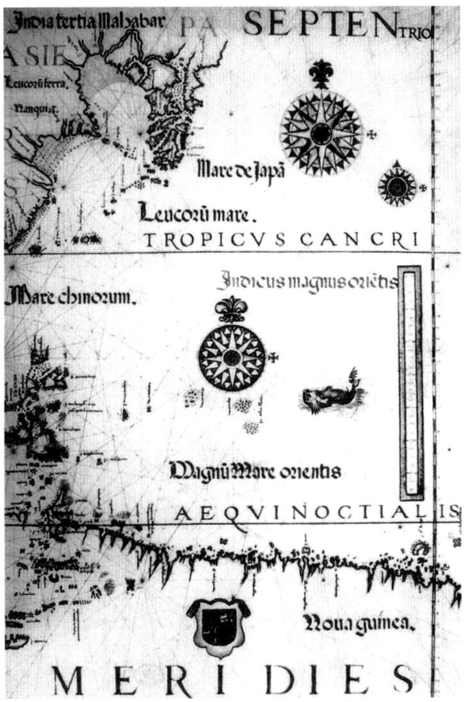

[Plate 2] Diogo Homem's 1568 map of East Asia. It is explained that this map depicted China, Japan and Korea before Matteo Ricci, but no markings of China, Japan and Korea are made except some mythical country names. The name "Japan Sea" does appear, though, but there is no knowing which sea it refers to.

that even during the time the name was not mentioned in historical documents, the Jurchens were still using the name.

Now, let us examine some maps that interest us instead of all 50 maps presented in Chapter 2. [Plate 2], Diogo Homem's 1568 map of East Asia, which is contained in the *Portugaliae Monumenta Cartographica*, was selected to show that the name "Sea of Japan" appeared long before Matteo Ricci's map of 1602. The Commentators point out that the map displays not only China, Japan and Korea, but also Okinawa, Japan Sea and even "Leucoru Mare," which he says is a mistake for the Ryukyu Sea.

It is true that the west part of the map is presumed to be China, but it is only a fictitious hypothesis to interpret that what lies in the southeast of Nanjing ("Nanguil") is the Korean peninsula and the island countries in the shape of a peninsula in the Asian continent are Japan. The part protruding to the southeast of Nanjing may be interpreted as the Shandong province but can hardly be seen as Korea. It is also hardly understandable to see the peninsula in the form of islands as Japan. Moreover, "Leucoru Mare" cannot be interpreted as "Ryukyu Sea" because it is written that there is "Leucoru Terra" ("Leucoru Land or Territory") in the Chinese continent. Also, it is a too far-fetched interpretation to regard the sea above the Leucoru Mare as "Japan Sea," not

[Plate 5] "Iaponiae insulae descriptio" by Luis Teixeira. The author was the one who raised a map-making family in Portugal. It was Jesuit priest Manuel Teixeira who went to Macau.

between the Korean peninsula and Japan, especially when there is no country that can be assumed as Japan.

[Plate 5], Luis Teixeira's 1595 "Iaponiae insulae descriptio" ("Description of Japan Islands"), is highly likely to have been influenced by the Gyogi-type maps as the Commentators explain. Like some European cartographers, he says Teixeira was a Jesuit priest who had been to the Far East, but material distributed by the Portuguese Cultural Center states that it was Manuel Teixeira, a Jesuit priest, who had been to Macau; and Luis Teixeira was the one who raised a map-making

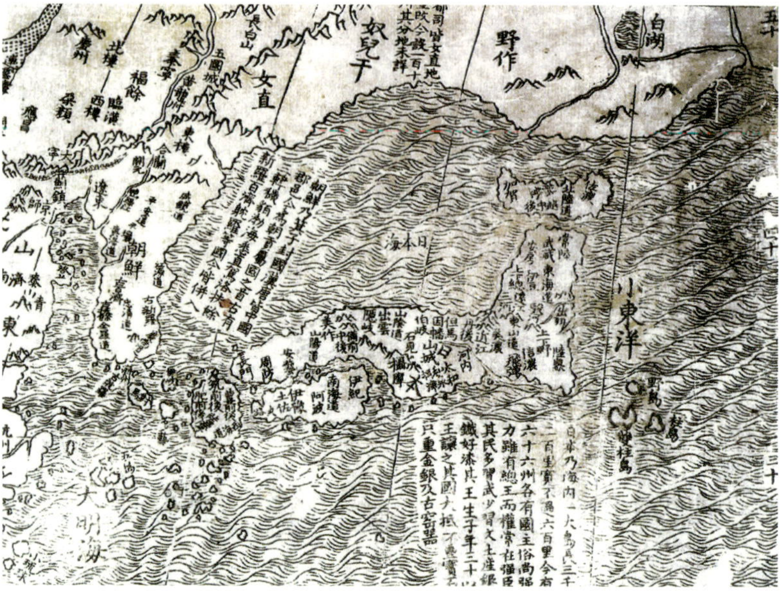

[Plate 6] Matteo Ricci's "Kunyu wanguo quantu" of 1602. Made in Chinese for the Chinese Imperial Household, the map had much influence on Japan. The Japanese themselves ignored Ricci's marking of "Riben Hai" (日本海) for a long time until, after 200 years, Ine Takago used the term "Japan Sea" in 1802 under the influence of European maps.

family in Portugal. Though the Korean peninsula is depicted as an island, the marking "Cory" on the south of it suggests that the map is related to Arab maps.

[Plate 6], Matteo Ricci's "Kunyu wanguo quantu" (坤輿萬國全圖, "A Map of the Myriad Countrie of the World") of 1602, or the first map where the notification "Riben Hai" (日本海, "Japan Sea") is marked on the East Sea, is the most favored and frequently used card that the Japanese put up on the table for the justification of the name "Sea of Japan."

The map, however, was made in Chinese for the Chinese Imperial Family and, although it had much influence on Japan, the Japanese themselves had no interest in the name "Riben Hai." In Japan, the name "Japan Sea" was first used 200 years after Matteo Ricci on Ine Takago's map of 1802. Furthermore, Takago's map is likely to have to do more with French or Dutch maps than with Ricci's map.

While commenting on [Plate 9], the Co-authors abruptly state that on Manuel Godinho de Erédia's 1615 map of East Asia, which is contained in Vol. 4 of the *Portugaliae Monumenta Cartographica*, the East Sea is marked as "Mar Coria" and interpret that it was because the Pacific Ocean to the south of Honshu was marked as "Japan Sea." They also point out that, as the "Japan Sea" is marked as "Mar de Syapon" on Plate map 419A in Volume 4 of the *Portugaliae Monumenta Cartographica*, the same author made different markings in different maps.

However, a closer look at the map discloses that the name of Japan is written "Iapon" and the sea area above Japan is clearly marked "Mar de S. Vapon," which the Commentator claims to be "Mar de Yapon." We cannot readily agree with the Commentators' claim that it is the marking for the "Sea of Japan." It is all the more incomprehensible that he gave the comment in the middle of explaining about another map

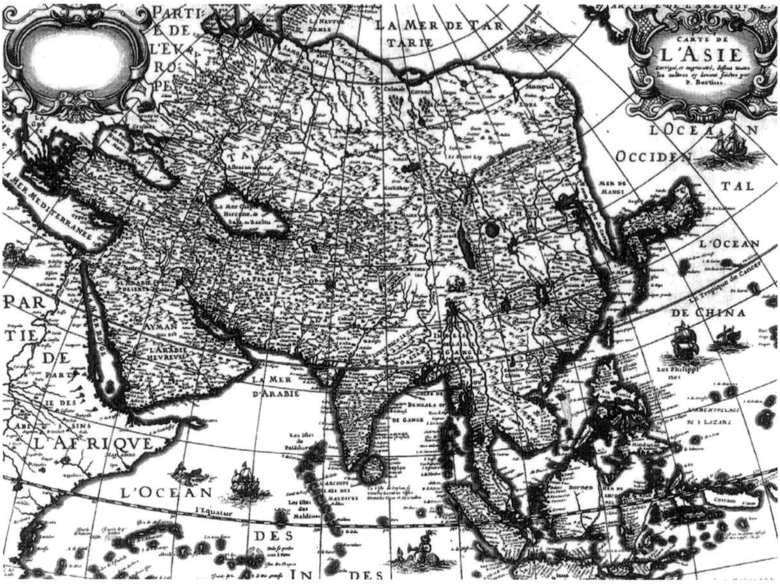

[Plate 9] P. Bertius's map of Asia of ca. 1640. Commenting on this map, the Co-authors draw upon Manuel Godinho de Erédia's 1615 map of East Asia. On the map, Erédia marked Korea as "Coria" and the East Sea as "Mar Coria." On an unfinished map he made in the same year, he marked Japan as "Iapon" and the East Sea as "Mar de S. Vapon." The Co-authors wrongly assert that it reads "Mar de Syapon."

and at that, without showing the map he was talking about.

Robert Dudley was a Great Britain-born oceanographer who became naturalized as an Italian for personal motives before settling in Florence. In 1646, he published the first maritime atlas of the world, the three-volume *Dell'Arcano del Mare* (*Secrets of the Sea*). He then arranged a reprint of the atlas with some corrections, which was published posthumously in 1661. After a calculation on its own,

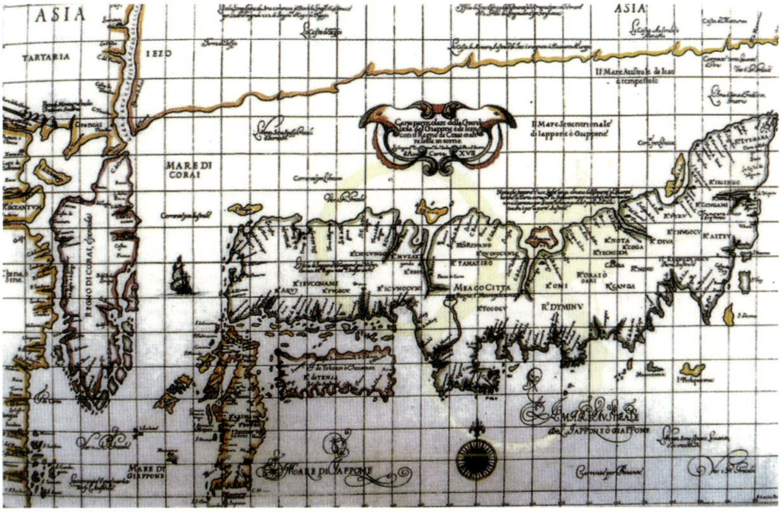

[Plate 12] R. Dudley, a map of Korea and Japan in Dell'Arcano del Mare (reprint edition of 1661), the world's first atlas of charts. The "Sea of Korea," written in square letters, is marked close to Korea and the "North Sea of Japan" and "Sea of Hokkaido" are marked in cursive letters.

the Commentators show "Carta particolare della Grande Isola del'Giapone è di Iezo con il Regno di Corai et altre Isole in torno" ("Detailed Map of the Big Island of Japan and Hokkaido with the Kingdom of Korea and Other Nearby Islands") of the reprint version in [Plate 12]. The said map in the first and second prints does have a few, if not fundamental, differences. One of the most noticeable differences is that in the first print, the marking of "Mare di Corai" for the East Sea was made close to the center of the map, while in the reprint, the cartouche with a long title was placed at the center, pushing the marking closer to the

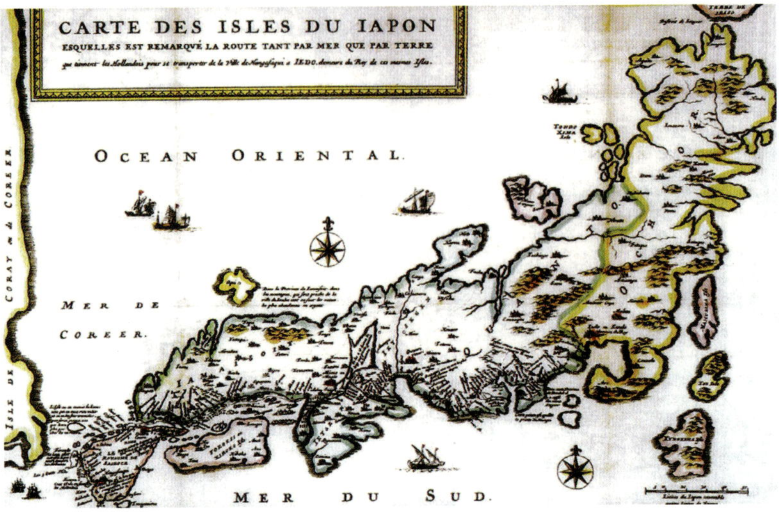

[Plate 15] "Carte des Isles du Iapon" of 1679 by Jean Baptiste Tavernier, a traveler and historian. Here, the East Sea is marked as "Océan Oriental" with another name "Mer de Coréer" in smaller letters in the south of the East Sea.

Korean Peninsula. Pointing out this fact, the Commentators emphasize that it was written in small letters and other markings are made in the East Sea. However, it is clear enough that the "Mare di Corai" is written in the largest square letters, with the "Mare Settentrionale di Iappone o Giappone" ("North Sea of Japan") in the northeast, closer to Japan, and "Mare di Iezo" ("Sea of Hokkaido") in the northeast, both in smaller letters. Moreover, the "Mare di Corai" has no article, while the two markings are made with an article each. How should then we interpret it? It is our judgement that the name in the larger letters without an article is the main title of the sea, while the names in the smaller letters with an article are subordinate and explanatory names.

Among the maps of the 1600s, the first maps with the markings of the "East Sea" or "Sea of Korea" include Father Pierre Briet's "Royaume de Japan" ("Kingdom of Japan") of 1650 where the East Sea is marked as "Océan Orientale," and a 1669 tourism map of Japan for the Dutch by Arnoldus Montanus where he marked the sea as "Mer de Corée." The Co-authors of the *Origin* excluded the two maps and put in only Jean Baptiste Tavernier's "Carte des Isles du Iapon" ("Map of Japan Islands") of 1679 as [Plate 15]. This map has the marking "Ocean Oriental" in the middle of the East Sea and "Mer de Coreer" in the southeast, apparently exhibiting the influence of both Briet and Montanus. However, Montanus' map from his book, which was a huge sensation that swept the European readership, and Briet's map, which contained the information that Briet obtained from his colleague missionaries to Beijing and translated in French in the map, cannot be excluded in terms of importance.

Although it is not clear whether he had been to Beijing, Father V. M. Coronelli made his name known in Venice as a maker of maps and astronomical charts. In his "Isola del Giapone e Penisola di Corea" ("Island of Japan and the

Korean Peninsula"), the Korean peninsula seems to have been influenced by M. Martini but the regions are not clearly identified. In the East Sea and and in the south of Japan, "Oceano Orientale" is marked in large type and across the seas off the southern coast of the Korean peninsula and off the northern part of the eastern coast is marked "Mare della China," indicating that many names were used for the East Sea until the end of the 17th century. The name "Mare del Giapone" is marked in small type in the sea off the south of Japan. One clear thing is that the interpretation, as the

[Plate 20] P. Schenk's "L'Asie" of 1708. It must have been influenced by de Fer's 1705 map of East Asia. The markings of this map are made in French, and Schenk too labeled the East Sea as "Mer Orientale."

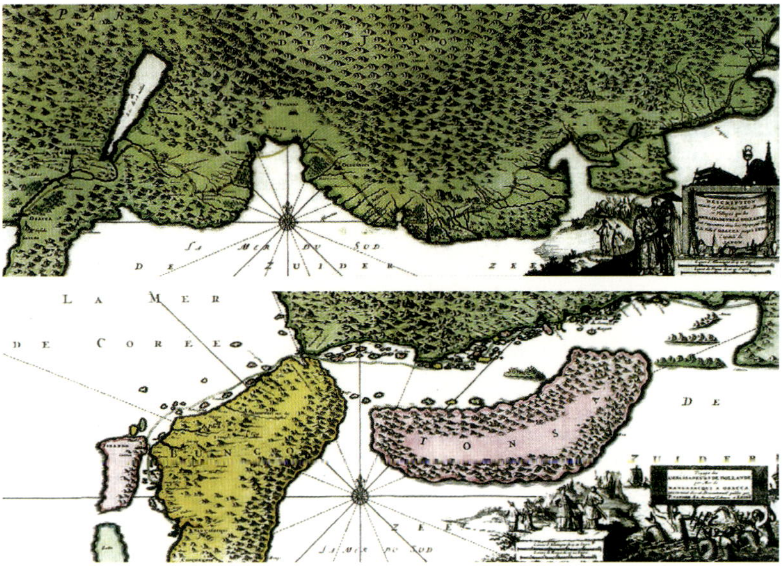

[Plate 21] Van der Aa's 1706 map of Japan. In fact, it is a copy of the map which was contained in Montanus' 1669 book on Japan where the East Sea is marked as "Mer de Corée."

Commentators argue, "Sea of Japan" covers not only the sea off the south of Japan but also the sea off the north of Japan is totally groundless.

[Plate 20] is the 1708 "L'Asie" by Peter Schenk of the Netherlands. Written in French, this map must have been affected by the 1705 map of East Asia by Nicolas de Fer of France. Still, the two maps are different in that Schenk's map has the simple marking of "Mare Orientale," while de Fer's map has a notation stating, "The sea is little or not known to Europeans. The Manchus call it the 'East Sea.'" As such, de Fer's map is definitely indispensable for the study of the name of the East Sea, but the Co-authors excluded it and used Schenk's map instead.

Between the two maps of Pieter van der Aa, the one titled, "Entree des Ambassadeurs Hollandois a Mia, en Japon" ("The Arrival of the Dutch Ambassadors in Mia, Japan"), [Plate 21], was, in fact, an attachment to Montanus' famous book on Japan that shows the travel route of the Dutch trade delegation. Montanus' map marked the East Sea as "Mer de Corée" but apparently van der Aa's map does not clearly show that it is the name of the sea. Still van der Aa's map was chosen over Montanus' map. Montanus' "Mer de Corée" was the marking which, via the map of Antoine Thomas who hailed from the same hometown as Montanus, laid the foundation for the golden age of the "Sea of Korea" in the 18th century.

The maps by Dudley in [Plate 12], Nicolaes Witsen in [Plate 16], Leonard Valk in [Plate 18], Matthäus Seutter in [Plate 22], and Isaak Tirion in [Plate 27] and [Plate 28] all mark the East Sea as "North Sea of Japan" and de Fer used the name twice. Some may have followed the examples of other map-makers, but most of them, either having some knowledge about Japan or having obtained relevant information, knew that the sea was called "North Sea" in

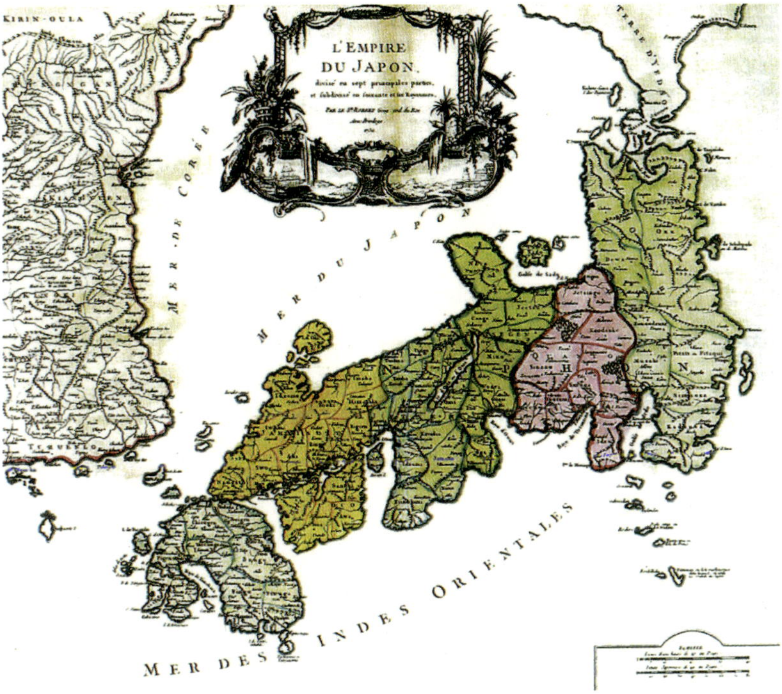

[Plate 29] Gilles Robert de Vaugondy's "L'Empire du Japon" of 1750. On this map, he marked "Mer de Corée" along the east coast of the Korean Peninsula and "Mer du Japon" above Japan. He, however, used "Mer de Corée" alone in his other maps.

Japan and thus added "Japan" as an explanatory qualifier. Yet, the Co-authors did not make any comment on it in the explanations of these maps.

Gilles Robert de Vaugondy, who, as a descendant of Sanson, opened the Robert de Vaugondy family which distinguished itself the most in the mid-18th century, made the "L'Empire du Japon" ([Plate 29]) in 1750 where he marked “Mer de Corée” in the sea along the east coast of the Korean Peninsula and “Mer du Japon” above Japan, giving the impression that he attempted some impartiality. However, on most other maps, he marked the East Sea simply as “Mer de Corée.”

Great Britain was under heavy influence of France in the 18th century but, together with France, most active in map-making in Europe. The French influence on British maps was brought about by Jean-François de La Pérouse’s voyage around the world and exploration as far as the East Sea. On its part, Great Britain produced a number of famous explorers and made a great contribution to the making of more developed world maps. British royal survey boats made several visits to the East Sea and made a contribution to the making of charts in the 19th century. Despite these facts, it is truly far removed from the cartographical common sense to deal only with Emanuel Bowen’s 1747 map ([Plate 30]) from among such a large pool of 18th century British maps. Moreover, maps by John Senex, Herman Moll and Thomas Kitchin were excluded in spite of their reputations, probably because they made the markings of the East Sea in favor of Korea.

The map ([Plate 36]) in the atlas appendix to La Pérouse’s 1797 *Voyage de* La Pérouse *au tour du Monde* marked the

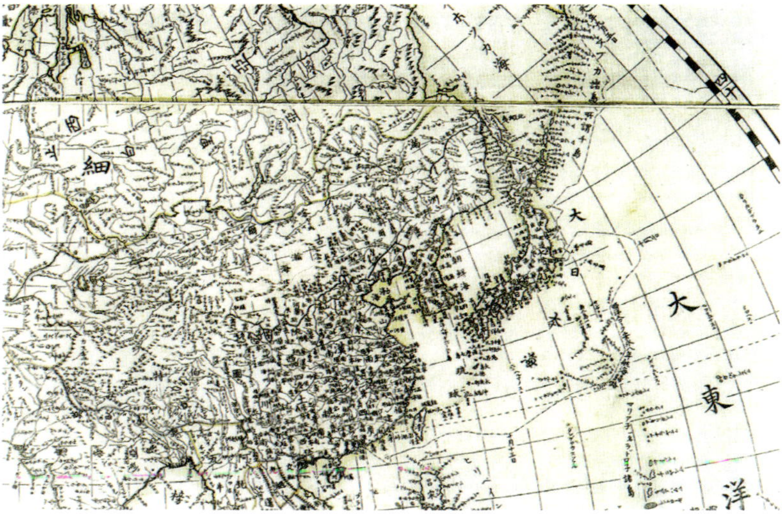

[Plate 35] "Shintei bankoku zenzu" (新訂萬國全圖, "New and Revised World Map"), 1810, by Takahashi Kageyasu, head of the Astronomy Institute of the Shogunate. Produced at the instruction of the Shogunate, the map has the marking "Josen Kai" for the East Sea and "Great Japan Sea" for the Pacific Ocean side of Japan.

East Sea as "Mer du Japon" along with a few other maps which were also contained in the appendix. Together with the map ([Plate 36]), which was included in Adam Johann von Krusenstem's atlas, the map did a lot in drawing the name of the East Sea toward "Sea of Japan" in the 19th century, with La Pérouse's map playing a more important role.

However, paradoxically enough, many important maps of the 19th century Japan marked the East Sea as "Josen Kai" ("Joseon Sea" or "Korean Sea"). The question is — why?

The first one who used the marking "Josen Kai" was Takahashi Kageyasu, a renowned astronomer and cartographer in charge of the Tenmongata (天文方, Astronomy Institute) of the Shogunate. On the Shintei bankoku zenzu (新訂萬國全圖, "New and Revised World Map") ([Plate 35]), which was made under the influence of European maps, he marked the East Sea as "Josen Kai" and the sea off northeast Japan across the sea off the southwest coast of Japan as "Dainihon Kai" ("Great Japan Sea"). Presumably he called the East Sea the "Sea of Korea" because, once he had named the Pacific Ocean side of Japan "Great Japan Sea" in an apparent attempt to show Japan's rising spirit to expand toward the rest of the world, he could not give the East Sea the name "Japan Sea" again. In fact, he had already marked the East Sea as "Josen Kai" on the "Nippon henkai ryakuzu" (日本邊界略圖, "Simplified Map of Japan's Periphery") that he made in 1809. The difference between the two maps is that the 1809 map does not have the marking "Dainihon Kai." What caused this to happen? Two lines of assumption are possible: The first is that he was affected by the European maps which he referred to as they marked the East Sea as "Sea of Korea" or "Mer de Corée;" the second is that he made the decision at his own discretion that the sea should rightly be called "Joseon Sea" on the basis of the shapes of the Northeast Asian countries

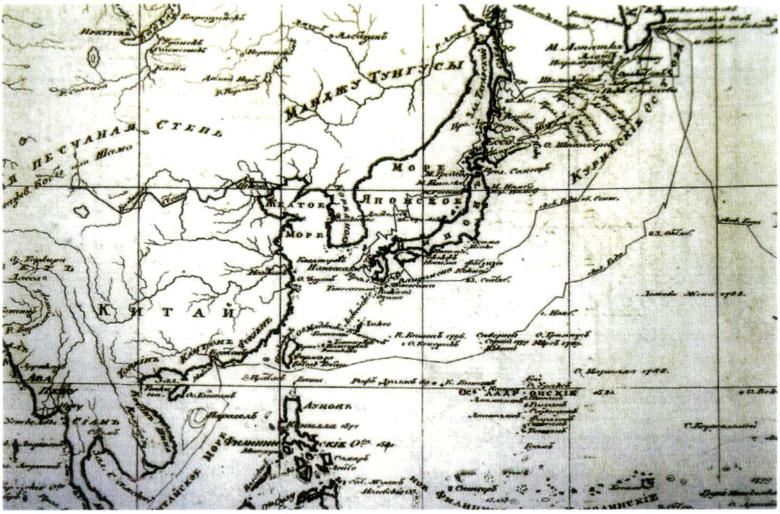

[Plate 36] Russian Admiral A. J. von Krusenstern's 1808 map of North Asia. In his Voyage round the World, he used both "Sea of Korea" and "Sea of Japan" for the East Sea, but on the map he marked "Sea of Japan" alone for the reason that Japan has a longer coastline.

and the general naming patterns. Whatever the truth may be, Takahashi and his students marked the East Sea as "Josen Kai." Such a move was made through the maps of about 20 Japanese map-makers in Japan until the 1870s — in other words, during the period when a considerable number of European maps were calling the East Sea "Japan Sea," - a fact that the Co-authors of this book never mention.

Probably in a bid to give the impression that all 19th-century British maps used the marking "Japan Sea" for the East Sea area and the name has thus been established internationally, the Co-authors of the *Origin* present as examples of the 19th century only those British maps that serve their purpose. Among the maps published by Aaron Arrowsmith, an important British map-maker in the late-18th to the early-19th centuries, the Co-authors present in the *Origin* only the map ([Plate 36]) that fit their purpose; They completely ignore the fact that other maps that Arrowsmith made in the late 18th century marked, like other British maps of the day, the East Sea as "Sea of Korea." William Faden, who took over the map business from the renowned map-maker Thomas Jefferys and was appointed the royal geographer, called the East Sea "Gulf of Korea," a name that Great Britain conceived, even after La Pérouse – for example, on the "Asia" of 1808. In Italy in 1820, Bonatti and Pietro marked, like Faden, the East Sea as "Gulf of Korea" on the "Asia," a map they made in English. James Wyld too used the marking, "Gulf of Korea," on the 1827 "Map of Asia." These maps are excluded altogether in the *Origin*.

Concerning the Russian maps, the same pattern appears. The *Origin* contains three Russian maps, or Krusenstern's 1808 map of East Asia ([Plate 36]), a 1826 map by the Russian Admiral Department ([Plate 38]) and B. Hassenstein's "Japanische Reich" ("Japanese Empire") ([Plate 49]), all of which show the marking of "Japan Sea."

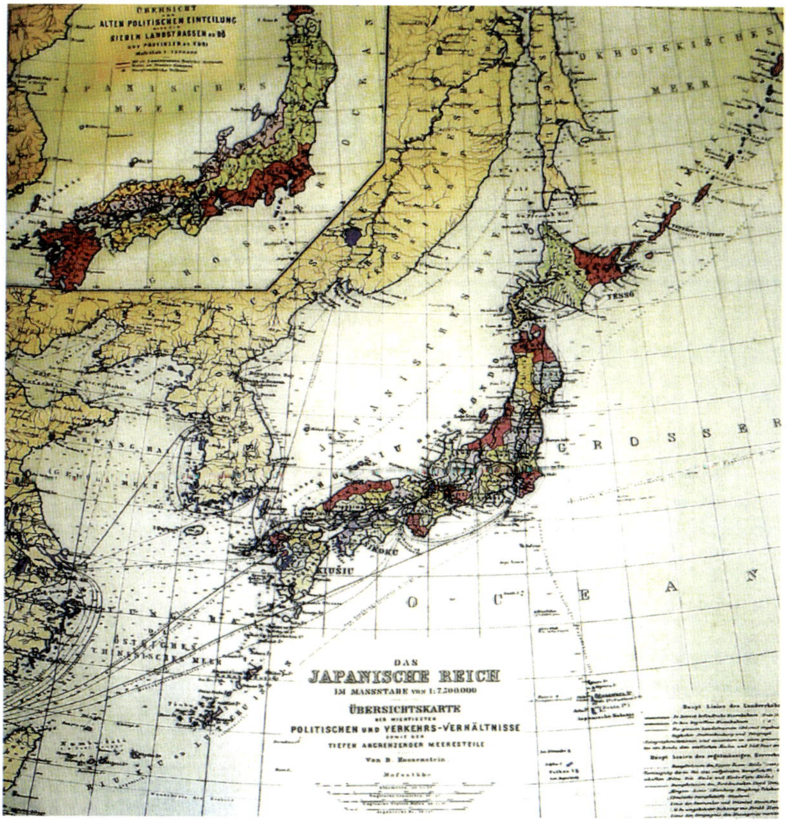

[Plate 49] B. Hassenstein drafted this map, "Japanische Reich," ("Japanese Empire") based on a map of Japan made in the late 19th century. The East Sea is shown as "Japanisches Meer" ("Japan Sea").

Now, let us take a wider and more accurate picture. Joseph-Nicolas Delisle had a great influence on the development of the Russian map industry, which began as late as the 1730s. After the death of his brother Guillaume Delisle in 1726, he was invited by the Russian Tzar and was appointed head of the St. Petersburg Observatory in 1727.

He was in charge of producing cartographers in Russia and supervising the Russian government's map-making. Our primary interest lies in what he thought about the notation of the East Sea and how he and his Russian colleagues did the marking of the sea area.

Having a historian as father and influenced by his brother Guillaume Delisle, a renowned geographer and cartographer of his days, J. N. Delisle was an astronomer who studied cartography as well. Whereas his brother called the East Sea "Mer Orientale" from the information he had gathered, J. N. Delisle decided that "Sea of Korea" was a more fitting name. Guillaume Delisle also used the name on the two maps that he made before he died, but apart from these exceptions, he stuck to "Mer Orientale" for the East Sea. When he was working in Russia, J. N. Delisle emphasized his choice on his students and followers. However, the Commentators fail to provide a full picture here too. Among the 19th century Russian maps, they say, "there is one map by Maxivibich (1826) with "Korean Sea" as Japan Sea, while there is another by the same author in the same year with the name "Japan Sea." There is also a map by the [Russian] Admiral Department with the inscription "Korean Sea" published in 1844. This map continued without altering the name in the subsequent editions (1860, 1864, and 1871) until it was changed to "Japan Sea" in the 1879 edition."[1]

Unlike in the Western Europe, it was rarely the case that individual map-makers produced maps in Russia. Except for some foreign map-makers, the state or public organizations made maps to satisfy the needs of the state. It was because the map-making did not target ordinary customers in the market. And only a limited number of old maps, about 20 or so versions, were produced. Under these circumstances, V. Kirilov was a cartographer in the early days of the Russian map-making who learned cartography properly. On "Asiae Recentissa Deliniatio" ("Latest Map of Asia") in 1734, he labeled the East Sea as "Sea of Korea." The "China, Korea and Japan" of 1737, a collection of the State Archive of the Russian Federation also marks the East Sea as "Sea of Korea." Another "China, Korea and Japan," which was made in the same year and is now in the collection of the Russian State Library, named the East Sea as the "Eastern Sea." The Planisphere of the Globe, also a collection of the Russian State Library, is not an exception in referring to the East Sea as the "Sea of Korea." The "Map of Asia" of 1739 in the State Archive of the Russian Federation also has the marking of "Sea of Korea" for the East Sea. Another "Map

1) Hiroshi Tanabe et al., *Origin and Functions of Geographical Names – Study on the Geographical Name "Japan Sea,"* p.92, Teikyo University Research Group on Geographical Names, 2010.

of Asia," now at the Russian State Library, used the same name. Yet another "Map of Asia," which is presumed to have been made in 1790 and is in the collection of the Russian State Library, marked the same. Still another "Map of Asia" of 1810 at the same place also used the marking of "Sea of Korea." The 1811 "Complete Map of the Korean Peninsula" at the Russian State Naval Archives also marked the East Sea as the "Sea of Korea."

The Korean Cultural Center at the Korean Embassy in Russia conducted a survey of major organizations and libraries in Russia in 2002. The result showed that from among the total of 21 maps, there were three unmarked maps, two "East Sea," eight "Sea of Korea," five "Sea of Japan," two "Sea of Korea/Sea of Japan," and one "Pacific Ocean." In a nutshell, 12 maps had Korea-related markings and seven had Japan-related ones. These statistics provide important information for the study of the name of the sea area.

Another noteworthy fact is that among those maps which shifted from "Sea of Korea" to "Sea of Japan" in the 19th century, some marked instead the sea area stretching from the south of Jeju Island to the East China Sea as "Mer de Corée," in what may presumably be a compensation for such a change. This phenomenon can be observed especially in France, where many maps had the markings of "Mer Orientale" in larger letters and "Mer de Corée" in smaller letters together, including Brué's 1821 "Map of Asia," Levasseur's 1847 "Historical Map of Oceania," Lapie's 1832 "Map of Asia" and Guillaume-Henri Dufour's 1836 map of Asia.

3. Conclusion

The Co-authors presented the same number of maps ranging from the 16th to the end of the 18th centuries with the markings of the sea area at issue either in favor of Korea or Japan, ostensibly showing a perfect balance between the two countries. However, it rather gives the impression that they elaborately balanced the number of the maps for each country from careful calculation. The fact that from among such a large number of old maps available, the selection of only 50 maps hints at the possibility that they may not be a realistic or accurate representation of the true picture; and it may be all the more so when it comes to the fact that they are so evenly distributed between the two nations. More importantly, a number of maps which are meaningful for the Korean side are excluded from the selection.

For example, Briet's map of East Asia of 1650, which provided an important opportunity for the names of "Sea of Korea" and "East Sea" to be introduced, and the 1669 "Map of Japan," which was contained in Montanus' book, were not dealt with. We have already pointed out that many European maps, especially French and British ones, in the 18th century, marked the sea area as "East Sea" based on the local information that the makers had acquired. To ignore the maps of Guillaume Delisle and his brother Joseph-Nicolas Delisle attests to the fact that the selection of the maps for the *Origin* was not made in a fair and transparent manner.

Guillaume Delisle, the chief royal geographer and the most respected scholar in the geographical and cartographic community in Europe of the day, received a good deal of information from a multitude of sources. He learned from missionaries who had been to Beijing that the "East Sea" was the endonym and stuck to the name for his life. The Co-authors did not mention a word about him. Many important British map-makers used the name "Sea of Korea," but only one map, Bowen's 1747 map, was presented.

Many foreign scholars, including some Japanese ones, do not hesitate to recognize that the 18th century was the "golden age" for Korea, but the Co-authors made a selection of only 15 maps from among so many 18th century maps, curtailing the rightful proportion of the maps in favor of Korea. Presenting the maps of the 19th century which are in favor of Japan, the Co-authors seemingly attempted to lay the ground for arguing that the balance broke in the 17th to 18th century and then the name "Sea of Japan" was established in the 19th century.

Dealing with old maps for the past 40 years, one of the authors of this book, Suh, has realized two things:

First, the most important historical material in the study of the history of sea names is old maps; and second, in many cases, the preference or dominance of a certain name can vary according to different places in different times.

Scholars are supposed to be fair and not biased in their study and ready to accept the reasonable argument of those on the other side rather than unilaterally asserting themselves. The old maps should be handled in such a way as to promote the friendship and peace between the two countries rather than sowing the seeds of mistrust and discord.

Chapter 2

Why We Object to the Use of the Name "Sea of Japan" Alone?

Soh Jeong-Cheol
Professor Emeritus, Hankuk Univ. of Foreign Studies

1. Introduction

Today, we are living in an age of globalization. Anything taking place in a remote corner of the global village can be recognized and popularized internationally if it is worthwhile. The barriers that have till now blocked free communication across different countries and regions have been brought down. This phenomenon has been apparent not just in political and economic areas, but in other fields as well.

Globalization, however, does not mean a unilateral, unconditional unification. Anything that has been generalized across the world must be subject to adjustment and supplement if it is found to have been lacking justification or historicity and/or causing regional conflicts. The issue of the naming of the East Sea is one of such problems.

Since the 1990s, the body of water largely between Korea and Japan, which is generally called "Sea of Japan" internationally, has increasingly been marked in two names, or "Sea of Japan" and "East Sea." Still, a majority of nations are still using the single name of the "Sea of Japan." Can "Sea of Japan," then, be justified as the name of the sea area? We will discuss the validation of the name from three points of view.

Whatever name they may be – those of nations, cities, regions or seas, place names were often marked first on old maps. It was because maps of the same place were competitively published, sometimes over several times in the same year. That is why old maps are the primary source in the study of geographical names. This study also uses old maps as the most important basic source.

2. The Reasons for the Objection

2.1 Regional Perspective

The East Sea is bordered by the coastlines of not only Japan but South Korea, North Korea and Russia as well.

China was also a coastal state of the sea until the 1860s and is still near it. Japan contends that the East Sea was formed by Japan blocking the Pacific Ocean but, if Korea did not exist, could the Sea of Japan still be accepted and used as is? If the name of a country had to be part of the sea name, the sea is most likely to have been called "Sea of China" as China is the largest in the neighborhood and has been known to the rest of the world far longer than any other in the area.

Russia and China did not seem to have any interest in the East Sea. However, having aspired to secure an ice-free port from a long time ago, Russia has been working hard to develop the Far East in order to utilize the East Sea as a channel for the transportation of goods and resources after Gorbachev's Vladivostok Speech in 1986. Russia has used the single name "Sea of Japan" following the decision of the IHO, but many scholars and intellectuals increasingly think that the name should be reconsidered in tune with the times.

China too has a strong interest in the East Sea. With Manchuria close to the East Sea, it cannot afford to be indifferent to the sea. Fully aware of the economic value of the East Sea in terms of resources and logistics, China has recently been making a huge investment in the development of the Rajin-Sonbong area in North Korea. Regarding the name of the East Sea, China has been in compliance with the decision of the IHO. However, immediately before World War II broke out, a great movement was initiated by intellectuals to point out the inappropriateness of the name "Sea of Japan" and change it and there are some embers still left. And most scholars view that the name of the sea should be "East Sea" from the historical and cultural perspectives. Putting the name of a country in the name of a sea which is shared by many countries would not be easily accepted by the other countries. If the Mediterranean should be called "Sea of Italia" or "Sea of France," could it be agreed by the neighboring countries that share the sea?

2.2 Inappropriateness of the Name, "Sea of Japan"

As stated above, to give the East Sea a name with the name of a country would be inappropriate internationally. Now let us examine the reason from the historical and linguistic perspectives.

2.2.1 Historical Review

In China in ancient times, the "East Sea," "West Sea," "North Sea" and "South Sea" were used to refer to the bearings and the regions in those directions. The "Yellow Sea" then came into being in consideration of the color of the sea. The "East Sea" was imagined as a place of dreams and ideals and was sometimes used to refer to the sea to the east of China. Since the modern times, the sea area to the southeast of China has been called "East China Sea."

In contrast, in Japan, there were no names that referred to the seas for a long time. As the simple mentioning of "the sea" was enough for both the speakers and the hearers to understand what sea was being referred to, no inconvenience was felt even when there were no names for the seas. The extra-linguistic context allowed them to infer which sea "the sea" was referring to.

Probably due to this tradition, when Matteo Ricci's "Kunyu wanguo quantu" (坤輿萬國全圖, "A Map of the Myriad Countrie of the World") of 1602 was introduced to Japan and had a significant influence on their world view, the Japanese themselves did not take any interest in Ricci's naming of the East Sea as "Riben Hai" (日本海, "Japan Sea"). It was 200 years after the publication of the "Kunyu wanguo quantu" that the first Japanese map where the East Sea was marked as "Japan Sea" appeared in Japan by Shiba Kokan and Ine Takago. However, even in the 19th century, Takahashi Kageyasu, who, as head of the Tenmongata (天文方, Astronomy Institute) of the Shogunate, was in charge of the publication of maps, marked the East Sea as "Josen Kai" ("Joseon Sea") on the "Nippon henkai ryakuzu" (日本邊界略圖, "Simplified Map of Japan's Periphery"), which he made in

1819 at the request of the of the Shogunate, and on the 1810 "Shintei bankoku zenzu" (新訂萬國全圖, "New and Revised World Map"). His students and map-makers who followed him continued to identify the East Sea as "Josen Kai" until 1870.

According to Dr. Lee Sang-Tae, until the 1870s, more than 20 Japanese maps labeled the East Sea as "Josen Kai" and four to five maps marked both names, or "Japan Sea" and "East Sea." In addition, over 10 official documents also used the name "Josen Kai."

It seems that the marking of "Josen Kai" was an unavoidable choice from the logical perspective. Japan already marked the Pacific Ocean side of Japan as "Great Japan Sea" and then could not give the East Sea the same name. Whether Japan wanted it or not, there was no escaping and the Shogunate must have known it at the time.

On the other hand, Japan seems to have had the tradition of calling the East Sea "Northern Sea" or "North Sea." It was because from the southern and southeastern regions of Japan, the East Sea was in the north, albeit the residents of the regions on the east coast called it simply "the sea." Now let us find out the traces of "North Sea" on old maps.

For example, Bernardino Ginnaro, a Jesuit priest who was

sent to Japan where he studied its history and geography, produced a map of Japan in 1641 where he marked the East Sea as "Oceano Boreale." Interestingly, "Boreale" originally meant the north wind in Greek mythology and then, as an adjective, referred to the natural conditions in the north. Later, it simply meant the north. Ginnaro asked what the East Sea was called to the locals who, after hesitation, answered "the sea in the north," which he translated for the map.

Robert Dudley, an expert in marine charts, also marked the East Sea as "Il Mare Boreale del Giappone" ("North Sea of Japan") on the 1647 "Carta particolare della Grande Isola del'Giapone è di Iezo con il Regno di Corai et altre Isole in torno" ("Detailed Map of the Big Island of Japan and Hokkaido with the Kingdom of Korea and Other Nearby Islands"). Obtaining geographical information from a relative who had trade with Yokohama, de Fer also identified the East Sea as "Mer Septentrionale du Japon" ("North Sea of Japan") on a map of Asia in 1696. "Septentrionale" originated from the mythology about the seven plow oxen working at the North Pole and is used as an adjective referring to "of the North." On a map of 1703, de Fer marked the East Sea as "Mare Orientale" and added an unusual note in the margin of the map, explaining that it was the local name. Two years later, however, in 1705, he went back to the previous notation and marked the sea as "North Sea of Japan" on a map of Asia as he did in 1696. These examples suggest that in Japan, such names as "North Sea" or "North Sea of Japan" were used to refer to the East Sea.

The fact that the East Sea was called "North Sea" in Japan remains in historical records. According to the research of Dr. Shim Jeongbo, many Japanese textbooks, dictionaries, newspapers, historical books and geographic books at the end of the 19th century referred to the East Sea as "Hokkai" ("North Sea"). The authors were so accustomed to the name "Hokkai" that they used sometimes "Japan Sea" and other times "Hokkai" in the same materials to refer to the same sea. These examples attest to the fact that the East Sea was called "North Sea" in Japan – a fact that Japanese scholars and the Ministry of Foreign Affairs of Japan alike have kept silence about presumably for fear that it might do harm to the standing of the name, "Sea of Japan." They instead consider that "North Sea of Japan" is another notation of "Sea of Japan."

2.2.2 Linguistic Review

Linguistics has a branch that deals with the name. It is largely divided into onomasiology and onomastics, which are closely inter-related. Almost all proper nouns are derived from common nouns. For example, the "East Sea" is composed of "the adjective ("East") + the common noun ("Sea")," with the two components retaining their respective etymological meanings.

However, when the two components are combined and used as a proper noun, like a name, the adjective loses its etymological meaning and merges into the combination to become one unique proper noun.

Therefore, the interpretation that the "East Sea" refers to "the sea area to the east of the Korean Peninsula" and thus it is something that can be referred to by those to its west is but an etymological analysis on the onomasiological level. The proper noun "East Sea" is a name that can be used anywhere in the world – be it Europe in the west, Australia in the south or Russia in the north – to refer to the sea area. It has dropped the etymological meaning.

However, it becomes a different matter when a proper noun is involved in the first place. For example, the "Bering Sea" and the "Philippine Sea" can mean "the sea which has a special relationship with Bering" or "the sea dominantly adjacent to the Philippines" on the onomasiological level. Still, when they turn proper nouns, the meanings do not change because "Bering" and "Philippines" are proper nouns from the beginning, remaining to mean "the sea which has a special relationship with Bering" or "the sea dominantly adjacent to the Philippines."

When this is applied to the "Sea of Japan," the appellation indicates that it is "the sea which has a special relationship with Japan" or "the sea dominantly adjacent to Japan" both on the onomasiological and onomastic levels. However, as the East Sea is the sea area shared by the four countries and a free waterway where ships of any country can pass freely, the name "Sea of Japan" for this sea area is totally inappropriate at its source.

2.3 Appropriateness of the Name, "East Sea"

2.3.1 Korean People's Perceptions and the Cultural Tradition

Although, as a peninsular state, Korea is surrounded by the seas on the three sides, the East Sea has especially been impressed with special meanings in the hearts of its people from a long time ago. For example, the Korean national anthem starts with "Until the day when the East Sea's waters and Mount Baekdu are dry and worn away, God protect and preserve us; Long live our nation." It is because that mountain and that sea representatively symbolize Korea from among the many mountains and seas and are deeply rooted in the consciousness of the Korean people.

King Munmu of Silla, who unified the ancient three kingdoms, left the will where he wanted to be buried in the East Sea to protect the country. The subjects followed his will and buried him under the rock called, "Great King's Rock." Other kings of Silla also left a will that they wanted their ashes to be scattered over the sea. It was because to protect the East Sea was thought to be the first step toward, and tantamount to protecting, the whole nation. Some might figure that it was because Silla principally faced the East Sea, but it also had a sea to its south and, after the unification, to the west as well. Still, the East Sea remained the most important sea with special meanings.

The strange, abnormal natural phenomena taking place in the East Sea became the materials for many myths, prompting the imagination of the Korean people with their symbolic meanings. The natural disasters occurring in the East Sea caused a great awe about nature in the hearts of the people. To the kings, as a voice of heaven, they provided an opportunity to reflect on the politics that they were practicing.

Due to its location, Goryeo had a greater interest in the West Sea which it faced. Still, it was not unlike Silla in holding the East Sea sacred and standing in its awe. In the spring and fall, the state-administered rituals dedicated to the East Sea were institutionalized.

During the Joseon Dynasty, the rituals for the East Sea continued, especially in Yangyang, Gangwon Province, that touches the East Sea. In Joseon, an agricultural country, when a drought struck, it was interpreted as the wrath of heaven expressed on earth. It was taken as an opportunity for the state to make sure there were no innocent prisoners and ensure the fair and speedy treatment of the trials. The politicians were resolved to practice moral, virtuous politics. The rituals were a representation of such interpretations and resolutions.

The East Sea as the object of folk beliefs and exaltation has been expressed in traditional Korean oral literature, folk songs and poetry. *Hanguk gubi munhak daegye* (韓國口碑文學大系, *Compendium of Korean Oral Literature*), published by the Academy of Korean Studies, contains about 800 items that relate to the East Sea. The Folklore Society at Kwandong University collected some 130 folktales about the East Sea. If those in the North Korea could have been added, the number would have been far greater. The East Sea also frequently appears as an important motif in many folk songs of fisher men along the shores of the East Sea as well as *sijo*, traditional three-line Korean poems, and *gasa*, vernacular narrative verses. Dr. Lee Sang-Tae, who studied the epitaphs, discovered over 120 tombstones with the inscription that mentioned the East Sea.

What is important in this respect is that the folklore pieces were consumed by people in all walks of life, from the highest ruling class down to the lowest, exhibiting how deeply the East Sea has been established in the lives and hearts of the Korean people.

2.3.2 Historicity of the Name, East Sea

As is known, in the section on King Dongmyeong in the "Goguryeo's Records" of the *Samguk sagi* (三國史記, *History of the Three Kingdoms*), a divine dream is recorded according to which the capital of Bukbuyeo was moved to Gaseopwon in the vicinity of the shores of the East Sea. It corresponds with 59 B.C., indicating that the Korean people have used the name "East Sea" from before 2,000 years ago. In addition, such Chinese scholars as Wu Songdi, Gu Renhe and Cheng Long have discovered from Chinese historical documents the accounts that the Manchus mentioned "East Sea" over 2,000 years ago. These facts attest that the name "East Sea" has been used by not only the Koreans but also the Manchus for over 2,000 years now.

The name "East Sea" was used quite frequently in the ancient times. It is mentioned in *Samguk sagi* 15 times and *Samguk yusa* (三國遺事, *Memorabilia of the Three Kingdoms*) 14 times, proving that it was an important name to the Koreans historically. The Gwanggaeto Stele is a monument with 1,775 Chinese characters which was built in 414 to extol the achievements of King Gwanggaeto (374-412?). On its fourth side, "Donghaego" (東海賈, also reads "Donghaega") is mentioned in relation to "東海" ("Donghae" or "East Sea") as one of the many places where the guardians of the tomb were requisitioned from.

These accounts attest to the fact that the name "East Sea" has never ceased to be used throughout the history of Korea for over 2,000 years. The English name "East Sea" (or "Eastern Sea") is an English translation of the Korean sea name "Donghae" by the Korean government for better understanding of foreigners. As much as "Donghae" is an endonym, "East Sea" should also be treated as an endonym.

In contrast, the "Sea of Japan" started to replace "East Sea" from La Pérouse's 1897 accounts of his voyage and was used increasingly since. It was accepted as the name of the sea at the International Hydrographic Organization (IHO) in 1928 while Korea had no voice as it was under Japanese colonial rule at the time. The name "Sea of Japan" is therefore essentially an exonym with a history of only over 100 years since foreigners first started to use it. Now it would be clear how inappropriate to maintain the name "Sea of Japan" alone.

3. Conclusion

Amidst Japan's recent conservative swing, the Japanese seem to take the name of the "Sea of Japan" as a matter of national pride. However, as we have surveyed, the "Sea of Japan" was not the name that Japanese used only 100-plus years ago. They called the Pacific Ocean side of Japan "Great Japan Sea" but, as the name was not accepted by foreign countries, they started to call the East Sea "Sea of Japan" – a name which was established in Japan from the end of the 19th to the early 20th century.

We are opposed to the solitary use of the name "Sea of Japan" because it lacks justification both historically and logically. It may be hard to expect the IHO and the international community to to the right thing and change the name in the near future but history has evolved toward universality and justice has prevailed slowly but steadily. The demands for the name "East Sea" will certainly be heard, and the name will surely be recognized for its validity sometime in the future.

References

Ahmad, S. Maqbul, "Cartography of al-Sharif al-Idrisi," *Cartography in Traditional Islamic and South Asian Societies* (David Woodward & John Brian Harley, eds., *The History of Cartography*, vol. 2), Chicago, University of Chicago Press, 1992, p.156.

Atoui, Brahim, "'Donghae,' 'Nihon Kai,' 'Sea of Japan' or 'East Sea': Is it a Question of Qualification and Categorization in Exonym, Endonym, Allonym or Translated Name?" The 17th International Seminar on Sea Names, 2011, The Society for East Sea/Northeast History Foundation.

Chen, Cai & An, Hu Sen, "Our View on the Origin of the Geographical Name of the Sea of Japan (East Sea)," The 1st International Seminar on Sea Names, 1995, The Society for East Sea.

Cheng, Long, "East Sea in Chinese Historical Documents of Late Qing Dynasty," The 12th International Seminar on Sea Names,

2006, The Society for East Sea.

Cheng, Long, "Research on Relationship between the Name of 'East Sea' and the Local Non-Han Government of Northeast China after Tang Dynasty," The 11th International Seminar on Sea Names, 2005, The Society for East Sea.

Cheng, Long, "Yuan Wei (1794-1857), His Research and Maps about East Sea," The 16th International Seminar on Sea Names, 2010, The Society for East Sea.

Choo, Sungjae, "Recent Progress for Restoring the Name East Sea and Future Research Agenda," The 13th International Seminar on the Naming of Seas and East Sea, 2007, The Society for East Sea.

Deng, Hui, "From the four seas to the four oceans: Changes of Chinese ocean views since the 10th century," The 15th International Seminar on Sea Names, 2009, The Society for East Sea.

Ganzei, S. & Baklanov, P., "Russian Geographical Investigations of Seas of North-Eastern Asia in XVII-XVIII Centuries," The 2nd International Seminar on Sea Names, 1996, The Society for East Sea.

Gu, Renhe, "Eastern Sea Area of Korea Peninsula should resume the Original Name: Donghai, Orient Sea," The 7th International Seminar on Sea Names, 2001, The Society for East Sea.

Han, Maoli, "'East Sea' and 'Korean East Sea': Records about the Sea Area to the East of Korean Peninsula on Chinese Literatures during the Last 1000 Years," The 13th International Seminar on Sea Names, 2007, The Society for East Sea.

Han, Maoli, "The Naming of the Sea Area to the East of the Korean Peninsula according to the Ancient Chinese Literatures," The 14th

International Seminar on Sea Names, 2008, The Society for East Sea.

Harley, J. B. & Woodward, *Cartography in the Traditional Islamic and South Asian Societies*, The University of Chicago Press, 1992.

Hishiyama, Takehide and Nagaoka, Masatoshi, "*Changing the Name of the "Japan Sea,*" quoted in Shim, Jeongbo, "Ilboneseo Ilbonhae Jimyeonge Gwanhan Yeongu Donghyang" ("Research Trends in Japan on the Place Name 'Sea of Japan'"), *Journal of the Korean Cartographic Association*, 2007, no.2: 18, Korean Cartographic Association.

IHB, Report of Proceedings, p.47, 1926.

Jing, Tian, "Recent Research Progress on a Study of the Sea Name on East Sea and Japan Sea in China," The 8th International Seminar on the Naming of Seas, Special Emphasis Concerning the North Pacific Ocean, 2002, The Society for East Sea.

Kadmon, Naftali, "Endonym or Exonym – is there a Missing Term in Maritime Names?" 9th United Nations Conference on the Standardization of Geographical Names, New York, 21 - 30 August 2007; United Nations, New York, E/CONF.98/ 6/Add.1, quoted in P. Jordan, "Is 'Exonym' an Appropriate Term for Names of Features Beyond any Sovereignty?" The 16th International Seminar on Sea Names, 2010, The Society for East Sea/Northeast History Foundation.

Kim, Heung-kyu, "The Seas as Shown in Korean Old Sijo," The "Floating Seminar" on the Sea of Dokdo Island, 1997, The Dokdo Institute.

Kim, Jong-Wee, *Jungse Islam Munheone Bichin Hanguksang* (*Images of Korea as Reflected in Medieval Islam Documents*), Korea International Economics Institute, 1977.

Kivelson, Valerie, *Cartographies of Tsardom: The Land and Its Meanings in Seventeenth-Century Russia*, Cornell University Press, 2006.

Lee, Ki-suk, "IHO and the Formalization of the Name 'Sea of Japan,'" The 4th Academic Conference of the Society for East Sea, 1997, The Society for East Sea.

Lee, Sang-Tae, "Even Japan Used the Name East Sea and Sea of Joseon, not Sea of Japan," The 13th International Seminar on the Naming of Seas and East Sea, 2007, The Society for East Sea.

Lee, Sang-Tae, "Sea of Chosun Appeared in Old Japanese Maps," The 16th International Seminar on Sea Names, 2010, The Society for East Sea/Northeast Asian History Foundation.

Liang, Er Ping, *Segyesaui Unmyeongeul Bakkun Haedo* (*Charts that Changed the Fate of the World History*), tr. Ha Jin-Ee, Myungjin Publishing Co., 2011, pp.306-314.

Liu, Xin Jun, "Ancient Books of China Records and Narrate about East Sea/Japanese Sea," The 12th International Seminar on Sea Names," 2006, The Society for East Sea.

Park, Chan-Hong, "Donghaewa Dogdoui Jayeongwahagjeog Gachi" ("The Value of the East Sea and Dokto Island in Natural Science"), *Donghaewa Hanguginui Salm* (*The East Sea and the Life of the Koreans*), Society for East Sea and Korea Institute of Ocean Science & Technology, 2011.

Pelletier, Philippe, "LES CARTOGRAPHES FRANÇAIS et la DENOMINATION de la 'MER DU JAPON' (MER DE L'EST) aux XVIIe et XVIIIe siècles," The 8th International Seminar on the Naming of Seas, Special Emphasis Concerning the North Pacific Ocean, 2002, The Society for East Sea.

Pelletier, Philippe, "The Role of French Geography in the Naming of the Sea between Korea, Japan and Siberia from the 17th to Early 19th Century," The 8th International Seminar on Sea Names, 2002, The Society for East Sea.

Postnikov, Alexei & Pospelov, Evgenii, "The History of Russian Names for Seas, with the Special Reference on the Development of the Korean (Japanese) Sea Presentation on Maps (Seventeenth through Nineteenth Centuries)," The 1st International Seminar on Sea Names, 1995, The Society for East Sea.

Raper, Peter E., "Interpreting United Nations Resolutions on Geographical Names," The 16th International Seminar on Sea Names, 2010, The Society for East Sea/Northeast History Foundation.

Raper, Peter E., "The UN and Standardization of Geographical Names," The International Seminar on the Standardization of Geographical Names, Session I, 1997, The Society for East Sea.

Shim, Jeongbo, "Ilboneseo Ilbonhae Jimyeonge Gwanhan Yeongu Donghyang" ("Research Trends in Japan on the Place Name 'Sea of Japan'"), *Journal of the Korean Cartographic Association*, 2007, no.2, p.18, Korean Cartographic Association.

Statues, Rules of Procedure and Resolutions on Geographical Names, 2002, UNGEGN.

Tanabe, Hiroshi et al., *Origin and Functions of Geographical Names – Study on the Geographical Name "Japan Sea,"* p.92, Teikyo University Research Group on Geographical Names, 2010.

Watanabe, Kohei & Yaji, Masataka, "Study on the Geographical Name "Japan Sea," The 16th International Seminar on Sea Names, 2010, The Society for the East Sea.

Woodman, Paul, "Maritime Feature Names: The Role of UNGEGN during its First Decade," The 16th International Seminar on Sea Names, 2010, The Society for East Sea/Northeast History Foundation.

Woodman, Paul, "The See of the Three Endonyms," The 15th International Seminar on Sea Names, 2009, The Society for East Sea/Northeast History Foundation.

Xi, Guo Jin, "Nationalities in the Eastern Part of Northeast China in History and Changes in the Name of the Sea of Japan," The 1st International Seminar on Sea Names, 1995, The Society for East Sea.

Yang, Bo Kyung, "The Names of the East Sea in Old Korean Maps, 17th to 19th Centuries," Academic Seminar on the Naming of East Sea, 2002,The Chosun Ilbo & Kyung Hee Univ.

Yang, Tae Jin, "A Study on the Meaning of 'East Sea', especially based on the National Emotion," The 8th International Seminar on Sea Names, 2002, The Society for East Sea.

Yee [Lee], Sang-tae, "A Study on the Understanding the East Sea (Donghae) in the Chosun Dynasty (14th C – 20th C)," The 8th International Seminar on Sea Names, 2002, The Society for East Sea.

Yuan, Shuren & Huang, Yangun, "Our Opinion on the Geographical Name of the Sea of Japan," The 2nd International Seminar on Sea Names, 1996, The Society for East Sea.

Zhu, Shiguang, "On the Transformation of the Geographical Name in the Area of the Sea of Japan (The East Sea) from a Perspective of Historical Documents," The 3rd International Seminar on Sea Names, 1997, The Society for East Sea.